WITHDRAWN

GREAT IDEAS
FOR TEACHING
ABOUT AFRICA

GREAT IDEAS
FOR TEACHING
ABOUT AFRICA

EDITED BY
MISTY L. BASTIAN
& JANE L. PARPART

LYNNE
RIENNER
PUBLISHERS

BOULDER
LONDON

Published in the United States of America in 1999 by
Lynne Rienner Publishers, Inc.
1800 30th Street, Boulder, Colorado 80301

and in the United Kingdom by
Lynne Rienner Publishers, Inc.
3 Henrietta Street, Covent Garden, London WC2E 8LU

© 1999 by Lynne Rienner Publishers, Inc. All rights reserved

Library of Congress Cataloging-in-Publication Data
Great ideas for teaching about Africa   /   edited by Misty L. Bastian and
    Jane L. Parpart.
        p.   cm.
    Includes bibliographical references and index.
    ISBN 1-55587-815-6 (hardcover   :   alk. paper).
    ISBN 1-55587-816-4 (pbk.   :   alk. paper)
        1. Africa—Study and teaching—United States.   I. Bastian, Misty
    L., 1955–   . II. Parpart, Jane L.
    DT19.9.U5G74   1999
    960'.07'073—dc21   98-49639
                                                                            CIP

British Cataloguing in Publication Data
A Cataloguing in Publication record for this book
is available from the British Library.

Printed and bound in the United States of America

       The paper used in this publication meets the requirements
 ∞ of the American National Standard for Permanence of
       Paper for Printed Library Materials Z39.48-1984.

     5 4 3 2 1

CONTENTS

PART 2
CONTROVERSIAL SUBJECTS AND CURRENT ISSUES

PART 3
NEW TECHNOLOGY IN THE CLASSROOM

PART 4
BROADER APPROACHES
TO TEACHING ABOUT AFRICA

Acknowledgments

First, we are grateful for email and email lists such as NUAfrica and H-Africa, which shaped the emergence, process, and completion of this book. Email allowed the editors to keep in touch with each other and with our contributors across the globe as the chapters went through various revisions.

Born as an idea floated by Jean Hay at an annual ASA lunch, *Great Ideas for Teaching About Africa* blossomed as a possibility (though a daunting one!) over another lunch between the editors. Our first task was the identification of potential authors. Rather than following the usual pattern of calling authors and convincing them to contribute, we needed to discover innovative teachers in African studies, many of whom we did not know personally. The Internet came to our rescue. We put out a call for papers via email and received many fascinating replies. Clearly we had an embarrassment of riches.

The Africanist community responded with philosophical ruminations on teaching as well as more concrete, practical suggestions for teaching in the classroom. We decided to focus on the practical, as various books have already explored the broader philosophical issues. Our thanks go out to this community and to the contributors (including those whose chapters could not be included in the final version of the book) for their fresh insights and practical approach.

Jane would like to thank Jean Hay for the idea of the book and for endless support, critiques, and comments on the manuscript. This book would not and could not have happened without her. Thanks go also to colleagues and friends who spent endless hours discussing pedagogy, particularly the gender and development group at Dalhousie and Saint Mary's Universities. Special thanks go to her coeditor, Misty, for her friendship, her insights, her lively prose, and her collegiality—she has been the ideal collaborator. Jane also thanks Misty's husband, John Svatek, whose publishing and computer skills made the manuscript's production possible, and Tim Shaw and her children for their patience and support.

Misty would also like to acknowledge Jean Hay's patience and perseverance, particularly with sometimes very elusive (or do I mean evasive) and busy academics. Jane has been more than a collaborator; she has also been a mentor and friend, two roles that will long survive this phase of our work together. It is impossible to thank everyone who has discussed teaching African topics with me over the years, but I would like to mention—besides the contributors themselves—Doug Anthony, Andy Apter, Mark Auslander, Tim Burke, Jean and John Comaroff, Debra Durham, Mariane Ferme, Rosalind Shaw, Amy Stambach, Brad Weiss, Eiman Zein-Elabdin, the members of the email lists mentioned, as well as the many student and faculty colleagues at Tufts University and Franklin and Marshall College who have taught me so much about what I'm supposed to be teaching them. Finally, I would like to thank John, who should, by now, take on the honorary title of Africanist.

—*The Editors*

INTRODUCTION: TEACHING AFRICA IN A NEW MILLENNIUM

MISTY L. BASTIAN AND JANE L. PARPART

Three scholars began their 1993 overview of African studies by imagining a job candidate at a major research institution who was asked what part the study of Africa had played in her discipline and what it could add to the university as a whole (Bates, Mudimbe, and O'Barr 1993: xi). Since 1993 this scene has been enacted again and again in real-life academic situations. The relevance of regional or area studies has come under attack as postsecondary education in North America and beyond has responded to demands from the "marketplace"—either for more localized or more global programs that will prepare students for a professional life in corporate bodies that transcend national or regional boundaries or for academic inquiry that is more free-floating, less territorially or culturally based (see Guyer 1996). Ironically, the current interdisciplinary and innovative approach in African studies (and other area-based scholarship) is elsewhere being trumpeted as the solution to globally sensitive research and teaching. Thus African studies as a discipline is being challenged at the very moment when its methods have become most celebrated.

Indeed, academic responses to controversial subjects and new technologies have inspired even more innovation in the Africanist classroom. The present volume demonstrates how a number of committed university-level instructors bring African issues and topics into their classrooms, breaking down stereotypical notions about the continent and engaging students with the variety, scope, and potential of societies on one of the largest continents of the world. The chapters are practical and down-to-earth, offering ideas that can be adopted by teachers both inside and outside the African studies rubric. They provide tips for integrating more African mate-

1

rials into classes within both the disciplines and other, more multidisciplinary programs (such as cultural studies or programs on globalization and
political economy). The contributors also illustrate how African materials,
in their specificity, can illuminate some of the most important, universally
relevant questions facing the world today—notably human rights; environmental concerns; the usefulness of nongovernmental organizations and
multinational corporations for "development"; the place of popular culture
and increasingly globalized media in contemporary consciousness; racial
categories and cultural stereotyping; worldwide epidemiological fears;
peacekeeping, mediation, and peacemaking; and gender and its multiple
meanings as well as the impact of new, information-based technologies on
global communication and understanding.

The volume is designed for undergraduate curricula both in universities with well-developed African studies programs and where Africa is a
relatively marginal institutional concern. (For a more general guide to
African studies, see Zell and Lomer 1997.) The separate chapters deal with
specific African and Africanist texts, films, case studies, popular culture
materials, and other, Africa-based scenarios, all meant to enliven the reader's own undergraduate courses whether on Africa or the world.
Contributors also discuss their personal experiences as teachers and students of African topics, lending a more intimate tone to many of the chapters than normally encountered in conventional academic publications and
offering glimpses into the rewards and frustrations associated with introducing innovations into the classroom.

The academic reader can move easily through the chapters, either looking for answers to a particular question (i.e., how to talk about female circumcision with a class or how to find Internet sites dealing with Africa) or
simply browsing, seeking ideas that might spark a new course or help transform an old one. Trainers and development specialists will find many ideas
that can be adapted for workshops and short courses on Africa and global
change. High school teachers will also find material useful for their global
studies courses. Nonacademic readers may look to the chapters for a
glimpse of state-of-the-art undergraduate teaching at the beginning of a
new millennium and learn something about how contemporary academic
culture operates, at least in English-speaking contexts.

THE SECTIONS

We begin the volume with the section "The Arts as Resources for
Teaching." Arts and aesthetics, of course, have been recognized as an area
where Africans and people of African descent have made a great contribution to the world of the twentieth century, and we foresee no decline in

African artistic vibrancy in the century to come. Indeed, many contributors whose chapters fall in other sections (such as Austen, Bastian, Daddieh, Keim, and Ray) pay tribute to the importance of African arts for their own teaching, and most of the other contributors would agree that African aesthetics have influenced their work in some manner. Those contributors whose chapters clearly belonged in this section bring a wide variety of African arts to their pedagogy: cinema, the plastic arts, staged drama, popular music, and various forms of literature.

Dickson Eyoh's chapter on using African cinema to teach about culture and politics starts off the section. Film can be a powerful tool for teaching contemporary students about Africa (as several other authors in the volume aver), since this is a medium students are both familiar with and heartily approve of. Eyoh uses film in his class to give students a better feel for African political life, and he offers several suggestions for using films to introduce North American young people to the intersection of culture and political action.

Rosalind Hackett and Elizabeth Isichei bring their expertise on using the plastic arts for teaching about African religions into this mix. In Chapter 2, Hackett demonstrates the strong connection between religious practice and performance or aesthetics; in Chapter 3, Isichei discusses how she brings art and its relationship to African religions into her courses in New Zealand, using a multimedia approach to interest students who might otherwise be alienated from African topics. Both Hackett and Isichei show how African cases can be used to enliven courses that take religion seriously, as well as the pedagogical gains to be made by integrating African material culture into any course on Africa.

Adeline Masquelier's lively Chapter 4 on popular music in the classroom demonstrates how someone with little musical training can help students listen and think constructively about the place of music in African and other societies. Besides giving the teacher an African popular discography that can be purchased in most major urban centers in North America, Masquelier discusses how particular genres of African music can tell us a great deal about the separation of rural and urban experiences in various countries, youth subcultures in Africa, and resistance to colonial and neocolonial oppressions. Popular music, as she demonstrates, can bring out the best in students, helping them to envision and analyze life in other cultures—and, perhaps, even imagine themselves listening and dancing to this music in Kinshasa, Soweto, Nairobi, or Lagos.

Natalie Sandomirsky, a comparative literature specialist, turns to West and East African literature for her teaching. In Chapter 5, Sandomirsky takes us for a tour of some of the best of West African fiction (with a brief detour at the beginning of the chapter for Kenya's Ngugi), providing teachers with suggestions for how to bring the colonial period or the angst of postcoloniality alive for students through their engagement with a series of novels whose themes build on each other rather dramatically. Sandomirsky's choice of a regional set of readings is designed to inspire others to develop other sets, focusing on other parts of the continent or on different topical questions.

The second section of the volume, "Controversial Subjects and Current Issues," expands our focus on contemporary issues in Africa and beyond to take into account how lecturers are confronting and commenting on controversial subjects in the classroom. Here the contributors confront truly challenging problems and show how African topics require engagement with some of the most thorny questions plaguing North American and European teachers today.

Because of the racial history of the United States, in particular, the editors realized that this volume would have to concern itself with the past and contemporary politics of racial identity in the classroom. To that end, in Chapter 6 Curt Keim gives us the benefit of his long experimentation with using primary documents to teach North American students about the Atlantic slave trade, making suggestions about which documents work well—and which do not—for effectively teaching about these events.

Bill Bravman's chapter on teaching students about African ethnicity, using one case that some students might think they knew about (the Maasai) and another they probably have not heard of (the Taita), is a good corollary for Keim's work. Bravman outlines a course that demonstrates how African ethnic groups have been constructed through the colonial encounter as well as in the postcolonial state, giving students an opportunity to compare and contrast this ethnic construction with those they may be more familiar with at home.

Beyond questions of race, ethnicity, and history, two of our contributors explore new ways to teach about HIV/AIDS in Africa (Stewart) and female circumcision, or "female genital mutilation" (Kratz), in such a way as to overcome stereotypes and misinformation so common among North American and European students. A third contributor (Parpart) considers how best to teach about the concatenation of gender and development. Teachers with a special interest in gender and sexualities will find these three chapters indispensable.

In Chapter 8, Kearsley Stewart lays out a course syllabus that not only problematizes "African AIDS" but also requires the teacher and his or her students to confront their own cultural baggage about disease in general and HIV/AIDS in particular. Along the way, she touches on stereotypes relating to sexuality in Africa, the history of how "African AIDS" has been represented by Western media and current epidemiological debates concerning field tests of all sorts on the continent.

Corinne Kratz's chapter provides much needed guidance on another contentious topic. She takes on the questions that more and more students have about those female operations known as female circumcision or female genital mutilation (FGM), showing with great sensitivity how the debate over these operations has been shaped from both within the continent and outside. Reviewing most of the current literature, Kratz clears a path for teachers to develop their own instructional modules about female circumcision—or simply to answer questions as they arise from students in the classroom. She and Stewart both offer excellent guides to the films and videos that will make classroom presentation on these topics more palatable and productive for all concerned.

Jane Parpart's chapter on teaching about gender and development in a hands-on fashion continues the tone developed by others in this section. In her course, students are required to develop a familiarity with a particular African country and learn about its past and present social conditions as well as current political and economic status. As the students research and work on their own models for development in the African countries they have chosen, they also attend lectures, are involved in small-group work, and engage in structured discussions on broader problems in the development and gender literature. This combination of general information and theoretical modeling paired with working up (and writing up) a viable, gender-focused development project enables students to learn a good deal about the process while developing critical skills that allow them to analyze the larger project of "development" as it is practiced in the late twentieth century.

Continuing Parpart's and Stewart's focus on global issues within an African context, Sandra MacLean, Katherine Orr, and Timothy Shaw use techniques that come from courses developed with peacemaking and peacekeeping professionals in mind. Chapter 11 begins with a concise critique of the idea of security, particularly in relation to Africa, and the contributors suggest that this discussion of recent theoretical transformations in the field is an essential first step for any consideration of peacekeeping and peacemaking materials. The chapter then describes how professional peacemakers' teaching modules can be adapted to modules better suited for undergraduate teaching. These modules combine fairly serious reading, very little lecture, and a good deal of small-group discussion and problem solving, using cases drawn from current African "emergency" situations.

In the third section, "New Technology in the Classroom," the contributors use specific African issues to discuss how to integrate technological innovations in teaching. Chapters in this section are most concerned with computers and the new media generated by computers—particularly how to use (or not to use) the Internet and the World Wide Web to expand students' access to African materials and to the wider world of scholarship now electronically available. The authors grapple with the fact that such scholarship has become both more welcoming—in the sense that more people are able to access academic information—and more daunting because of the sheer volume of information and questions about its accountability.

Tamara Giles-Vernick discusses in Chapter 12 how to bring both high-tech (computer/Internet) and low-tech (foodstuffs and other objects of African material culture) approaches into a class on African environmental history. Whether using scanned images of Africans at work in their local environments or preparing dishes from different parts of the continent with students, she demonstrates how the environment must, on some level, be experienced firsthand before students can begin to comprehend the enormity of the task of preserving it. Her emphasis on student-controlled debates and roundtables on environmental issues and their historical and social contexts provides a model for a much more participatory and immediate teaching style that reinforces students' interests in the topic.

Benjamin Ray and Robert White bring the reader to a new set of virtual pedagogical spaces: the cybermuseum and the email-driven classroom. In Ray's Chapter 13, we learn how he and his students at the University of Virginia developed virtual exhibitions of African art. Students in this course were encouraged to bring their own sense of aesthetics and topical interests to the study of African art—eventually mounting miniexhibitions on the course Web site, made up not only of the images they found most compelling but of labels and small essays on the objects, their social and cultural contexts, and why the students felt these objects spoke to one another. Besides learning Web-building skills, the students found out about the often unspoken criteria that a curator must address when putting together an exhibition. In Chapter 14, White tells the reader how he developed a virtual class on African politics and societies that raised student computing skills enormously while also spurring their (lasting) interest in the continent of Africa. White's chapter is particularly useful as a cautionary tale, however: Technology can swallow the course content; lecturers may find themselves teaching the students more about the nature of the new media than the material in the syllabus.

In Chapter 15, Garth Myers, Jack Livingston, Aimee Stewart, and Sarah Signiski discuss how sophisticated geophysical technologies can be carefully integrated into coursework on Africa. Realizing that the average reader might not be familiar with these technologies but finding them potentially useful for many classroom contexts, Myers and his collaborators discuss, in great detail, what these technologies do and how to bring them to more traditional exercises in geography or environmental studies such as statistical analysis, graphing, and charting from physical data. The authors evaluate the utility of geophysical data about Africa on the Internet, giving some sense of what exactly is "out there" and how to download it once it has been found. They also acknowledge the difficulties inherent in using such large databases and caution the reader about the kinds of computer equipment needed to take advantage of these technologies. Finally, they warn against an uncritical embrace of technology in the face of theoretical and ethical questions about gathering knowledge indiscriminately, especially knowledge that Africans may have no access to themselves.

In the final section of the volume, "Broader Approaches to Teaching About Africa," the contributors move back to a more general level of discussion and consider teaching about Africa at the beginning of the twenty-first century from various broad perspectives. These perspectives have one real commonality: The teacher of African materials must not only bring an understanding of current issues to the seminar table or podium but also deal with the multifarious histories of Africa and African studies in order to make the culturally constructed content of those issues more transparent for students.

In Chapter 16, Ralph Austen looks at a long and productive career of teaching the African civilizations sequence at the University of Chicago and gives the reader a tripartite model (inventing, proclaiming, and deconstructing Africa) of how African studies have been taught since World War II. He then moves on to discuss how his teaching of the African civilizations course has been transformed by his own evolution as an Africanist historian as well as by changes in student interest and understanding of the continent. Austen's solution to these changes has been to move to a "culture area" approach, looking specifically at a region where it can be demonstrated that African people have been engaged with one another for a long period of time. Austen explores the connections and interactions of the peoples in a region through its literature and some carefully chosen scholarly readings.

In Chapter 17, Cyril Daddieh brings another method to the survey, echoing Parpart's claim that country "adoption" helps to focus North American student attention on the realities of life on the continent. Daddieh's pedagogical interest, however, is on having students concentrate on the continent as a whole, engaging them in a learning experience that encompasses the great variety of African social and political experience. He does this, at first, by allowing the students to uncover what they already know about the continent, using a set of ingenious exercises that place Africa within its material and social contexts. Gradually, as the course progresses, the instructor and students collaboratively fill in the empty spaces on the map with which they began. Individual students add immensely to the development of the course by "adopting" a country and reporting on it to the class at large, thereby also becoming responsible for some of the course's content. Eventually the students are asked to take part in a final exercise that mirrors the first one, demonstrating to them concretely the scope of what they have learned.

Philip Zachernuk's chapter could be said to "deconstruct" certain North American notions about the continent as well, but he does this rather differently than Daddieh or Austen. He describes a course that focuses on African intellectuals and how those intellectuals have transformed the world's understanding of Africa and its people. Zachernuk makes a strong case for the necessity of teaching North American and European students about the various intellectual movements that have originated in Africa or among people of African descent in the Black Diaspora. As Zachernuk notes, an active engagement with the products of these intellectuals can destabilize any too-comfortable understanding that North American or European students hold about Western theory versus African emotional knowledge.

It is, perhaps, fitting that Misty Bastian's chapter should end the section that began with Ralph Austen's meditation on his tenure at Chicago, since he was her first undergraduate professor in African studies. Bastian's chapter suggests that we as teachers and "lifelong learners" need to bring a constantly refreshed perspective to our often-obligatory survey courses about Africa. To this end, Bastian discusses how she uses African as well as Africanist scholarly writing, film, and literature in the course. She also gives an example of role playing gone slightly awry to comment on how the Africa survey refuses to become isolated from the North American or European world that surrounds it. Indeed, she believes we should make a virtue out of this necessity, recognizing the power that our own cultures exercise over the imagination of both our students and ourselves as we investigate the societies of Africa.

Each contribution and section of the volume builds on the one before it, demonstrating the power and usefulness of teaching African materials. While the contributors explore African cuisine as a way to understand the relations between people and their environment, take us on a tour of a virtual African art museum, demonstrate how to involve students directly in development planning, or discuss how film and music can engage image- and style-conscious students, we see that the current state of African studies teaching is healthy. These techniques present complex and important information about Africa in ways that attract and hold student attention. They are practical and accessible to most teachers and are easily transported into a variety of teaching contexts while being unashamedly innovative and interdisciplinary.

We live—and teach—in a world where no region is physically so separate from the rest as to be unreachable or in "need" of colonial modes of exploration. The institutions where we work, whether as practicing academics or consultants and development experts, are trying to adapt to the new claims of globalization by demanding courses and training that are more interdisciplinary but less regionally specific. As our contributors demonstrate, teaching and research about Africa continue to be highly interdisciplinary in nature.

Whether focusing on the world at large or on Africa in particular, the techniques developed to teach the complexities of Africa have much to offer those trying to teach about other cultures and our connections to them. The very techniques and innovations developed to explain the complexities of Africa and to counter the unrelievedly negative stereotypes promulgated about the continent are needed if we are to enrich our students' understanding of the wider world in which they must inevitably take their place.

SUGGESTIONS FOR FURTHER READING AND RESOURCES

Bates, Robert H., V. Y. Mudimbe, and Jean O'Barr, eds. 1993. *Africa and the Disciplines: The Contributions of Research in Africa to the Social Sciences and Humanities.* Chicago: University of Chicago Press.

Guyer, Jane I. 1996. *African Studies in the United States: A Perspective.* Atlanta, Ga.: African Studies Association Press.

Zell, Hans M., and Cecile Lomer. 1997. *The African Studies Companion: A Resource Guide and Directory,* 2nd rev. ed. London: Hans Zell.

PART ONE

The Arts as Resources for Teaching

1

TEACHING CULTURE AND POLITICS WITH AFRICAN CINEMA

DICKSON EYOH

Political relations and processes in all places and at all times are culturally mediated. Thus the understanding of politics in any society is bound to be incomplete without a good grasp of that society's cultural makeup. Because the basic business of comparative politics is the study of what is universal and particular about politics in different societies, commonalities and differences in the cultural organization of societies are crucial to that explanation. Teachers of African politics who want students to appreciate how politics is shaped by the cultural relations and symbolic systems of societies that are different from their own are obliged to deal with a number of related problems. I focus in this chapter on two.

The most obvious problem has to do with the relative "cultural illiteracy" of students, as most students taking courses on African politics have neither visited nor lived in an African society. Students differ in levels of sophistication in their knowledge about Africa, and the knowledge they possess is in no small measure formed by representations of Africa and Africans in the Western popular media. Considerable time separates us from the sensationalist travelogues of Victorian explorers and other, colonialist representations of the continent; yet the imagery of Africa in Western popular media continues to be marked by a fascination with the "exotic," the "bizarre," the "abnormal." With a fleeting attention span and fixation on the ingredients of political instability (wars, famines, corruption, communal strife, etc.), reporting of African political affairs in the Western popular media is overburdened by an appetite for stereotypes that accent the "difference" of African societies vis-à-vis Western society. For teachers of African politics, improving the cultural literacy of students means nurturing in them an awareness of the diversity and dynamism of African cultures. But this task is not easily discharged by simply noting and discussing the negative stereotypes of Africa. This problem leads to a second, more significant and vexing one having to do with the conceptual frameworks of political analysis and what can loosely be referred to as the limits of "cultural relativism."

Our lived experiences and internalized conceptions of the proper organization of society and politics are powerful points of reference for how we read, write, and speak about politics in societies different from those into which we were born or with which we are most familiar. Students come to the study of politics in Africa having been socialized into an assumption of the inherent superiority of "Western" over "non-Western" societies. Despite a generalized awareness of the dangers of ethnocentrism, standard models of political analysis do little to challenge this common view. On the contrary, these models are anchored in the presumption that the "Western experience" is the repository of universal standards for evaluating the politics of other regions. This is particularly so in the subfield of political development, which is the orientation of the study of politics in Africa. The concept of political development itself implies a process of maturation from a situation of relative political infancy (the condition of African and other postimperial nation-states of this century) to one of political adulthood (the condition of Western societies).

It may no longer be academically fashionable to designate as primordial the cultural attributes of so-called developing societies, but the logic of primordialism dies hard because it is grounded in a developmentalist paradigm. This paradigm predisposes us to evaluate the ways in which belief systems and culturally embedded notions such as kinship, community, and political participation order individual and collective political practices in relation to how much they facilitate or impede the tortuous march toward political modernity, Western style. The centrality of the state in comparative political development only compounds the problem. It underscores the preoccupation with large-scale political processes (especially economic development and class formation) and ignores or underplays the ways in which the political behavior of individuals and groups is rooted in everyday social practices. The bias implicit in the paradigm is further compounded by a tendency always to resort to the binary constructs of "modernity" and "tradition" when discussing African cultural forms and identities.

AN APPROACH TO CULTURE
AND POLITICS IN POSTCOLONIAL AFRICA

For the past eight years, I have been using films by African directors and African literary works as pedagogic tools that, through images and dialogue, provide a better feel for the texture of everyday life and politics. I do this both in an introductory course on African politics and in an upper-level seminar on political liberalization. This approach is used to counter the tendency in political science scholarship to focus on the building and validation of universal theories rather than on cultural specificities and practices.

The organizing premise of both courses is that frameworks of political inquiry are analytical and ideological models built on implicit or explicit assumptions about desirable pathways to some ideal political system. These assumptions orient explanation of the influences of cultural forces on political relations and processes. Inquiry into the cultural contexts of politics in Africanist political science is conducted through three umbrella topics.

First, we review the modernization and dependency paradigms in order to consider the extent to which they shared a vision of what development entailed and how this vision accounted for the preoccupation with nation-state building and the practices of Westernized elites in the analysis of politics. We explore the way these paradigms encouraged a tendency to project indigenous cultural forms and identities as obstacles to nation-state construction.

Second, we examine debates about the causes or political ramifications of African development crises. We focus on the global political changes that are responsible for the current interest in democratization within international and comparative politics, that is, the extent to which both the widely shared consensus about the political foundations of the crises of African societies and the common use of terms such as "neopatrimonialism," "prebendalism," "overdeveloped" to characterize the postcolonial state presuppose that the liberalization of economies and politics is required to transcend the impasse in African development. We also focus, during this part of the course, on the current popularity of the notion of "civil society" and the related, scholarly emphasis on "associational life" in the analysis of the dynamics of political change within Africa.

In dealing with these issues, we consider how the dominant analysis of political transitions or liberalization condition explanation of the cultural bases of political responses to the African crises. The key question we pose here is the extent to which the heightened attention to the political activities of urban-based middle classes and civic associations, which are seen as the driving force in the resurgence of civil society, is informed, implicitly and explicitly, by a reliance on a pluralist–interest group model of politics and an assumption that African middle classes are bearers of the "universal values" associated with liberal democracy. We examine diverse responses to the crises in order to assess the potential costs of these assumptions for understanding the significance of culture and identity change in shaping the political behavior of different social groups. These responses include the resurgence of communal mobilization and conflict (ethnic, regional, and religious); the mushrooming of fundamentalist spiritual movements on the continent (e.g., American-style evangelical churches); the resilience of witchcraft and sorcery discourses in popular evaluations of the uses of political power; and increased social violence, for which the ever-expanding legions of destitute and alienated urban youth bear substantial responsibility.

The third set of topics is designed to encourage a more discerning analysis of the ways in which the various and often contradictory political responses to African crises are conditioned by the dynamics of culture and identity change. Literature that is influenced by the postmodernist/post-structuralist turns in social and cultural theory and, in particular, writing within the rubric of postcolonial criticism make up the bulk of the readings for this section. Special attention is given here to the reflections of African scholars on the legacies of the colonial encounter and the postcolonial experience. The reason for this is straightforward. Even as their meditations are couched in the language of "universal theory," African scholars bring a deep, socially internalized knowledge to discussions of the meanings and significance of cultural syncretism in their societies; only the most ethnographically sensitive external scholars can arrive at these meanings. We also rely on case studies of colonialism and postcolonial crises to illustrate specific, culturally encoded responses to the pressures of state expansion and economic change.

EXPLORING ISSUES OF CULTURE AND POLITICS THROUGH FILMS

To help prepare students to engage in the discussion of issues and literature with which they often are unfamiliar, we screen films by African directors at the end of the second set of topics. Among the most popular are *Saaraba* by Ahmadou Saaloum Seck (1988) and *Guelwaar* by Ousmane Sembène (1992). Both directors are Senegalese, and the dialogues of their films are in Woolof and French (with English subtitles). In similar but also in divergent ways, their films are commentaries on the travails of postcolonial Senegal and represent African intellectual meditations on the postcolonial experience.

According to a popular Senegalese myth, Saaraba is a utopia. Seck engages this myth to explore the alienation of youth and their quest for escape from the material and moral depredations of postindependence life. Tasmir, the main character, is a young man recently returned to Senegal after a seventeen-year sojourn in France. The society he reenters is one mired in unrelenting poverty and presided over by an economic and political elite for whom state power is a means to the corrupt acquisition of wealth. His businessman uncle is emblematic of this elite, the self-styled agents of the modernization program of postcolonial states. The struggles for survival of the majority of citizens, who are denied the gains of independence, are enacted in urban spaces in which the icons of modernization (luxury cars, multistory office buildings, wide tree-lined boulevards, the comforts of Western-type middle-class homes, etc.) are rudely mocked by the chaos and improvised character of much of the postcolonial city. A barren Sahelian landscape whose capacity to sustain material life appears to have been exhausted centuries ago is the canvas on which the harshness of rural life is etched. In his quest to make sense of the vulgarities of postcolonial life and the struggles against the corrupt elite, Tasmir rejects Westernization in favor of indigenous social practices. His journeys back to his ancestral village lead him to realize the impossibility of a return to an idealized past. The forces of modernization have thoroughly penetrated traditional (rural) society, compounding its material hardships and corroding its value system. Villagers understand who are the agents and beneficiaries of a modernization program of which they are the casualties but seem incapable of organized resistance. Their contempt for predatory elites is combined with a grudging admiration for the possibilities represented by elite ill-gotten wealth. Organized religion and indigenous belief systems offer the poor a rich vocabulary to articulate their moral indignation at ruling elite practices. But these belief systems also require their adherence to the dictates of tradition, which excuse the subordination of women, advise spiritual escape from the problems of the contemporary world, and recommend submissiveness to established authority. Overwhelmed by the contradictions of postcolonial society, Tasmir takes to the world of alienated urban youth. Drugs, casual sex, and the pulsating rhythms of Western popular music provide succor to these anguished youths surrounded by the stench of shantytowns. In this world, the icons of Western popular culture are the referents for identities, and the glitter of Western materialism offers a means for Tasmir to escape to a different life. In the film's final scene, Tasmir survives a motorcycle accident in which his fellow traveler, a village mechanic finally on his long-dreamed-of journey to Saaraba, perishes. The mechanic's parting words bring out the film's message: Confronting the realities of the present, rather than escaping into the past or into dreamworlds, is the only effective path toward a less malign future.

Usually advertised as a comedy, *Guelwaar* is an economical film with, in characteristic Sembène style, a simple plot. It turns on the events surrounding a funeral in a provisional town, the sort of place where city and village forms and lifestyles effortlessly merge. Being buried is Pierre Thioune, popularly known as Guelwaar (the noble one), a community leader and a Catholic who has devoted his life to battling political corruption and external dependency. When his family, led by his son Barthelemy—home from Paris for the funeral—arrives at the morgue to collect Guelwaar's corpse, it cannot be found. Police are brought in to investigate. The initial suspicion is that the dead body has been stolen by "fetishists," but it is later discovered that it has been mistakenly handed over to a Muslim family from a neighboring village and already interred in a Muslim cemetery.

At the heart of the struggle over Guelwaar's corpse is the clash of systems of belief (Christianity, Islam, and witchcraft), social identities, and cultural practices that is the legacy of colonialism and the substance of communal conflict in postcolonial Senegalese society. To leaders of the Muslim community, whose religion mandates burial within twenty-four hours after death, the demand to disinter a corpse suspected to be Guelwaar's becomes a Christian or "infidel"-led affront. Guelwaar's son, who considers himself more French than Senegalese, can barely contain his disdain for "traditional" ways of life that make resolution of a matter so straightforward as ownership of a corpse the object of interminable negotiations.

As events progress, the moral claims of representatives of both communities are revealed to be as much about advancing individual and class interests as defending community religious and cultural practices. The local mayor has been using food aid to enrich himself. In his steadfast opposition to foreign charity as a manifestation of the collective debasement of Senegalese society, Guelwaar had positioned himself as the mayor's nemesis. The Muslim leaders who approach the mayor to back their case against Guelwaar's family represent an opportunity to fortify his political coalition against the opponents of food aid. Both parties implicitly understand that improved allocations of food aid to the leaders of the Muslim community are part of the political bargain. Guelwaar's life is a metaphor for the moral ambiguities of postcolonial subjects caught in the vortex of state expansion and commercialization of economic relations. A justifiable indignation at the consequences of external dependence motivated his opposition to food aid and refusal to accept any for his family. To sustain this opposition, at the cost of much pain to his wife, Guelwaar obliged his family to rely on financial support from his daughter, who worked as a prostitute in Dakar. Through the involvement of a motley crew of policemen, petty bureaucrats, and corrupt politicians, the film fashions poignant commentaries on how the organization and exercise of state power is complicated and easily overwhelmed by the contending rationalities, identities, and values of the plural communities that inhabit postcolonial nation-spaces.

As these summaries suggest, the kaleidoscopic images of differently ordered social spaces and places—of dress styles that symbolize the haphazard (and sometimes calculated) blending of local and external influences, diverse religious and ritual practices, and the polyphony of public discourse that is sustained by constant shifts in linguistic registers—make these films by African directors rich sources for discussions of the social tensions induced by identity and cultural change on political relations and processes. These two films have been particularly effective in enabling critical class discussions of the ways in which class relations and political practices in African societies are conditioned by their hybrid cultural and symbolic systems.

However labeled, middle classes and other elites have always been privileged as the primary agents of change in past and current frameworks of political analysis. These films provide a way to rethink these assumptions. We begin by soliciting students' views of the main factors used to distinguish middle classes and ruling elites from other social groups in the films they have just watched. Invariably, higher levels of education and the socioeconomic status conferred by education are the most commonly identified factors. We then confront the question, again using the films as our data, of whether the emphasis on higher levels of education is, indeed, an adequate premise for drawing conclusions about the constitution of the social and political identities of elites and their everyday interactions with subordinate groups.

In addressing this issue, we focus on a salient theme in the reflections of African intellectuals on the postcolonial experience: the ways in which the knowledge and experiences defining the social and political identities of intellectuals and their middle-class compatriots alienate them from the majority of their fellow citizens who are consigned to the margins of state power. The archetypes of elites in these films convey powerfully how elite identities are molded by their implication in the material world associated with (Western) modernity as well as the vibrant "indigenous" cultural traditions of their societies. Separated from the subordinate classes by their Westernization, African elites nonetheless remain bonded to these classes by ties of kinship, language, religion, and ethnicity.

Scenes from the films are used to orient discussion of ways in which the plural identities of citizens and the hybrid cultural forms of postcolonial societies shape everyday encounters between elite and subordinate social groups. An example is scenes from *Saaraba* of Tasmir's uncle in his well-appointed (typically Western) business offices, at home, and in meetings in the village to deal with an arranged marriage of a young woman—made pregnant by Tasmir—to a wealthy, educated, urban politician. In the latter scenes, it is obvious that traditional precepts of honor (the requirement that one must stand by agreements entered) inform the young woman's parents' insistence that she must marry the politician. Tasmir's uncle appears uncomfortable with an arrangement that threatens to deny the union of two young people in love. Contrary to what might be expected of a man with his education and wealth, he comes across as a person with a deep sensitivity to the values of his ancestral community. The high esteem in which he is held by villagers is an acknowledgment of the dignity and respect that mark his interactions with them. Although his intention is to make possible the marriage of Tasmir and the young woman, his interventions in the deliberations proceed from an assumption that the system of values mandating the arranged marriage has to be accommodated, if not defended. The urban-centered universe of state power within which he operates demands that he cater to the sensibilities of the politician, a class ally and an asset to the advance of his business, which is dependent on public contracts. Like all characters in both films who are representative of different segments of postcolonial elites and middle classes, Tasmir's uncle epitomizes individuals whose concept of self involves maintaining a balance between the social relations and cultural practices that define them as different from villagers (or subordinate classes) and those that must be respected in order to preserve good standing in the smaller "traditional" village worlds in which they began their life journeys. For subordinate groups and elites, everyday life requires negotiating overlapping social, cultural, economic, and political networks.

We concentrate on specific problems to elaborate the implications for rational-scale political organization and behavior of the tensions and ambiguities that surround interactions across class and spatial boundaries. Two examples will suffice. We consider the extent to which the European-derived languages of state constrain easy political conversation between ruling elites and the vast majority of their fellow citizens, who are illiterate or lack facility in these languages. More specifically, students are asked to reflect on how the language barrier, which is symptomatic of the elite-mass cultural gulf, constitutes a major handicap on the ability of elites to communicate the values of the universal ideologies to which they are drawn or to mobilize support behind collective national objectives. Scenes that comment on the equation of development with Westernization by middle classes and ruling elites are invoked to elucidate the many dimensions of this problem. Another example is the ways in which plural systems of belief and indigenous modes of political organization entail conflicting premises for evaluating the morality or legitimacy of political authority. We consider the difficulties these differences present to the management of state power, which rests on European-derived judicial norms and institutions. *Guelwaar*'s evocative scenes of state officials and security agents— who must deal seriously with the suspicion that a corpse has been stolen by fetishists and mediate the rival claims of Christians and Muslims over ownership of the corpse—throw into bold relief the ordinariness of these tensions.

Discussions of these and related issues set the stage for reconsideration of biases in the analysis of the resurgence of civil society and political change. The unflattering characterizations of political and economic elites in these films accord with their generally negative representation in explanations of the roots of the crises of development and the postcolonial state. They also reinforce the intuitive belief of students in the imperative of democracy for development and their identification with the ambitions of social groups that are portrayed as leading the struggles for political reform. To dissuade from simple-minded assumptions about the capacity of middle classes to engender radical shifts in state-society relations, we use opposed characters from films, for instance, Tasmir in *Saaraba* and Barthelemy in *Guelwaar*. Tasmir elicits easy admiration because of his apparent disgust with the corruptions of postcolonial life and a program of social change that is informed by the "traditional" values of his society. In contrast, Barthelemy's initial appearance is always greeted with derisive laughter, and the disapproval of his character is unabated at the end of the film. The analysis of both characters allows for inferences about the type of values that lead to protest against and that are conducive to the reproduction of the postcolonial political malaise. Evaluation of the behavior of both characters in the context of their interactions with "ordinary" people also affirms that regardless of how middle-class elements are ideologically positioned, they share a common alienation from subordinate classes.

As younger or aspirant members of middle classes and ruling elites, these characters and their travails are good material with which to frame discussions of the role of youth in contemporary politics. Literature that addresses the demographic preponderance of youth in African countries, the bleak material prospects that presently confront even the best educated among them, and the ways in which the identities and political practices of urban youth are inflected by international and other cultural flows makes apparent the sources of youth alienation. Students, understandably, identify easily with the alienation and rebelliousness of other youth. We engage *Saaraba*'s representations of how this alienation is enacted in everyday life to debate the question of whether youth alienation and political practices should be perceived as a force for desirable political change (however defined), as support for the status quo, or as an ambivalent phenomenon. In a manner not so different from scholarly work, these representations point to the ambiguity of the identities and behavior of youth: their discomfort with existing social orders but subscription to the materialism that drives the corruption in their societies.

Both courses conclude with the vexing question of whether the institutional protocols of liberal democracy (multiparty elections, the protection of individual rights, freedom of expression, etc.) are a sufficient condition to redress the crisis of postcolonial state legitimacy. This question is never resolved. My hope, which is satisfied by class comments, is that students leave with a strong awareness of the diversity and complexities of Africa's shifting cultural forms and social identities, the ways they imprint political relations and processes, and their continuation as significant, if not determinant, factors in the ongoing struggles of Africans to transform inherited nation-spaces into viable (national) political communities and to fashion more legitimate systems of governance. The quality of class discussions and the comments of students over the years confirm that films contribute significantly to their appreciation of the relation of culture, identity, and the production of politics in postcolonial African societies. Films ease the complexity of issues that are dealt with in the relevant, and usually very theoretical, scholarly literature.

SUGGESTIONS FOR
FURTHER READING AND RESOURCES

PRINTED MATERIAL

El-Kenz, Ali. 1996. "Youth and Violence." In *Africa Now: People, Policies, Institutions,* ed. S. Ellis. Portsmouth, N.H.: Heinemann; London: James Curry.

Eyoh, Dickson. 1998. "Social Realist Cinema and Representations of Power in African Nationalist Discourse." *Research in African Literatures* 19, 2 (Summer): 112–127.

Irele, Abiola. 1992. "In Praise of Alienation." In *The Surreptitious Speech: Presence Africaine and the Politics of Otherness, 1947–1987,* ed. V. Y. Mudimbe. Chicago: University of Chicago Press.

Jegede, Dele. 1995. "Popular Culture in Urban Africa." In *Africa,* 3rd ed., ed. P. Martin and P. O'Meara. Bloomington: Indiana University Press.

Mbembe, Achille, and Janet Riotman. 1996. "Figures of the Subject in Times of Crisis." *Public Culture* 7, 3: 323–352.

Nixon, P. J. "'Uneasy Lies the Head': Politics, Economics, and Continuity of Belief Amongst the Yoruba in Nigeria." *Comparative Studies in Society and History* 33, 1: 56–85.

Triulzi, Allesandro. 1995. "African Cities, Historical Memory, and Street Buzz." In *The Post-Colonial Question,* ed. I. Chambers and L. Curti. London: Routledge.

Samoff, Joel. 1994. "Triumphalism, Tarzan, and Other Influences: Teaching About Africa in the 1990s." In *African Studies and the Undergraduate Curriculum,* ed. A. Samatar et al. Boulder: Lynne Rienner.

Schatzberg, Michael. 1993. "Power, Legitimacy, and 'Democratization' in Africa." *Africa* 63, 4: 445–461.

FILMS

Seck, Ahmadou Saaloum. 1988. *Saaraba.* Senegal/France coproduction. 86 minutes in French and Woolof with English subtitles. San Francisco: California Newsreel.

Sembène, Ousmane. 1992. *Guelwaar: An African Legend for the 21st Century.* Senegal/France coproduction. 115 minutes in French and Woolof with English subtitles. New York: New Films; and Vancouver: Idera.

2

TEACHING AFRICAN RELIGIONS THROUGH ART AND LITERATURE

ROSALIND I. J. HACKETT

IN MEMORY OF KOFI E. AGOVI

Teaching about religion, about the ways in which people conceptualize and act upon the places, events, and individuals they hold to be sacred, has never presented itself as an easy task. Teaching about African religions—I include here the many indigenous traditions of Africa, Christianity, Islam, and the African-derived religions of the New World—constitutes an even more daunting challenge given the prejudices and lack of knowledge about Africa that most students in North America and Europe bring to the classroom. Mobilized by these concerns, a group of us in the African Religions group of the American Academy of Religion assembled a few years ago to discuss the pedagogical challenges of our field. Our combined efforts were published in the AAR's *Spotlight on Teaching* (Houchins and Wickler 1993). (See also an earlier foray in a special issue of *Religion* [Lewis 1990]). In this chapter, I present some of the salient features of these discussions together with reflections and suggestions from my own teaching and research experiences in the United States, Africa, and Europe over the past twenty years. By so doing, I hope to make a case not just for a more critical lens on the teaching of African religions but also for the inclusion of such a rich and challenging subject in any African studies curriculum.

One of the primary concerns for any scholar or teacher is creating academic space and legitimacy for the subject matter. Religion is perceived by many outsiders as a minority subject. This perception belies not only student interest but the undeniable political and cultural significance of religion as a global phenomenon. African religions generally suffer the indignity of being cast into the pit of "primitivism" with its attendant exotic and ahistorical connotations, leaving little room for exploration of the historical forces that have shaped Africa's complex religious landscape. Furthermore, scholars with training in other (Western or Eastern) religious traditions may be put off by the absence of written texts. So it is imperative to address at an early stage the underlying stereotypes that inform many Western, whether academic or media, perspectives on the subject. This can be done in a number of ways. One can read texts that address underlying notions of primitivism in Western thought and culture such as that found in Clifford (1988). He delivers a forceful critique of a controversial exhibition held at the Museum of Modern Art in 1984 entitled *"Primitivism" in 20th Century Art: Affinity of the Tribal and the Modern*. There is also Lutz and Collins's *Reading National Geographic* (1993). These provocative pieces seek to reveal the racist and sexist underpinnings of Western representations of (and yearnings for) the primitive "other." Students may rethink their viewing of Tarzan movies, but most say they will not cancel their *National Geographic* subscriptions!

Alternatively one could home in on African critiques of Western and Western-influenced interpretations of African religions through the trenchant work of the cultural nationalist Okot p'Bitek. In *African Religions in Western Scholarship* (1971), he argued vehemently that anthropology was a colonialist and imperialist enterprise. Less ideologically charged is the useful historical analysis by David Westerlund (1985) of the evolution of Africanist scholarly discourse on African religions and the more recent publication *The Study of Religions in Africa* (Platvoet, Cox, and Olupona 1996), which contains several important contributions by African scholars. One appreciates, for example, the pressures of political and cultural nationalism on scholarship to articulate and legitimate African religious systems in terms of their unity rather than their ethnographic diversity. The founding fathers of scholarship on African "traditional" religions, notably John Mbiti, E. Bolaji Idowu, and Geoffrey Parrinder, were motivated in part by a desire to frame and justify the study of Africa's indigenous religious heritage for a wider scholarly audience. In doing so, and in part because of their theological lenses, they employed homologies drawn from Western Christian thought. As Rosalind Shaw (1990) has so significantly shown, the resultant concepts and structures were recycled in African popular discourse. All of these provide important entry points for students to gain insights into the politics and power relations of a subject.

The issue of the unity (i.e., common themes) and diversity of African traditional religions never fails to generate discussion. It also leads to questions of cosmological structure, namely the monotheistic or polytheistic character of African traditional religious thought and praxis. Evans-

Pritchard's (1956) work on the Nuer of Sudan is popular for its emphasis on the high god concept, as is Bolaji Idowu's (1973) notion of "diffused monotheism" for its explanation of Yoruba thought regarding the relationship between the supreme being and lesser divinities (which he posits as "lieutenants" or emanations of the supreme being). Ultimately these imported labels, particularly of the dichotomous variety, are misleading in terms of illustrating the fluid diversity (this point is made by Ikenga-Metuh [1981]) and unhelpful in avoiding the pitfalls of essentialism and generalization. A text that does more justice to the fluidity and complexity of African religious ideas and praxis is Wendy James's *The Listening Ebony* (1988).

In my own course on African religions, I address in a number of ways the challenge of dealing with a continent of more than fifty countries with more than 2,000 ethnic groups and their attendant distinct cultures and religions. I particularly like Basil Davidson's film *Mastering a Continent* (of his *Africa* series) for the way it looks at different African societies with reference to significant historical developments and geographical factors while highlighting the powers of Africans to adapt successfully, even if in culturally diverse ways, to their environments. Davidson's message that there is no correlation between technological sophistication or "civilization" and religious complexity registers forcefully with many students. I find that after students have viewed this film, it helps to tackle some of the key themes of ancestors, concepts of evil and personhood, ritual practice such as sacrifice and spirit possession, and the diversity of conceptions of the divine. (Ben Ray's [1976] textbook *African Religions* is helpful here, as is his "African Religions" in the *Encyclopedia of Religion* [1987].) The topic of witchcraft never fails to elicit interest, but it must be treated sensitively and "unexotically," as my late friend and colleague Professor Kofi E. Agovi insisted. In fact, he was highly influential in alerting me, early on in my career, to the significance of my choice of subjects and terms as a teacher and scholar. Several years of teaching in Nigerian universities and schools also made me rethink many of the concepts and premises I had been programmed with (namely "primitive" and "primal"). Perhaps that is why I like the work of I. M. Lewis (1986), who helps turn many notions of African witchcraft on their head by discussing Europeans' own connections to witchcraft (even if he failed to apply the same critical lens to his discussion of gender issues). The ethnographic film *Witchcraft Among the Azande* provides a useful base for discussing the multidimensional and multidisciplinary aspects of the phenomenon of witchcraft. Misty Bastian's (1993) perceptive analysis of articles about witchcraft in the Nigerian popular press reveals how the idiom may give meaning to urban life experiences such as political corruption and economic deprivation.

Ultimately, however, I spend more time focusing (with varying degrees of emphasis) on specific peoples such as the Zulu, the Akan, the Yoruba, and the Igbo. These are in part chosen because of my own experience with the Yoruba and Igbo in Nigeria over many years, and more recently with the Akan in Ghana and the Zulu in South Africa, but also because of the available literature. For example, E. Thomas Lawson's (1986) small text on the Zulu and the Yoruba, *Religions of Africa,* is both reliable and useful. Yoruba scholars themselves have produced numerous critical renderings of their own religious, philosophical, and artistic worlds. Such accounts not only encourage students to work with indigenous categories such as *ase* (the power to make things happen) but, because of their sheer complexity and depth (see Abimbola 1986 for an example), tend to dispel very quickly any lingering notions of "primitive," small-scale societies. The various diasporan transformations of Yoruba religion and culture, whether as Santeria or Vodou, further endear the Yoruba to students as a primary case study. As a footnote to any case studies, there should be a healthy class discussion of the constructed and contested notions of "the Yoruba," "the Igbo," and so on.

I am pleased that students tend to prefer the opportunity of exploring religious ideas and practices in particular cultural contexts. Such an approach also offsets the risks of resorting to overgeneralization and essentialization. It does not take long to persuade them that the reified category of religion as they have generally understood it is challenged by what they learn regarding the African context. By the same token, conventional approaches to the study of religion, which privilege the written text and doctrinal formulations, reveal themselves to be inadequate for understanding the connections between religious and political activity, between religious and social structure, and between religious expression and material culture in the predominantly oral cultures of sub-Saharan Africa. A multidimensional and multimedia approach does more justice in this regard whether it is in the form of films, novels, slides, primary sources such as newspapers or magazines, artifacts, or speakers. Novels such as Chinua Achebe's *Arrow of God* (1969) and Ngugi wa Thiong'o's *The River Between* (1965) give students an unforgettable window onto the disruptive effects of colonialism and Christianity on traditional African lifestyles. Several of my students claim never to have read a more influential novel than Cheik Hamidou Kane's *Ambiguous Adventure* (1972). Excerpts from Wole Soyinka's (1985) amusing play *Requiem for a Futurologist* go down well when trying to explain the religious pluralization of many parts of Africa today. There are all manner of audiovisual and print materials available on the burgeoning revivalist Christian movements in many parts of Africa—several of which have strong connections with North American evangelists. The multilateral spread of Pentecostalism and its transformations in the African context—whether manifested as popular videos depicting warring good and evil forces or best-selling gospel tapes—both surprise and engage students.

Another genre of book has its pedagogical uses: the culture broker's account of "traditional" culture for a Western readership. Two of the more reliable accounts are by the Kongo scholar Simon Bockie (1993), who pays special attention to issues of death and evil in his *Death and the Invisible Powers,* and by Malidoma Patrice Somé (1994), who has really developed his intermediary status to professional levels, not least in his *Of Water and the Spirit: Ritual Magic and Initiation in the Life of an African Shaman.* This type of account calls for instructors to raise the critical issue of authorship and readership. They may find that there are students in the class who can helpfully relate these questions to the Native American situation, which has an impressive range of propagandist and analytical texts by "insiders" and "outsiders" alike.

Because of a particular project I was invited to undertake some years ago, namely the volume *Art and Religion in Africa* (Hackett 1996), I have come to view the artistic dimension as especially revealing and useful for the scholar and teacher of African religions. Although appreciative of the visual and performing arts in Africa from an early stage (not least because I was exposed to their importance while living in West Africa), I was not trained to "see" the iconic and aniconic forms of religious expression. Yet African art is an art of ideas. It is an important medium for communicating, sometimes in appropriately oblique ways, knowledge about the spirit world. Because many African cultures are predominantly oral and nonliterate, the various art forms provide important points of entry into people's conceptual worlds. They are not bound by resemblance and may experiment with form to make visible the force or meaning. Whether shrine sculptures or masquerades or divination objects, they are not only expressive but also transformative.

My book *Art and Religion in Africa* is subdivided into manageable topics for a class period or two. There is also discussion of and reference to the work of many others, which could be followed up for research and other projects. Each chapter can be illustrated with the films that are available—for example, the Chicago Art Institute's *The World Began at Ile-Ife* (Marriott 1990) underlines the importance of creation myths and their performance—in this case for the Yoruba. *Ethos, Cosmos, and Hierarchy* can be accompanied by *Kingdom of Bronze* (Attenborough 1975), both in *The Tribal Eye* series. The fact that African artworks do not just represent but are believed to make present spirit forces or ancestors, for example, comes across well in the film *Yaaba Sore: The Path of the Ancestors* (produced by the University of Iowa). Masquerades held to facilitate the transition of individuals from one status to another or from this world to the next is conveyed by the film on the Dogon *Behind the Mask* (Attenborough 1975), also in the *Disappearing World* series. A feature film such as *Yeelen* may serve to illustrate the role of Bamana secret societies.

Even with no training in art studies, students soon start to see the connections among form, symbol, and myth in the ritual context. They will discern the religious significance of the form of images—as in the kneeling woman who symbolizes for the Yoruba the correct attitude of devotion and submission vis-à-vis the deity or in the superhuman appearance of the *egungun* ancestral masquerades, also of the Yoruba, with their voluminous cloth structures. Likewise, they learn about the choice of materials employed to construct the image—as in the aggressive Kongo *minkisi,* whose apotropaic qualities that drive away evil spirits are expressed in the multiple metal wedges and nails driven into the wooden human or animal form. An accumulation of materials—beads, rope, cloth, feathers, packets of medicine, shells—connotes the mysterious powers of an object, as in the case of Fon *bocio* figures. The Basinjom masquerade of the Ejagham and Efik peoples of the Cross River region of Nigeria and Cameroon is distinguished by its movements and its composite form, gliding darkly and threateningly through the community in search of witches. Many African artworks combine an ensemble of symbolic devices condensing a range of meanings, some known to the whole community, some known to specific groups defined by initiation or gender, for example. Furthermore, a complex variety of agents and processes may be required to activate the objects for ritual use.

Focusing on material and expressive culture is salutary in that it reveals to students that power may be concealed or embodied in the least attractive host, and not in the most prominent or colorful piece. But it is that very concealment or containment that reveals the power of the object or the person with whom it might be associated. This type of perspective is particularly important in relation to understanding gender issues. The caricaturing and humoring of women, notably those older women whose powers may turn into the destructive force of witchcraft, is a central feature of the Gelede festival of the Yoruba of western Nigeria. But it is also a recognition of the central importance of women's procreative powers to the smooth functioning of society, and the ritual drama constitutes a forum for the resolution of male-female relations. Atop Yoruba staffs and crowns often sits a bird, the symbol of transformative power and nighttime activities—associated in particular with powerful women or witches and their integral role in constituting authority. This image is readily available in the growing repertoire of books and catalogs on Yoruba and African art. It hardly needs stating that a trip to a museum to see some African art will be a high point of any course—especially if the students have prior knowledge of the pieces.

So just as a focus on art and performance invites the student to a more nuanced as well as embodied perspective on religious ideas and practices, it also permits an understanding of religious change by revealing how people might incorporate or reject new elements, whether Islamic or Christian (this is treated in the conclusion to my book). By studying the African-derived religions in the New World, for example, Santeria or Vodou, students can get a real sense of the transformative capacities of African religions. By reading texts such as Karen McCarthy Brown's (1991) acclaimed *Mama Lola: A Vodou Priestess in Brooklyn* or Joseph M. Murphy's (1988) *Santería: An African Religion in America* or viewing films such as *Legacy of the Spirits* (1986) or *Bahía: Africa in the Americas* (Brewer 1988), students are quick to perceive the dissonance between the images of religions generated by practitioners and those, more negative, representations constructed by the media and Hollywood in particular.

The books by Murphy and Brown also have the added bonus of raising the controversial question of subjectivity in academic discourse with their respective "initiations" into the objects of their study. The anthropologist Michael Jackson (1989) sought to steer a middle path between subjectivism and objectivism in his lucid and moving account—*Paths Toward a Clearing*—of Kuranko daily life and thought in Sierra Leone. Paul Stoller (1987) claims he went further by developing his magical powers through initiated apprenticeship to a Songhay sorcerer in Niger. There is never a student in the class who does not have an opinion about which scholar went too far or which one did not go far enough!

In sum, the religious dimension affords teachers and students a magnificent opportunity to explore not just African belief systems and ritual practices but also artistic expression, cultural trends, political power, and social relations. Resources are abundant now in terms of films, books, and CD-ROMs. Students can "visit" an African art collection at their leisure and at virtually no cost. Likewise they can communicate on the Internet with African religious specialists and bookstores via their Web pages. Studying religion in Africa involves not just utilizing a treasure trove of sources but also "seeing" Africa in a wealth of important new ways. This approach can provide much-needed counterimages to the pictures of suffering humans in war-torn zones or happy animals in serene, open spaces that regrettably dominate the Western popular media.

ACKNOWLEDGMENT

I wish to thank Professor Ulrich Berner and members of the Religionswissenschaft seminar on method and theory at the University of Bayreuth for their most helpful comments on this chapter.

SUGGESTIONS FOR
FURTHER READING AND RESOURCES

PRINTED MATERIALS

Abimbola, Wande. 1986. "An Appraisal of African Systems of Thought." In *The Arts and Civilization of Black and African Peoples*, vol. 2, ed. J. O. Okpaku et al. New Rochelle, N.Y.: Third Press International, 11–29.

Abiodun, Rowland. 1994. "Ase: Verbalizing and Visualizing Creative Power Through Art." *Journal of Religion in Africa* 24, 4 (November): 294–322.

Achebe, Chinua. 1969. *Arrow of God*. New York: Anchor Books.

Bastian, Misty L. 1993. "'Bloodhounds Who Have No Friends': Witchcraft and Locality in the Nigerian Popular Press." In *Modernity and Its Malcontents: Ritual and Power in Postcolonial Africa,* ed. Jean Comaroff and John Comaroff. Chicago: University of Chicago Press, 129–166.

Baum, Robert M. 1993. "Teaching the History of African Religions." *Spotlight on Teaching* 1, 2 (May): 3–4.

Blier, Suzanne Preston. 1995. *African Vodun: Art, Psychology, and Power*. Chicago: University of Chicago Press.

Bockie, Simon. 1993. *Death and the Invisible Powers: The World of Kongo Belief*. Bloomington: Indiana University Press.

Brown, Karen McCarthy. 1991. *Mama Lola: A Vodou Priestess in Brooklyn*. Berkeley and Los Angeles: University of California Press.

Clifford, James. 1988. "Histories of the Tribal and the Modern." In *The Predicament of Culture*. Cambridge: Harvard University Press, 189–214.

Drewal, Henry John, and Margaret Thompson Drewal. 1983. *Gelede: Art and Female Power Among the Yoruba*. Bloomington: Indiana University Press.

Drewal, Henry John, and John Pemberton III with Rowland Abiodun. 1989. *Yoruba: Nine Centuries of African Art and Thought*. New York: Center for African Art.

Evans-Pritchard, E. E. 1956. *Nuer Religion*. Oxford: Oxford University Press.

Hackett, Rosalind I. J. 1996. *Art and Religion in Africa*. London and New York: Cassell.

Houchins, Sue, and Kathleen O'Brien Wickler. 1993. "African Religions and Their Literary Representations." *Spotlight on Teaching* 1, 2 (May): 2–3.

Idowu, E. Bolaji. 1963. *Olodumare: God in Yoruba Belief*. New York: Praeger.

———. 1973. *African Traditional Religion: A Definition*. London: Longman.

Ikenga-Metuh, Emefie. 1981. *God and Man in African Religion: A Case Study of the Igbo*. London: Geoffrey Chapman.

Jackson, Michael. 1989. *Paths Toward a Clearing: Radical Empiricism and Ethnographic Inquiry*. Bloomington: Indiana University Press.

James, Wendy. 1988. *The Listening Ebony: Moral Knowledge, Religion, and Power Among the Uduk of Sudan*. Oxford: Clarendon Press.

Kane, Cheikh Hamidou. 1972. *Ambiguous Adventure*. Westport, Conn.: Heinemann.

Lawal, Babatunde. 1996. *The Gelede Spectacle: Art, Gender, and Social Harmony in African Culture*. Seattle: University of Washington Press.

Lawson, E. Thomas. 1986. *Religions of Africa*. New York: Harper and Row.

Lewis, I. M. 1986. *Religion in Context: Cults and Charisma*. Cambridge: Cambridge University Press.

Lewis, James R. 1990. "Images of Traditional African Religions in Surveys of World Religions." *Religion* 20 (October): 311–322.

Lindsay, Arturo, ed. 1996. *Santería Aesthetics in Contemporary Latin American Art*. Washington and London: Smithsonian Institution Press.

Lutz, Catherine A., and Jane L. Collins. 1993. *Reading National Geographic*. Chicago: University of Chicago.

Murphy, Joseph M. 1988. *Santería: An African Religion in America*. Boston: Beacon.

———. 1990. "Black Religion and 'Black Magic': Prejudice and Projection in Images of African-Derived Religions." *Religion* 20 (October): 323–338.

Ngugi wa Thiong'o (James Ngugi). 1965. *The River Between*. London: Heinemann.

Nooter, Mary H., ed. 1993. *Secrecy: African Art That Conceals and Reveals*. New York: Museum for African Art.

p'Bitek, Okot. 1971. *African Religions in Western Scholarship*. Nairobi: Kenya Literature Bureau.

Platvoet, J. G., J. L. Cox, and J. K. Olupona, eds. 1996. *The Study of Religions in Africa: Past, Present, and Prospects*. Cambridge: Roots and Branches.

Ray, B. 1976. *African Religions*. Englewood Cliffs, N.J.: Prentice-Hall.

———. 1987. "African Religions." *Encyclopedia of Religion*, Vol. 1. New York: Macmillan.

Shaw, Rosalind. 1990. "The Invention of 'African Traditional Religion.'" *Religion* 20 (October): 339–354.

Somé, Malidoma Patrice. 1994. *Of Water and the Spirit: Ritual Magic and Initiation in the Life of an African Shaman*. New York: Tarcher.

Soyinka, Wole. 1985. *Requiem for a Futurologist*. London: Rex Collings.

Stoller, Paul, and Cherly Olkes. 1987. *In Sorcery's Shadow: A Memoir of Apprenticeship Among the Songhay of Niger*. Chicago: University of Chicago Press.

Thompson, Robert Farris. 1983. *Flash of the Spirit: African and Afro-American Art and Philosophy*. New York: Vintage Books.

Westerlund, David. 1985. *African Religion in Western Scholarship*. Stockholm: Almqvist & Wiksell.

FILMS AND RECORDINGS

Art and Life in Africa Project. 1996 (rev. 1998). University of Iowa.

Attenborough, David. 1975. *Behind the Mask,* part 2 of the series *The Tribal Eye.* New York: Time-Life Films.

———. 1975. *Kingdom of Bronze,* part 6 of the series *The Tribal Eye.* New York: Time-Life Films.

Brewer, Geovanni. 1988. *Bahía: Africa in the Americas*. Berkeley: University of California Extension Media Center.

Marriott, Celia. 1990. *The World Began at Ile-Ife: Meaning and Function in Yoruba Art*. Chicago: Art Institute of Chicago.

Witchcraft Among the Azande. 1984 (*Disappearing World* Series).

3

AFRICAN "TRADITIONAL" RELIGIONS: A MULTIDISCIPLINARY AND MULTIMEDIA APPROACH

ELIZABETH ISICHEI

I teach two courses on Africa in a religious studies department in New Zealand: a second-year course on "traditional" religion in black Africa and a third-year course on new religious movements, which includes neotraditional/syncretistic movements such as Mumbo in Kenya and Mbiti in Gabon as well as the Aladura and Zionist churches and the Brotherhood of the Cross and Star, which falls somewhere in between. This chapter focuses on the first of these courses. (For an introduction to the new religious movements, including courses on various aspects of Christianity in Africa, see Isichei 1995).

WHOM AM I TEACHING?

The class consists predominantly of white New Zealanders with some Maoris, Pacific Islanders, and students of Asian descent. The course always proves attractive to our North American exchange students (none of whom, as yet, have been African Americans). Teachers in other countries teach a different ethnic and cultural mix of students; what we have in common is that students probably know very little about Africa when we start. The challenge is twofold—to make the material intelligible to those with little background knowledge and to make it interesting and life enhancing.

To some extent one can tailor the course to one's students. If I were teaching a class that included African Americans or African Caribbeans I would do a lot more on black religions in the New World. When I talk about creation myths I briefly outline the Maori version. When we go on to African agricultural myths, such as the buried person resurrected as a yam (Isichei 1983: 24), I mention the Pacific Islands version with coconuts.

Many students have been influenced by what is loosely called New Age. They may already be involved in dream journaling, alternative holistic healing, or divination (tarot cards)—all of which relate to some aspect of Africa's traditional religions. The fields that interest them most are healing, witchcraft, spirit possession, and dreams. I often assign essays in these areas.

A MULTIDISCIPLINARY APPROACH

My own background is in history, but I teach the religion course largely from anthropological literature. African religion is clearly a field that benefits from a multidisciplinary approach, but this does create problems; in particular, what is the source of the theoretical focus? This is clearly not the place for a history of anthropology. It is an excellent opportunity for students, especially those who are not anthropology majors, to read some of the classics—Evans-Pritchard, Lienhardt, Victor Turner, Douglas, and so on. But one cannot discuss these texts without considering how the subject has moved on. In Lienhardt's famous study (1961) of Dinka religion, for instance, women are almost invisible.

THE SEARCH FOR A TEXTBOOK

The basic approach I use is to introduce a general issue such as witchcraft or divination and explore it in two or three case studies.[1] The textbook I use is Ray's (1976) *African Religions,* chosen because it employs this approach and because students find it clear and readable. It is over twenty years old, however, and understandably shows little awareness of gender issues. In addition, certain themes—notably witchcraft—are neglected. Because of this, I distribute supplementary readings, often from my own work.

African Religions was written in reaction to earlier books that saw Africa's traditional religions through Christian spectacles. It is important to be clear about this, as these books are still on library shelves and students often track them down. Idowu (1973), Mbiti (1969, 1970, 1975), and Parrinder (1954) wrote in reaction to an older missionary tendency to condemn indigenous religions as demonic and tended to emphasize these religions' "Christian" elements—the high god rather than spirit possession.

They also tended to conflate different religious traditions into a continent-wide "African religion" that never existed. Mbiti's (1970) *Concepts of God in Africa*, for example, includes data from 270 ethnic groups. These authors tended to see "traditional" religions as static and unchanging, as did many anthropologists. Some may well find information and insights of value in these studies, but in general, the study of traditional religions in Africa has moved on.

Many older collections of case studies are still useful. Middleton and Winter's (1963) *Witchcraft and Sorcery in East Africa* is an example. More recent work adds new insights but does not necessarily render earlier studies obsolete. Older studies do often show an inadequate awareness of gender issues, however, and do not appreciate the continuing dimension of change in African religion—and in particular how religion continues to take new forms in the postcolonial situation.

There is no good recent textbook or general survey. Hackett's (1996) *Art and Religion in Africa* is excellent but focuses on the visual arts. The journals *Africa* and the *Journal of Religion in Africa* are invaluable, ongoing resources.

The study of black religions in the New World contrasts with the current African situation. A number of good general surveys—not necessarily intended or suited for textbooks—have appeared in the past few years (e.g., Murphy 1994; Hurbon 1995; Thompson 1984). In the study of African "traditional" religions, there is a need for a new synthesis.

Where is good recent interpretative material to be found, and how should the teacher make use of it? Much excellent material can be found in edited collections. The Comaroffs' (1993) *Modernity and Its Malcontents* is an outstanding example. It is unsuited for a textbook and was not intended as one. Like much work influenced by postmodernism, its essays tend to be written in a rich and allusive but difficult style, and it does not cover many aspects of "traditional" religion. The best way to use it is to refer students to particular chapters—Bastian on witchcraft, Masquelier on spirit possession, Kaspin on masking cults, and so on. Other valuable collections, which can be used in the same way, are Jedrej and Shaw (1992) on dreams, Peek (1991) on divination, and a whole African issue of *Social Science and Medicine* (1981) on healing.

METHOD: THE NEED FOR CLARITY

I begin with a class that knows virtually nothing about Africa. It is important to remember this; an introductory class is not the place to explore the latest discussion of the interface between literacy and orality. One needs to paint with a broad brush; the finer details can be added at a more advanced stage. It is pointless to discuss the invention of ethnicity with students who have never heard of the Yoruba and could not locate them on a map.

Two tools are particularly useful in making sense of a body of new information. One is reinforcement—returning to the same case studies from different but mutually confirming points of view. The second is to locate the data firmly in space (and where possible, in time). Each student has a map of Africa with national boundaries and old and new names, for example, Northern Rhodesia and Zambia. I use the frontispiece map in Isichei (1995)—feel free to do the same! I use the same map as an overhead. I make it a rule never to refer to a place or an ethnolinguistic group without locating it on this map. I also use local ethnolinguistic maps. Students are encouraged to write in each ethnolinguistic group on their own map of Africa.

The course consists of lectures supplemented with tutorials—small, structured discussion groups. In my first session, I distribute a detailed outline of the whole course with the date on which each topic will be discussed. I display this outline overhead at the beginning of each class so that students have a strong sense of where we have been and where we are going. For every class, I prepare about eight computer-generated overheads. Each section of the data is summarized—where possible in diagrams—and all direct quotations are reproduced. This is essential if students are to deal with unfamiliar words, spellings, and concepts.

METHOD: ON LITERATURE AND ART

I illustrate virtually everything I discuss with art slides or colored overheads and video clips. I usually read at least one poem a lecture—sometimes a modern one on a relevant theme, sometimes a traditional one. I sometimes play tapes, such as songs taped in the field. (Material in an unfamiliar language should not go on for long!) I think more than anything else, it is the richness of the multimedia presentation that attracts students. I use the same approach in my non-African courses; when I lecture on Hildegard of Bingen, I show slides of her painting and play some of her (Latin) songs; the caveats about unfamiliar languages apply here too.

In the first module, I discuss general and theoretical issues. Why study traditional religions in Africa? There are millions of believers in so-called primal religions worldwide (I emphasize their variety). I discuss the rediscovery of these religions in the West (for example, the attraction of many European Americans to Native American religious traditions) and the close links between primal religious traditions and ecological awareness. I point out "traditional" religions' links with great art and oral literature. I contrast primal religious traditions with so-called world religions, which many in the class have already studied. African primal, or "traditional," religions are part of an oral culture; how does this affect the way they are understood and transmitted? I compare them with Judaism, Christianity, and Islam as "religions of the book." African primal religions have no founder and African languages lack a word for religion—it is part of the continuum of life. African religions are inclusive, ready to accept new ideas, new elements. We all discuss the pros and cons of the various labels that have been used (primal-traditional, ethnic-primitive).

I deal briefly with the question of the invention of African primal religion. I try to develop visual aids even in theoretical discussions, where they do not seem to have an obvious place. I show the class several slides of antique maps of Africa. One of these places stone castles and white-mitered bishops in the middle of the Sahara (Davidson 1978)—an example of the outsider's misunderstandings—but they all have fairly accurate coastlines. I then show them examples of writing from African cultures, such as *nsidibi*, an indigenous form of southeastern Nigeria (Isichei 1983: 333–335), which are unintelligible to outsiders without an interpreter. Finally, I talk about the strengths and weaknesses of the various approaches to primal religion, discussing famous studies by historians, anthropologists, and religion specialists.

The first tutorial deals with these issues. Each group is given a set of readings that includes a passage from Okot p'Bitek criticizing the distortions of African religions by those who see them through Christian spectacles and an extract from one of his poems, *The Song of Lawino* (1967) ("The things they shout I do not understand . . ."). Another extract is from a small book by black South African church leaders who complain about the distortions of outsiders' accounts. A whole issue of *Religion* deals with these issues, and the article by Shaw (1990), in particular, makes an excellent discussion paper. We also discuss the ethnographer's assumption (an assumption I do not share) that the spirit world of primal religion does not exist. There are several possible sources here. One is a short extract from Jackson (1989: ch. 7), a superb exploration of Kuranko (Sierra Leone) religion. Another is an extract from the latter portion of Somé (1994), a personal account of Dagara (Burkina Faso) initation that describes supernatural experiences as real.

I sometimes joke to colleagues that I specialize in *son et lumière*! My extensive use of slides, videos, sound recordings, myths, poems, and so on involves a great deal of extra work and very careful organization. I am beginning to use colored overheads of artwork rather than slides; they can be filed with computer-generated overheads, and one avoids the complexities of using too many machines at once. However, there is a further consideration. Each section of the course needs a solid theoretical underpinning; it should not degenerate into entertainment or a pastiche of visual and literary treasures.

My second module is concerned with spiritual beings, divinities, and ancestors. An older model—with a good deal of evidence to back it up—stressed the remoteness of the High God and the closeness of ancestors and nature divinities to daily life. I illustrate this model with several of the many African myths about how God was once close but withdrew to the sky (there is a moving example in Ray 1976) and with the Yoruba creation story, where Oludumare *delegates* the work of creation to Obatala (Beier 1980; also Ray 1976: 42–43). The theoretical model comes from a famous paper by Horton (1975) suggesting that local gods dominate the small world of village life and that as people move into a wider world, a more generalized divinity meets their needs. It explains why some people—such as the Ijebu Yoruba—were converted both to Christianity and Islam at the same time and sheds light on the oracle of Chukwu (God), run by Aro (Igbo) long-distance traders. But it does not fit in with a lot of other evidence—like the modern spread of spirit-possession cults.

My next theme is gender. I show slides of the Western God the Father, complete with beard (using a drawing by Blake, but Michelangelo's Sistine Chapel rendering would do equally well). I then point out that among the Fon (Aja) of Dahomey (now Benin), the supreme divinities are Mawu (female) and Lisa (male)—the latter is never found alone (Argyle 1966). Among the Kalabari of the Niger Delta, the supreme divinity, Tamuno, is seen as female (Horton 1970).

I move on to the concept of the earth as Mother, using Chapter 9 of my thematic *History of Nigeria* (1983). It includes a beautiful invocation to Innah (the Earth, greatest of the Hausa spirits, or *iskoki*) and Igbo and Idoma debates on whether God or the Earth is supreme. There is splendid visual material here in the sculptures erected by Owerri Igbo in *mbari* houses in honor of the Earth (Cole 1969, 1983). The supremacy of the Earth was also the secret of the Yoruba Ogboni society (Morton-Williams 1964). (There are also visual materials relating to this in the society's bronze sculptures, *edan*. See Roache 1971.)

In choosing poems, I allow myself to go beyond the day's case studies. There is a wonderful one in Mbiti (1975), identified as "Pygmy," which students love. (Later in the course I point out that "Pygmy" will not do for the people who call themselves Baka and so on.) It begins:

In the beginning is God . . .

Lienhardt (1961: 38) offers another, particularly poignant poem about the remoteness of God:

Great Deng is near, some say 'far' . . .
Do you not hear, o Divinity?

Finally, there is a profound Fulbe poem about the creation of the world (Mapanje and White 1983: 113–114).

I discuss nature and other "departmental" divinities in terms of Yoruba and one other religious system. Yoruba religion is much studied and lends itself particularly well to visual representation and storytelling. Ogun, Shango, Eshu/Elegbara—each has his characteristic iconography, for example, Ogun's cutlass and projecting hair, Shango's double-headed axe. Thompson's (1971) *Black Gods and Kings* is an excellent introduction and source of illustrations. Each divinity is the focus of many poetic invocations and myths (Beier 1966, 1980; Thompson 1971). A number of theoretical dimensions come in here. One can point out that spirits do not live in watertight ethnic—or other—compartments. The divinity of the sea, Olokun, is common to the Yoruba and the Edo (as are Orunmila, Eshu, and Ogun) and is sometimes male, sometimes female.

I stress the changing nature of primal religion and the way it crosses ethnic boundaries. Ogun, god of iron, becomes Gu in Dahomey and Ogou Feray (or other forms of Ogou) in Haiti (Barnes 1989). The teacher has to decide how far, if at all, to include the study of black religions in the New World. I mention it briefly here and there. There is already too much ground to cover; but there is splendid visual material on, for instance, Haitian folk art and earth paintings (Hurbon 1995).

One needs a contrasting case study to show that the Yoruba pattern (a vast number of divinities perceived in gendered terms) is not universal. One needs to point out, too, that Yoruba individuals and communities choose a particular divinity to serve (a point well made in Barber 1981). A single Igbo community—typically dominated by a water goddess—makes a good contrast (Isichei [1991c] on Asaba or Ubah in the Okigwe area). My anthology *Igbo Worlds* (Isichei 1977) includes several accounts of Igbo water goddesses, one of which goes into a handout to my class. There is also great material on Uhamiri, the goddess of Oguta Lake, in Flora Nwapa's novel *Efuru*:

> I got to the bottom of the lake and to my surprise, I saw an elegant woman, very beautiful, combing her long black hair with a golden comb. She used different kinds of fish as fire wood. (Nwapa 1978: 146)

> Efuru . . . dreamt of the woman of the lake, her beauty, her long hair and her riches. She had lived for ages at the bottom of the lake. She was as old as the lake itself. She was happy, she was wealthy. She was beautiful. She gave women beauty and wealth but she had no child. . . . Why then did the women worship her? (Nwapa 1978: 221)

These local water goddesses have been at least partly absorbed in the modern cult of Mami Wata. My handout here includes extracts from Murphy's (1994) essay on the Yoruba River goddess Oshun, who is also worshipped in the New World. He quotes some wonderful Yoruba and Cuban invocations to her. For a handout on Mami Wata there is good material in Salmons (1977), Drewal (1988), Jewsiewicki (1991), also Isichei in Drewal (in press). There is also great visual material on the West African version of Mami Wata in Salmons (1977) and Drewal (1988) as well as from Zairian popular paintings in Jewsiewicki (1991). There are at least two videos—one as much about traditional water goddesses as about Mami Wata—by Jell-Bahlsen and Wendl and Weise; they are described in Kasfir (1994).

The final part of this module deals with ancestors, "ghosts," and the soul. I discuss the importance of ancestral cults, and the elaborate mortuary rites that often reflect this in Africa, drawing on the quite similar material on the Yoruba and Igbo. Ideas of a future life are often shadowy, but Goody's account of the Lo Dagaa of northern Ghana (summarized in Ray 1976) is an exception. I read several stanzas in translation of the Senegalese poet Birago Diop's *Soufflés* (in Moore and Beier 1984):

> *Those who are dead have never gone away . . .*
> *The dead are not under the ground.*

Both peoples share a belief in the Returner, the child born to die— *ogbanje* in Igbo, *abiku* in Yoruba. There are two *abiku* poems in Moore and Beier (one by Soyinka, one by John Pepper Clark). Azaro, the spirit child of Ben Okri's (1991) novel *The Famished Road*, is an *ogbanje*. An account to which students will relate more easily is in Soyinka's *Ake* (1995), a wonderful (Abeokuta Yoruba) childhood memoir. It tells of an *abiku* spoiled by her doting mother and also of Uncle Sanya, who as a child was close to *oro*, forest spirits, and shared a feast with them. (For visual material on *abiku*, see Merlo 1975). At this point I show slides of *ibeji*—wonderful Yoruba wood carvings to commemorate dead twins (Houlberg 1973).

My third module focuses on places of encounter between humanity and divinity. There are four themes here: masking cults, spirit possession, ritual, and divination. The masker is in a state of transformation, temporarily becoming a supernatural being. Discussing the encounter between humanity and divinity follows on well from ancestors—some masks embody them (like Yoruba *egungun*) and some embody forest spirits (notably Ekpe on the Cross River). Gelede (Drewal 1974; Drewal and Drewal 1983) and *egungun* (Thompson 1974) are good examples of the expression of gender antagonism on the part of the anonymous male collectivity with the witch seen as female. A whole issue of *African Arts* (11, 3 [April 1978]) was devoted to *egungun*. Here, I reinforce a point made earlier with reference to water goddesses: Not all Yoruba have the same cults or divinities. (Gelede, for instance, is found among the southwestern Yoruba.) Nigerian masks are controlled by male secret societies, which have traditionally used them to maintain authority over women, children, and strangers. (A good short introduction is in Isichei 1983: 286–290.) Gelede is particularly interesting for the light it sheds on gender roles—it is intended to placate (female) witches. "On Masks and Audible Ghosts" (Isichei 1988) explores less well known central Nigerian mask cults; it is illustrated with line drawings. For a mask society controlled by women, one must turn to Bunde/Sande in Liberia (Tonkin 1983; d'Azevedo 1973).

There is a superabundance of visual material on masking. Thompson's (1974) *African Art in Motion* has fine text and illustrations. *African Arts* is an important resource for the whole course; it has published many articles on Nigerian and other masks. Masks, as Thompson reminds us, are art *in motion,* and videos are therefore especially valuable. I like to use a portion of a beautiful ethnographic film on the Baka, "Pygmy" hunter-gatherers of Cameroon, for this section (Aglund 1988). It shows the forest spirit Jengi appearing as a raffia mask in a community torn by witchcraft accusations. The only problem is that it can reinforce student-held stereotypes of an Africa peopled with hunter-gatherers living in rain forests. There is also good material on masks (and ritual in general) in the video made by Henry Drewal to accompany Margaret Drewal's (1992) *Yoruba Ritual.* There are no subtitles or voiceovers, so the instructor must make a careful prior study of both text and video as well as offer detailed explanations to students. It is, however, an authentic picture of the place of traditional religions in modern Nigerian urban life and valuable for that reason.

Space does not permit me to go through the whole course and the materials I use. I study the cognitive maps created in myth and in witchcraft beliefs, the role of religion in healing, and specialists in the sacred. I explore the world of symbolism in ritual and art. An outstanding source here is Thompson's (1970) "The Sign of the Divine King," which explores the varied significances of birds in Yoruba iconography; on the beaded crowns of Yoruba kings, on diviners' staffs, and elsewhere, birds are associated with witches and recur in Gelede invocations (Isichei 1983: 349–354).

Since the course has for the most part concentrated on particular themes, I end with a "total" picture of the changing religious life of one or more peoples. I always include the Kalabari (interesting both because of Horton's [1970] fine ethnography and because of the interaction with an aquatic environment). My studies of the Anaguta of central Nigeria (Isichei 1991a, 1991b), which include line drawings, are another possibility. In East Africa, Beidelman (1993) on the Kaguru or Willis (1968) on the Fipa are good choices. When a scholar has published both articles and books on a subject (Drewal on Gelede, Cole on *mbari*) students (and perhaps teachers) pressed for time will often fare better with the articles.

It is important to emphasize the way in which "traditional" religions have changed in the twentieth century. Their role in anticolonial resistance movements is well covered in Ray (1976: 155–170). For more recent surveys, see Wright (1995) on Maji Maji; Lonsdale (1990) and Green (1990) on Mau Mau. The cult of Mumbo (a water snake of Lake Victoria) is a good example of the reinvention of tradition (Wipper 1977). So, in the 1990s, is Alice Lakwena's uprising in northern Uganda (Allen 1991).

It is important to study the way in which witchcraft beliefs survive and flourish as a statement of "moral economy" (see Bastian 1993; Rosen 1981; Fisiy and Geschiere 1990; Austen 1993). An excellent example from the Nigerian literary canon of witchcraft can be seen through the eyes of Amos Tutuola (1981) (a Yoruba from Abeokuta, writing in pidgin, whose work Dylan Thomas called "grisly and bewitching"). Studies of religious change in modern village communities are illuminating—Willis (1968) and Stevens (1991) are good ones.

I would not encourage anyone to attempt to duplicate the course as I teach it. What I have to share is a basic approach of using the study of religion to enter more deeply into other peoples' cultures, to break free from the ethnocentric assumptions to which we are all heir. We learn to read other cognitive maps and find alternative ways of looking at the world.

I believe that humanities programs must be life enriching. We need to nurture those we teach with great literature, great art. By browsing in anthologies, each teacher will build up, as I have done, a collection of favorite poems that work in a class situation. One can also build up a slide collection—indeed, one need go no further than the back numbers of *African Arts*—and there are also good visual resources in coffee-table books on Africa. I constantly record educational programs on television, on anything I might conceivably teach. These videos have become precious resources. By reading African novels and autobiographies, one accumulates an ever-expanding database of possible teaching materials. (Achebe's novels are the most frequently used in this way, but there are many other examples—Elechi Amadi's [1970] *The Great Ponds* has wonderful material on Igbo ritual specialists. Camera Laye's [1994] *The Dark Child* describes the childhood of a "casted" goldsmith.) Teaching provides insights for writing, and research nourishes teaching—which is as it should be.

NOTES

1. As a Nigeria specialist I draw many, but not all, of my case studies from Nigeria and its neighbors. I concentrate on the Nigerian material in this chapter.

SUGGESTIONS FOR
FURTHER READING AND RESOURCES

Aglund, Phil. 1988. *Baka: People of the Forest.* Washington, D.C.: National Geographic Society. [film]

Allen, T. 1991. "Understanding Alice: Uganda's Holy Spirit Movement in Context." *Africa* 61, 1: 370–398.

Amadi, Elechi. 1970. *The Great Ponds.* Nairobi and London: Heinemann Educational.

Argyle, W. J. 1966. *The Fon of Dahomey.* Oxford: Clarendon Press.

Austen, R. 1993. "The Moral Economy of Witchcraft: An Essay in Comparative History." In *Modernity and Its Malcontents: Ritual and Power in Postcolonial Africa,* ed. Jean Comaroff and John Comaroff. Chicago: Chicago University Press.

Barber, Karin. 1981. "How Man Makes God in West Africa: Yoruba Attitudes Towards the Orisa." *Africa* 5: 724–745.

Barnes, S. 1989. *Africa's Ogun: Old World and New.* Bloomington: Indiana University Press.

Bastian, M. L. 1993. "'Bloodhounds Who Have No Friends': Witchcraft and Locality in the Nigerian Popular Press." In *Modernity and Its Malcontents,* ed. Jean Comaroff and John Comaroff. Chicago: University of Chicago Press.

Beidelman, T. O. 1993. *Moral Imagination in Kaguru Modes of Thought.* Bloomington: Indiana University Press.

Beier, U. 1966. *African Poetry.* Cambridge: Cambridge University Press.

———. 1980. *Yoruba Myths.* Cambridge: Cambridge University Press.

Cole, H. M. 1969. "Mbari Is Life." *African Arts* (Spring): 8–15.

———. 1983. *Mbari, Art, and Life Among the Owerri Igbo.* Bloomington: Indiana University Press.

Comaroff, Jean, and John Comaroff, eds. 1993. *Modernity and Its Malcontents: Ritual and Power in Postcolonial Africa.* Chicago: University of Chicago Press.

Davidson, B. 1978. *African Kingdoms.* New York: Time-Life.

d'Azevedo, W. 1973. "Mask Makers and Myth in Western Liberia." In *Primitive Art and Society,* ed. Anthony Forge. London: Oxford University Press.

Drewal, H. J. 1974. "Gelede Masquerade: Imagery and Motif." *African Arts* (Summer): 8–19.

———. 1988. "Mermaids, Mirrors, and Snake Charmers: Igbo Mami Wata Shrines." *African Arts* (February): 38–45.

Drewal, H. J., and M. T. Drewal. 1983. *Gelede: Art and Female Power Among the Yoruba.* Bloomington: Indiana University Press.

Drewal, M. T. 1992. *Yoruba Ritual.* Bloomington: Indiana University Press.

Ekpo, I. 1978. "Ekpe Costume of the Cross River." *African Arts* 12, 1: 72–75.

Fisiy, C., and P. Geschiere. 1990. "Judges and Witches, or How Is the State to Deal with Witchcraft?" *Cahiers d'Etudes Africaines* 118: 135–156.

———. 1991. "Sorcery, Witchcraft, and Accumulation: Regional Variations in South and West Cameroon." *Critique of Anthropology* 11, 3: 251–278.

Green, Maia. 1990. "Mau Mau Oathing Rituals and Political Ideology in Kenya: A Reanalysis." *Africa* 60: 69–87.

Hackett, R. 1996. *Art and Religion in Africa.* London and New York: Cassell.

Horton, R. 1970. "A Hundred Years of Change in Kalabari Religion." In *Black Africa: Its Peoples and Their Cultures Today,* ed. J. Middleton. London: Macmillan.

————. 1975. "On the Rationality of Conversion," part 1. *Africa* 45, 3: 219–235.

Houlberg, M. H. 1973. "Ibeji Images of the Yoruba." *African Arts* (Autumn): 20–27.

Hurbon, L. 1995. *Voodoo: Search for the Spirit.* New York: Harry N. Abrams.

Idowu, E. B. 1973. *African Traditional Religion: A Definition.* London: SCM.

Isichei, E. 1977. *Igbo Worlds: An Anthology of Oral Histories and Historical Descriptions.* Philadelphia: Institute for the Study of Human Issues.

————. 1983. *A History of Nigeria.* Harlow: Longman.

————. 1988. "On Masks and Audible Ghosts: Some Secret Male Cults in Central Nigeria." *Journal of Religion in Africa* 18, 1: 42–70.

————. 1991a. "On Being Invisible: An Historical Perspective of the Anaguta and Their Neighbours." *International Journal of African Historical Studies* 24, 3: 513–556.

————. 1991b. "Change in Anaguta Traditional Religion." *Canadian Journal of African Studies* 25, 1: 34–57.

————. 1991c. "Myth, Gender, and Society in Pre-Colonial Asaba." *Africa* 61, 4: 513–529.

————. 1995. *A History of Christianity in Africa from Antiquity to the Present.* London: SPCK.

————. forthcoming. "Mami Wata and Indigenous Cultures: Two Case Studies— Igboland and the Cameroon Coast." In *Mami Wata and Her Sisters in the New World,* ed. Henry Drewal. Los Angeles: Fowler Museum, UCLA.

Jackson, M. 1989. *Paths Towards a Clearing: Radical Empiricism and Ethnographic Inquiry.* Bloomington: Indiana University Press.

Jedrej, M. C., and R. Shaw. 1992. *Dreaming Religion and Society in Africa.* Leiden: Brill.

Jewsiewicki, B. 1991. "Painting in Zaire: From the Invention of the West to the Representation of Social Self." In *Africa Explores 20th Century African Art,* ed. S. Vogel. New York: Centre for African Art and Prestel.

Kasfir, S. L. 1994. "Review of Mami Wata Videos." *African Arts* (January): 80–82, 96.

Kaspin, D. 1993. "Chewa Visions and Revisions of Power." In *Modernity and Its Malcontents: Ritual and Power in Postcolonial Africa,* ed. Jean Comaroff and John Comaroff. Chicago: University of Chicago Press.

Laye, Camara. 1994. *The Dark Child.* New York: Hill & Wang.

Lienhardt, Godfrey. 1961. *Divinity and Experience.* Oxford: Clarendon Press.

Lonsdale, John. 1990. "Mau Maus of the Mind: Making Mau Mau and Remaking Kenya." *Journal of African History* 31: 393–421.

Mapanje, J., and L. White. 1983. *Oral Poetry from Africa: An Anthology.* Harlow: Longman.

Masquelier, A. 1993. "Narratives of Power, Images of Wealth: The Ritual Economy of *Bori* in the Market." In *Modernity and Its Malcontents: Ritual and Power in Postcolonial Africa,* ed. Jean Comaroff and John Comaroff. Chicago: University of Chicago Press.

Mbiti, J. 1969. *African Religions and Philosophy.* London: Heinemann.

————. 1970. *Concepts of God in Africa.* London: SPCK.

————. 1975. *The Prayers of African Religion.* London: SCM.

Merlo, C. 1975. "Statuettes of the Abiku Cult." *African Arts* (Summer): 30–35.

Middleton, J., and E. Winter. 1963. *Witchcraft and Sorcery in East Africa.* London: Routledge and Kegan Paul.

Moore, G., and U. Beier. 1984. *The Penguin Book of Modern African Poetry,* 3rd ed. Harmondsworth: Penguin.

Morton-Williams, P. 1964. "An Outline of the Cosmology and Cult Organization of the Oyo Yoruba." *Africa* 34: 243–261.

Morton-Williams, P., and J. Murphy. 1983. "Oshun the Dancer." In *The Book of the Goddess Past and Present: An Introduction to Her Religion,* ed. Carol Olsen. New York: Crossroad.

Murphy, J. 1994. *Working with the Spirit: Ceremonies of the African Diaspora.* Boston: Beacon Press.

Ngada, N. H., et al. 1985. *Speaking for Ourselves.* Braamfontein: Institute for Contextual Theology.

Nwapa, F. 1978 (1966). *Efuru.* Oxford: Heinemann.

Okri, Ben. 1991. *The Famished Road.* London: Jonathan Cape.

Parrinder, E. G. 1954. *African Traditional Religion.* London: Hutchinson.

p'Bitek, O. 1967. *The Song of Lawino: A Lament.* Nairobi: East African Publishing.

———. 1970. *African Religions in Western Scholarship.* Kampala: East African Literature Bureau.

Peek, P. M., ed. 1991. *African Divination Systems: Ways of Knowing.* Bloomington: Indiana University Press.

Pelton, R. D. 1980. "Legba: Master of the Fon Dialectic." In *The Trickster in West Africa: A Study of Mythic Irony and Sacred Delight,* ed. R. D. Pelton. Berkeley: University of California Press.

Pemberton, John. 1975. "Eshu-Elegba: The Yoruba Trickster God." *African Arts* 9: 20, 27, 66–70.

Ray, B. 1976. *African Religions: Symbol, Ritual, and Community.* Upper Saddle, N.J.: Prentice-Hall.

Roache, L. 1971. "Psychophysical Attributes of the Ogboni Edan." *African Arts* 4, 2 (Winter): 48–53.

Rosen, D. 1981. "Dangerous Women: 'Ideology,' 'Knowledge,' and Ritual Among the Kono of Eastern Sierra Leone." *Dialectical Anthropology* 6: 151–164.

Salmons, J. 1977. "Mammy Wata." *African Arts* 10, 3: 8–15.

Shaw, R. 1990. "The Invention of 'African Traditional Religion.'" *Religion* 20: 339–354.

Social Science and Medicine. 1981. 15 (special Africa issue).

Somé, M. P. 1994. *Of Water and the Spirit: Ritual Magic and Initiation in the Life of an African Shaman.* New York: Arkana.

Soyinka, W. 1995. *Ake: Years of Childhood.* London: Mandarin.

Stevens, L. 1991. "Religious Change in a Haya Village, Tanzania." *Journal of Religion in Africa* 21: 2–25.

Thompson, R. F. 1970. "The Sign of the Divine King: An Essay on Yoruba Bead-Embroidered Crowns." *African Arts* (Spring): 8–17, 74–78.

———. 1971. *Black Gods and Kings.* Los Angeles: Museum of Ethnic Arts.

———. 1974. *African Art in Motion.* Los Angeles: University of California Press.

———. 1983. *Flash of the Spirit: African and Afro-American Art and Philosophy.* New York: Vintage Books.

Tonkin, E. 1983. "Women Excluded? Masking and Masquerading in West Africa." In *Women's Religious Experience,* ed. Pat Holden. London: Croom Helm.

Tutuola, A. 1981. *The Witch-Herbalist of the Remote Town.* London: Faber.

Ubah, C. N. 1982. "The Supreme Being, Divinities, and Ancestors in Igbo Traditional Religion: Evidence from Otanchara and Otanzu." *Africa* 52, 2: 90–105.

Wescott, J. 1962. "The Sculpture and Myths of Eshu-Elegba, the Yoruba Trickster." *Africa* 32, 4: 336–353.

Willis, R. 1968. "Changes in Mystical Concepts and Practices Among the Fipa." *Ethnology* 7, 2: 139–157.

Wipper, A. 1977. *Rural Rebels.* Nairobi: Oxford University Press.

Wright, M. 1995. "Maji Maji: Prophecy and Historiography." In *Revealing Prophets,* ed. D. M. Anderson and D. H. Johnson. London: James Currey.

4

THE MEDIUM IS
THE MESSAGE: TEACHING
AFRICA THROUGH MUSIC

ADELINE MASQUELIER

Teaching African culture, history, and society in a quarter or a semester to undergraduate students who have had little or no exposure to anthropology is at best a challenging enterprise, at worst a logistical nightmare. As I was searching for a particular theme from which to introduce my students to the exciting multiplicity of African cultural forms, I hit upon the idea of using music to let the class experience Africa from a more intimate perspective, through a medium whose value undergraduates all inherently recognize in their own lives. From my research among Hausa speakers of southern Niger, I was aware that music, in particular praise singing (for a carefully contextualized historical study of praise poetry and possession songs in South Africa, see Vail and White 1991) and the songs sung to induce possession by spirits, is a privileged medium for altering the world and its people through the combined effects of words, rhythm, and melody. (See also Berliner 1978; Besmer 1983; Blacking 1995; Rouget 1985; Stoller 1989.) Just as blacksmiths' capacity to transform iron ore into metal makes them potent individuals not to trifle with, so musicians' mastery over words and sounds are feared in Mali, Senegal, or Niger because they are the catalysts of powerful transformations. (See Conrad and Frank 1995; Hebert 1993; Laye 1976: 39–40.) Music, I thought, would help students engage with the ethnographic material at the same time that it would serve as a platform through which to present important issues from spirit possession to colonialism to urbanization.

When I first experimented with this pedagogical approach to the study of Africa, I had my students listen to several distinct and even contrasting recordings of African music and asked them what was "African" about the music they heard. We would begin by noting the emphasis on percussion and complex rhythms and the steady tempo. Some students might remark that songs are often structured around repetitions and variations of short segments. I would also point out the strong connection that sometimes exists between music and the social context of its performance (e.g., work, political meeting, ceremony). After noticing the commonalities among distinct musical forms, my class would also become aware of the tremendous diversity of musical styles south of the Sahara. Most students rarely question the stereotypic view that African music is all drumming, just as they generally assume that Africa is an undifferentiated and wild continent plagued by poverty, disease, and tribal wars. As students become baffled by the multiplicity of genres of African music, as they fail to distinguish a pattern that underlies all the pieces, and as they recognize Western elements in recordings that otherwise sound distinctly "African," they realize that just as they can no longer talk about an essential African musical style, they cannot hold on to a generalized view of Africa as a single place, space, or culture. In other words, music becomes both the evidence they need to realize the inadequacy of their notion of an African unidimensional primitivism and the lens through which to reconceptualize Africa's multiple facets.

Juxtaposing the strange with the familiar might also help students outgrow some of their preconceptions and lead them to further insights concerning the nature of musical creativity and diversity south of the Sahara. For instance, when students listen to the reggae sounds of Alpha Blondy, they are reminded of Bob Marley at the same time that they are forced to acknowledge the inimitable style of the musician, the recognizably African content of his lyrics, and the fact that the songs are in French. For rap enthusiasts, the music of Positive Black Soul, a rap group from Senegal, might provide the flicker of recognition they need to appreciate and discern the complexity of African musical forms: all the usual rap sounds but with African drums and lyrics in French, English, and Wolof. A helpful guide to navigate through the ocean of musical styles is Bender's *Sweet Mother* (1991), in which the author sets out to "give the reader an incentive to listen to African music—especially modern African music—but also to provide a broad general survey" (xx). Though it is poorly organized and at times even confusing for students, the volume offers a wealth of information on the roots of musical styles, regional trends, groups and individuals connected to a particular genre, and the sociopolitical context in which these styles evolve. It contains wonderful photos of some album covers (that could provide the basis for students' discussion) and has a very helpful discography.

Like culture in its largest sense, music is neither static nor unchanging, and like the cultural forms we attempt to describe and define from an anthropological perspective, music's flexibility and susceptibility to multiple forces and influences challenge our mechanical models of change and history. In Africa, where music is a total performance involving bodily motion, facial expression, and singing (Bender 1991), its complexity and multidimensionality are not easily captured in the linear, bounded context of ethnographic writing. Yet because it is already an intimate part of students' lives, music is far more accessible to a class of undergraduates than a historical model of cultural transformations, and this is what enhances its appeal as a teaching instrument. Music is paradoxically so easy to hear yet so difficult to describe and dissect. It is hard to imagine packing rhythm, sound, and movement into words on a page so that the reader can "hear" and understand music in a fresh way. Partly because of this paradox, music provides a good medium through which to introduce students to the cultural complexity and plurality of the African continent. Its inherent sensorial primacy, structural dynamics, and diffuse character make it an apt icon for heterogeneous societies. After being exposed to multiple musical genres, students are less likely to reduce such societies to a unified social field limited by procrustean boundaries. In what follows, I want to briefly outline some of the ways that African popular music can be used to give texture and liveliness to the commentaries and analyses of African societies we bring to the classroom—especially noting how music can be used to highlight African people's reckoning of history, their resistance to colonial and postcolonial regimes, their embattled relationship with modernity, and their experience of migration.

Music plays an active role in the weaving of fabrics of "horizontal comradeship" (Anderson 1983: 16; see also Bender 1991) that help people feel part of what has been called an "imagined community." It is thus tempting to correlate musical expression with cultural tradition. Nonetheless, we must be cautious not to assume there exists a "one-to-one equation of musical style and cultural core" (Bohlman in Erlmann 1991: 19) that would allow for an identification of musical style on the basis of geographic, social, or ethnic units. Though music has undoubtedly actively promoted the evolution and definition of identity for countless Africans throughout the continent (Blacking 1995; Coplan 1987; Waterman 1990), the fact that it is never the product of a unique, discrete, and unidimensional tradition renders problematic any attempt to define a form of musical expression in terms of ethnic, cultural, or linguistic boundaries.

TRADITION AND MODERNITY
SEEN THROUGH THE MUSICAL PRISM

In dealing with students who are incorrigibly fond of defining Hausa, Mandinka, or Nuer practices as either "traditional" or "modern," I found it helpful to use music to help dispel the long-standing myth that throughout the African continent, the meaningful orders of the past are being replaced by a material economy of the present. The sound of Ghanaian highlife or Nigerian *juju,* to name but two musical genres, demonstrates more eloquently than any theoretical argument the uselessness of sustaining the opposition between modernity and tradition, an opposition that serves only to confine Africans in a conceptual space defined by negation or absence. Let me take the example of highlife. Highlife is a musical style popular throughout English-speaking countries of West Africa from Nigeria to Sierra Leone. When it is played by a dance band, horns are used extensively, and it has a Western, at times almost Caribbean, calypso flavor (Stapleton and May 1990). When played by a guitar band, highlife is leaner and less jazzy. Known as palm-wine music because it was originally played in palm-wine bars, this form of highlife lays stories and proverbs over indigenous rhythms, explaining why until recently it was considered rural, provincial, and common in contrast to its more sophisticated counterpart. Highlife developed in the western coastal regions of the continent, where indigenous instruments like drums, gongs, and various kinds of lamellaphone—the hand piano—were progressively combined with the guitar (Bender 1991). As Ghanaian musicians learned to play brass instruments in the European armies or at mission school, large brass bands emerged that combined Western dance tunes with local rhythms and those exported from Afro-Cuba (Stapleton and May 1990; see also Collins 1992).

Whether highlife is performed by dance orchestras for the urban elite or by acoustic guitar bands for the lower classes of the countryside or the city, the gentle blend of jazzy guitars, horns, and subtle, muted rhythms that characterizes highlife points to the complex dialectic of synthesis and innovation, cross-fertilization and hybridization, that makes up cultural encounters on the coast. Today, many guitar bands have turned electric or incorporated brass sections. Yet in all its localized and diversified versions, highlife retains an unmistakable West African rhythm. Firmly rooted in local musical legacies yet resolutely open to Western and other influences while constantly changing, highlife vividly demonstrates the subtlety and continuity of the interaction between "black" and "white" music.

More important, highlife music and its twentieth-century history shows the inherent difficulty of applying concepts such as modern or traditional in cultural contexts that defy simplistic and synthetic oppositions between the past and the present. Just as the rich and varied musical syntheses emerging from the recording studios of Lagos or Yaounde are inadequately described by notions of organic unity and accidental change, so the complex, fragmented realities of African life cannot be captured by old-time anthropological models of culture as an a priori, coherent whole occasionally disturbed by external forces. Tracing the emergence of highlife in cities, whose wider culture formed a base for professionalized musicians, and setting it in contrast to the palm-wine music performed in the countryside by semiprofessional artists who held on to day jobs is also a useful way of contextualizing the experience of many Africans caught between the dwindling resources of increasingly impoverished rural areas and the opportunities (and temptations) associated with expanding urban centers.

LISTENING TO MUSIC: AN ACTIVE EXPERIENCE

Like *juju* or afro-beat (for a discussion of how afro-beat's founder, Fela Anikulapo-Kuti, made it on the international pop charts and became one of the few African musicians known throughout the world, see Collins 1992: ch. 8; Bender 1991: ch. 3), highlife has been so massively exported to Europe and America that it is fairly easy to find samples of this musical style at the local music store. Prince Nico Mbarga's famous Nigerian English song "Sweet Mother" (1991), for instance, provides a good illustration of highlife. After I played "Sweet Mother" to my students a first time, I gave them a copy of the song's lyrics, and we listened to Prince Nico's music again. This led to an animated discussion of what the song meant to its author and what we could learn about West African practices (motherhood, nurturance, marriage) simply by paying attention to the words. Despite its infectious vivacity, the song also has an inescapable nostalgic quality that can be easily detected even without knowing what it is about.

Before being handed the lyrics, students can be asked to identify what instruments they hear, whether the song resembles any Western music they are familiar with, and what emotional qualities are being conveyed by the "grain" of the voice. Having to think for themselves imaginatively about where and in which contexts different musical genres might be performed and what these songs might mean to their intended audience, students are forced to go beyond their cultural stereotypes of African "traditional" performance and values to appreciate the music's tremendous creative vitality. Listening assignments such as the ones just described constitute an active learning experience that enables students to picture what everyday people in Accra or Onitsha really care or dream about, what they fight for or make fun of, and what they consider inventive or politically astute. Students can be asked to take notes on their personal reactions to the music they are listening to, or they can be given short written assignments around questions such as "What do you think (referring to "Sweet Mother") made this song into a bestseller?" or "In what way is this song political?" Students' reflections on such issues may pave the way for more general discussions of cultural aesthetics (see Chernoff 1979; Coplan 1994) or the role of music in politics (see Blacking 1995: ch. 7; Bender 1991).

Juju music, a local variant of the urban West African palm-wine guitar tradition, is another particularly rich musical style whose history is closely tied to the structural transformations experienced by the Nigerian society out of which it emerged in the 1930s. Tunde King, the Lagosian guitarist credited with initially popularizing *juju,* incorporated elements of Christian hymns, *asiko* drumming, and Yoruba poetic rhetoric into the labile palm-wine framework to create a musical style soon associated with the development of a "pan-Yoruba" identity (Waterman 1990: 55). Born out of the struggle of Yoruba migrant workers seeking to reconcile their visions of a past life with their present experience of proletarianization, *juju* ironically flourished under the patronage of a new urban elite looking for culturally sanctioned ways of confirming their *arriviste* status. The music of King Sunny Adé, one of the leading exponents of *juju,* is available everywhere (on Mango Records) and is nicely complemented by Adé's video *King Sunny Adé Live at Montrose.* The music of Sonny Okosun (1978) is also widely available in North America. Though it is perhaps a bit too complex for assigned undergraduate reading, Waterman's superb ethnography about *juju* contains several transcribed song texts that can easily provide written support to a *juju* music session—since most of the available compact discs or tapes rarely have transcriptions of the lyrics. In addition, *juju* is sold with a ninety-minute cassette tape that features the songs whose lyrics are transcribed in the book. In chapter 4, Waterman provides a very helpful and informative discussion of two superstars of the *juju* style, Chief Commander Ebenezer Obey and King Sunny Adé, focusing on their careers, their musical arrangements, their philosophies, and the messages of their respective music. Looking specifically at artists who have achieved international fame might help personalize and concretize a discussion of African music for the class as students realize that the star system is as firmly entrenched in Lagos or Abidjan as in North America.

POLITICS, CONSCIOUSNESS, AND THE MUSIC OF RESISTANCE

Students for whom the term "Africa" conjures up the image of emaciated faces of starving Somalian children or hordes of exhausted refugees fleeing Rwanda, and who regularly witness on television that survival on the continent is possible only because of the benevolent intervention of Western nations, often find it difficult to consider the possibility that Africans have struggled all along for self-determination. When we discuss the European colonization of the African continent, we focus on African encounters with Western musical styles to help dispel the assumption that people in Kenya, Senegal, or Zaire passively absorbed the values, categories, and practices of a foreign "metropole." Showing students how music in South Africa or Zimbabwe can borrow Western instruments, rhythms, sounds, or techniques but nonetheless become a message of resistance and subversion enables them to understand some of the processes through which Africans creatively reshaped and interpreted foreign elements and novel practices to refashion their own vision of an evolving world.

Bender (1991: chs. 3, 5, 6) provides a good account of how music can be used in the struggle against oppression and injustice. The case of Zimbabwe, which Bender discusses briefly, cogently illustrates the role of popular music in spreading the voice of ZAPU (Zimbabwe African People's Union) and educating and recruiting new fighters that would liberate the country from the oppressive Rhodesian regime. Thomas Mapfumo's (1984) subversive music, which was so popular during the Chimurenga period (the 1970s armed struggle that led to Zimbabwe's independence), was played with guitars, drums, and saxophones, but it was modeled on "traditional" *mbira* (lamellaphone) playing.[1] While listening to Mapfumo's singing, students can, for instance, ponder the ambiguities of the message contained in the song "We Are Sending Our Children to War" (transcribed in Bender 1991: 162) or debate the usefulness of assigning such labels as "modern" or "traditional" to Chimurenga-pop music. The film *Rhythm of Resistance* (Marre 1979), which chronicles the vibrant musical traditions of South Africa under apartheid, is especially appropriate for a discussion of music's contribution to the fight for independence and self-determination in colonial and postcolonial Africa. Because it represents South Africa during the apartheid regime, it is more useful as a historical document than as a commentary on today's musical scene. Students will get a clear picture of the politics of space and representation in the South Africa of the 1970s, but they must realize that even though opportunities for recording are still limited, contemporary black artists have a relatively easier time making and recording music now that censorship has eased. After students watch South Africans of twenty years ago attending musical performances in unofficial arenas (churches, rented halls late at night) and illicit clubs where both black and white patrons would squeeze in together, they can discuss the recent changes—freedom of expression, legitimation and dissemination of musical styles, availability of recording studios, and so on.

Besides showing music videos or documentaries to demonstrate the links between music and politics, one can once more use the resources provided by recordings of internationally acclaimed artists. For instance, the songs of Miriam Makeba, the South African singer who long criticized the injustices of the apartheid regimes in Southern Africa, are widely available. In her album *Welela* (1989), she sings about FRELIMO (Front for the Liberation of Mozambique), the Soweto 1966 massacre, and the fate of political prisoners in one terrible prison of Guinea-Bissau, among other things. Another well-known artist previously mentioned, Fela, built his career around the criticism of corrupt elites and an abusive government in Nigeria. His album *Zombie* (1977)—titled after the term used to refer to soldiers—became an instant hit even among the very army circles at whom Fela directed his verbal attacks. Incidentally, having the students listen to a musical sample of Fela's "James Brown Period" might also help further establish the legitimacy of African music on the global stage. Waterman's (1990: 225–226) ethnography of *juju* presents several of Fela's songs, which can provide the focus of a discussion on social inequality. Students can, for example, consider the cultural meanings of hunger (as an index of suffering, a metaphor for political oppression and social inequities) when discussing the song "No Bread," which contrasts sharply the natural wealth of the African soil and the utter poverty of the Lagosian night-soil carrier.

MUSIC, MIGRANCY, AND THE PROBLEMS OF EVERYDAY LIFE

Throughout Africa, economic conditions have for over fifty years dictated the massive departure of migrants to urban centers, plantations, or mines. From Dakar to Nairobi, from Khartoum to Durban, the migrant labor system fostered important changes in the lives of both those who left in search of work and those who stayed behind in the rural area. It has earned its place in the African studies curriculum. Yet, save for some notable exceptions, anthropological accounts of the migratory process have generally privileged sociological theory over cultural reflexivity to trace the social origins and consequences of cyclical migration. Turning to the musical scene that has developed around migrant communities is a profitable strategy when teaching undergraduates about the dehumanizing world of migrant labor because such an approach privileges human agency and local subjectivities.

As aesthetic formulations of the experience of migrancy, musical performances vividly capture what it is like to leave one's home and sell one's labor for economic survival. As Coplan (1987: 431) has demonstrated in his work on Basotho migrants' oral literature, the songs performed by travelers-poets struggling to redefine their human worth "in opposition to their identity as mere labor units in the political economy of South Africa" provide an eloquent and poignant testimony of the experience, problems, and aspirations of migrant laborers—which students can compare with their own dreams and difficulties. Because they both draw upon and are measured against the expressive traditions and authoritative values of Sotho historical culture, *sefela* and *lifela* performances, for instance, provide an easily graspable medium for understanding how Basotho migrants deploy culturally salient categories and concepts (initiation, marriage, war, cattle herding, chiefly authority, etc.) to make sense of and cast a critical eye upon their participation in the South African labor market.

Coplan's *In the Time of Cannibals* (1994; see also his *In Township Tonight!* 1985) is replete with Basotho men's and women's songs, which, thanks to the author's exegeses, provide a rich source of oral narratives from which the students can extract important cultural themes or uncover significant aspects of the social history surrounding the experience of migrancy and mining (poverty, unemployment, prostitution, homelessness, the trials of marriage and being away from one's family, etc.). When the texts are paired with the movie *Songs of the Adventurers* (Coplan 1986), which chronicles the performances of travelers responding to the challenges of everyday life with "complexly evocative word-music" (Coplan 1994: 8), students also become aware of the inseparability of verbal, sonic, and visual media. Like Barber's (1991) masterful study of Yoruba *oriki* praise texts, or Vail and White's (1991) historical exploration of southern African oral genres, Coplan's material lends itself well to a convincing demonstration of why it makes no sense to separate art from politics or history from representation when talking about African musical-oral performance. For instance, the familiar metaphor of cannibalism that structures a young migrant's song (Coplan 1994: 7) provides a good departure point from which to explore (1) what it means for people in South Africa or elsewhere to be "eaten up" by a host of economic, social, and political forces; (2) what history of violence (warfare, raiding, slavery) is conjured up through these images of wrongful consumption; and (3) the preponderance of the body in supplying graphic imagery that people can redeploy to comment on selfhood, society, and historical transformations.

There are, of course, other similarly rich musical traditions besides the Sotho songs described by Coplan that could be used in the classroom to discuss the impact of migrant labor on African societies. Erlmann's (1991) chapter on *isicathamiya* provides a good introduction to the history of this genre of Zulu male choral music (see also Coplan 1985; Bender 1991). Thanks to the appearance of Ladysmith Black Mambazo on Paul Simon's album *Graceland* and on the accompanying video, this genre of Zulu choir music is now better known outside of South Africa (see Erlmann 1989). Some of Ladysmith Black Mambazo's albums are now available in local music stores on the Shanachie label. Veit Erlmann has also produced two albums entitled *Isicathamiya: Zulu Worker Choir in South Africa* (1987) and *Mbube Roots: Zulu Choral Music from South Africa* (1986). A third album compiled by Kivnick (1987) also features a cross section of *isicathamiya* music performed in Durban, South Africa. Sections of Jeremy Marre's film *Rhythm of Resistance* (1979) again can be used to illustrate how powerful and rhythmically breathtaking men's choirs can be.

CONCLUSION

In this chapter, I have briefly outlined some of the potentially fruitful ways one can use African popular music as a lens through which to explore the culture and history of African people. Even the briefest study of music—what music is, what it does, what power it has, and how it is defined, performed, and appreciated—from various communities, nations, or regions of the continent yields insights into the culture, history, and struggles of African societies. Students may familiarize themselves with some of the ways Africans go about using words, rhythms, and melodies to make sense of their lives and to resist abusive governments, piece together the fragments of a shattered world, or comment on the trials of modernity. The rapid evolution of musical styles in the past ten or twenty years tangibly reminds students that they cannot look at culture as a stagnant group of "things." There are many musical genres I have not mentioned—such as the rich tradition of the *griots,* Sahelian bards who combine the roles of praise singers, messengers, and historians[2] (Conrad and Frank 1995; Zemp 1964; Bender 1991), or the jazzy music of Congo and Zaire that is sometimes referred to as *soukous* or *rumba*[3] (Bender 1991). *Soukous* could be used in the classroom to introduce students to particular facets of life in urban Zaire.[4] The point is that even if one is not an ethnomusicologist, there are easily available resources at the campus library and the local, urban music store that, when used to provide an entry into the lives, struggles, and aspirations of people in Conakry or Brazzaville or rural Tanzania, can lend stimulation, rhythm, and theoretical depth to a survey course on Africa.

ACKNOWLEDGMENTS

This chapter would not have been written without the intellectual support, editorial assistance, and patient advice provided by Misty Bastian, who also worked very hard to convince me that I could make a valuable contribution to this volume.

NOTES

1. For a thorough and sensitive account of *mbira* music in Shona society, see Berliner's *The Soul of Mbira* (1978). Though it was written before the nationalist aspirations of the country's Africans were to be realized through Zimbabwe's independence, it nevertheless provides a very helpful background to Bender's short description of *mbira*'s role in the Chimurenga. Berliner shows through telling, and sometimes moving, anecdotes that *mbira* music is an integral part of Shona identity

and culture and "a sacred gift from the ancestors" (245). He has produced two albums, *The Soul of Mbira* (1973) and *Shona Mbira Music* (1977). Available as well is an album produced by the Ephat Mujuru Ensemble (1986) under the title *The Mbira Music of Zimbabwe*.

2. A representative album available in the United States is Samuel Charters's *The Griots: Ministers of the Spoken Word* (1975). See also *The Wassoulou Sound: Women of Mali*.

3. A well-known figure of the Zairian music scene is Franco. His albums, such as *Le Grand Maître Franco et le Tout Puissant O.K. Jazz* (1990) are available at local music stores. I must mention also Tabuley Rochereau, the other Zairian giant, who recorded songs with the female singer Mbilia Bel. With Franco, he went on to record *Omona Wapi*.

4. The film *La Vie est Belle*, which takes us inside the vibrant music scene of Kinshasa in the early 1980s, can be used to lend visual support to a focus on *soukous* music. Directed by Ngangura Mweze and Benoit Lamy, it is available through California Newsreel.

SUGGESTIONS FOR FURTHER READING AND RESOURCES

PRINTED MATERIAL

Anderson, Benedict. 1983. *Imagined Communities: Reflections on the Spread of Nationalism*. London: Verso.

Barber, Karin. 1991. *I Could Speak Until Tomorrow: Oriki Women and the Past in a Yoruba Town*. Washington, D.C.: Smithsonian Institution Press.

Bender, Wolfgang. 1991. *Sweet Mother: Modern African Music*. Chicago: University of Chicago Press.

Berliner, Paul. 1978. *The Soul of Mbira: Music and Traditions of the Shona People of Zimbabwe*. Berkeley and Los Angeles: University of California Press.

Besmer, Fremont E. 1983. *Horses, Musicians, and Gods: The Hausa Cult of Possession-Trance*. South Hadley, Mass.: Bergin and Garvey.

Blacking, John. 1995. *Music, Culture, and Experience: Selected Papers of John Blacking,* ed. Reginald Byron. Chicago: University of Chicago Press.

Chernoff, John Miller. 1979. *African Rhythm and African Sensibility: Aesthetics and Social Action in African Musical Idioms*. Chicago: University of Chicago Press.

Collins, John. 1992. *West African Pop Roots*. Philadelphia: Temple University Press.

Conrad, David C., and Barbara E. Frank. 1995. *Status and Identity in West Africa: Nyamakalaw of Mande*. Bloomington and Indianapolis: Indiana University Press.

Coplan, David B. 1985. *In Township Tonight! South Africa's Black City Music and Theatre*. New York: Longman.

———. 1987. "Eloquent Knowledge: Lesotho Migrants' Songs and the Anthropology of Experience." *American Ethnologist* 14, 3: 413–433.

———. 1994. *In the Time of the Cannibals: The World Music of South Africa's Basotho Migrants*. Chicago: University of Chicago Press.

Erlmann, Veit. 1989. "A Conversation with Joseph Shabalala of Ladysmith Black

Mambazo: Aspects of African Performers' Lifestories." *World of Music* 31, 1: 31–58.

———. 1991. *African Stars: Studies in Black South African Performance.* Chicago: University of Chicago Press.

Hebert, Eugenia W. 1993. *Iron, Gender, and Power: Rituals of Transformation in African Societies.* Bloomington and Indianapolis: Indiana University Press.

Laye, Camara. 1976. *L'enfant noir.* Paris: Pocket.

Nketia, J. H. Kwabena. 1974. *The Music of Africa.* New York: W. W. Norton.

Rouget, Gilbert. 1985. *Music and Trance: A Theory of the Relations Between Music and Possession.* Chicago: University of Chicago Press.

Stapleton, Chris, and Chris May. 1990. *African Rock: The Pop Music of a Continent.* New York: Obelisk/Dutton.

Stoller, Paul. 1989. "Sound in Songhay Possession." In *The Taste of Ethnographic Things: The Senses in Anthropology.* Philadelphia: University of Pennsylvania Press.

Vail, Leroy, and Landeg White. 1991. *Power and the Praise Poem: Southern African Voices in History.* Carter G. Woodson Institute Series in Black Studies. Charlottesville: University Press of Virginia.

Waterman, Christopher Alan. 1990. *Juju: A Social History and Ethnography of an African Popular Music.* Chicago: University of Chicago Press.

Zemp, Hugo. 1964. "Musiciens Autochtones et Griots Malinké chez les Dan de Côte d'Ivoire." *Cahiers d'Etudes Africaines* 4, 3: 370–382.

FILMS AND RECORDINGS

Berliner, Paul. 1973. *The Soul of Mbira.* New York: Nonesuch Records, World Explorer Series H72077.

———. 1977. *Shona Mbira Music.* Nonesuch Records, World Explorer Series H72054.

Coplan, David. 1986. *Songs of the Aventurers.* Constant Spring.

Ephat Mujuru Ensemble. 1986. *The Mbira Music of Zimbabwe: The Spirit of the People.* Harare, Zimbabwe: Teal Record Company, ZML1003.

Erlmann, Veit. 1986. *Mbube Roots: Zulu Choral Music from South Africa, 1930s–1960s.* 33 1/3 disc. Cambridge, Mass.: Rounder, 5025.

———. 1987. *Isicathamiya: Zulu Worker Choirs in South Africa.* 33 1/3 disc. London: Heritage, HT313.

Fela Anikulapo-Kuti & the Africa 70. 1977. *Zombie.* London: Creole, CRLP511.

Franco (Luambo Makiadi). 1990. *Le Grand Maître Franco et le Tout Puissant O.K. Jazz.* Paris: Sono Disc, CD8476.

Kivnick, Helen. 1987. *Mbube! Zulu Men's Singing Competition.* 33 1/3 disc. Cambridge, Mass.: Rounder, 5023.

Mapfumo, Thomas, and the Blacks Unlimited. 1984. *Mabasa.* London: Earthworks/ Rough Trade, ERT1007.

Makeba, Miriam. 1989. *Welela.* New York: PolyGram Records.

Marre, Jeremy. 1979. *Rhythm of Resistance: Black South African Music.* Part of the PBS Beats of the Heart series. New York: Shanachie Entertainment, 1204.

Okosun, Sonny. 1978. *Fire in Soweto.* Paris: EMI Pathe Marconi 2C06482447.

5

TEACHING AFRICA
THROUGH LITERATURE

L. NATALIE SANDOMIRSKY

"Would you like to go to school?"

"O, mother!"—Njoroge gasped. He half feared that the woman might withdraw her words . . .

"You won't bring shame to me one day by refusing to attend school?"

"O mother, I'll never bring shame to you. Just let me get there, just let me." . . . "O mother, you are an angel of God, you are, you are."

Then he wondered. Had she been to see a magic worker? Or else how could she have divined his child's unspoken wish, his undivulged dream? (Ngugi 1987: 3)[1]

Why is going to school such an extraordinary event for the boy? Why does he think that his mother must have been inspired by a magic worker to send him to school? What, indeed, is a "magic worker?" The reader's interest is necessarily awakened by such a text. This dialogue is but one example of how African fiction allows outsiders to make direct cognitive and emotional contact with an unfamiliar culture. The novel, because of this facility, is the tool I chose to introduce students to the civilizations of western-central Africa in the course Negritude and Beyond, described in this chapter.

This course is a literature elective for third- and fourth-year North American undergraduates. Students do learn a few techniques of literary analysis during the term, but the main goal of the course is to acquaint them with modern West African literature and with the societies it portrays. Students are encouraged to develop a sense of relativism and an awareness of the similarities and differences between these cultures and their own. I also teach Negritude and Beyond as a required course for students in the honors college. In this case, it includes a stronger writing component. I selected the novels studied in accordance with three criteria: their literary merit, what aspects of African culture they reveal, and the fact that the problems they raise have universal resonance.

Since most North American students know little about Africa, however, I first briefly introduce the geography and history of this part of the continent. Geography, including climate and vegetation and the all-important distribution of ethnic groups, can be illustrated simply with the help of maps and charts. (See, for example, Gailey 1979.) History is a more complex matter, since it is important in any course on African topics for students to realize that the peoples who inhabit the continent have ancient cultures,[2] to be aware of the slave trade, and to know about the colonial and postcolonial periods. Therefore students are asked to read a book on African history in preparation for taking the course. (Texts I suggest include Bohannan and Curtin 1995; Curtin et al. 1994; Iliffe 1995; Oliver and Lafarge 1988; and Shillington 1995.)

In the introductory lectures I incorporate a presentation on oral African literature and on the relatively recent emergence of written literature in this part of Africa, using Abrahams (1983), Courlander (1996), or Johnson and others (1997) as sources. I also examine the reasons why most of this literature is still written in Western languages and the problems writers face in attempting to express their own cultures in words that carry foreign connotations.[3] These problems, which are the object of much controversy in African literary circles today, are discussed in greater detail later in the course when reading novels by Ahmadou Kourouma and Chinua Achebe.

The first readings are primarily African bildungsromans because they are closest to the students' own experience. There are many interesting ones to choose from. In the 1950s and 1960s, as West African writers sought to create a new literature reflective of their own cultural experiences, they often began their search by recapturing formative moments of their youth.

To set the stage and acquaint students with an African civilization in an accessible form, the first book we read for the class is an idyllic novel, Camara Laye's autobiographical *The Dark Child* (1954). In it Laye draws a picture of his family, meant to invalidate the stereotype of the African savage. (This is an appropriate place to briefly explain the Negritude movement and its ties to the Harlem Renaissance as well as to read a couple of poems by Senghor.) Readers encounter a deeply rooted, well-structured Guinean society in which the "child" grows into manhood, though not without some problems. The basic theme Laye develops is of the separation from family and the other ties of youth necessarily implied in the process of reaching adulthood. In Laye's case, there is also the conflict between his native society and the French-style education that eventually enabled him to become an internationally recognized writer. He learned a great deal in the process, but it required him to move away from everything and everyone who made him what he was. He has forfeited his right to discover the intimate secrets of his Mande culture, the same culture that he so fondly remembers and associates with his father. Was it worth it, he wonders; the students wonder with him.

Students thus begin their journey in the classroom by learning about a traditional African family, its daily life, its values and beliefs. They find themselves in quite a different world where there is no clear-cut distinction between the living and the dead, between humans and other creatures—a world where supernatural and magical powers are as real as the daily rising and setting of the sun. I sometimes point out here the resemblance between Laye's social milieu and that described by Nelson Mandela—an African all North American students are likely to have heard about—in his autobiography. It is also helpful here to show some video so that students can better visualize the landscape in this part of West Africa.

North American students clearly relate to Laye's experiences, often referring to their own family dynamics, their parents' attitude toward education, and the difficulties inherent in the transition to adulthood in our society. Every novel selected offers similar possibilities for comparative discussions while teaching students about African societies.

In the next novel, Ngugi Wa Thiong'o's *Weep Not, Child* (1987), students recognize some features similar to those in Laye's story. This, too, is the story of a young boy, Njoroge, whose family background and outlook appear at first very close to Laye's. Njoroge is also convinced of the importance of a Western-style education. He sees in it the path to a better life for himself, his family, and his people more generally. But the world in which he lives is, in many ways, shockingly different from Laye's. Whereas the white colonial administrator played only an incidental role in *The Dark Child,* Njoroge has to face the problems associated with European settler populations. This gives me the opportunity to explain the difference between colonial and settler societies on the continent during the earlier years of the twentieth century.

The havoc settlers cause occupies center stage in Ngugi's novel. Rebellion against British domination within Kenya appears inevitable and justified, yet Ngugi also shows how political and violent action causes disruption and grief for indigenous peoples. Njoroge's father becomes disoriented under the pressure of events he experiences. However valid his intentions, he fails to regain his ancestral land, the significance of which is one of the central themes of the novel. He is unable even to lead his family and, at the end, becomes a beaten man who seeks death. Njoroge is left without guidance. When his brothers' participation in the Mau Mau rebellion causes his expulsion from school, Njoroge sees his dreams of a better future based on education shattered by the maelstrom of history.

The impact of Western education is also the main theme of Cheikh Hamidou Kane's *Ambiguous Adventure* (1972). In this story of young Samba Diallo, Kane outlines a heartwrenching dilemma. Samba's people, the Diallobé of eastern Senegal, are abysmally poor, and in order to survive in the midst of enforced modernization, they must acquire Western skills. These same skills may also someday enable them to stand up to the French invaders. Yet as one of their rulers, the Most Royal Lady, says: "The school in which I would place our children will kill in them what today we love and rightly conserve with care"—their spiritual values (Kane 1972: 46).

Samba, the most talented scion of the local ruling aristocracy, is sent to France by his family and is subsequently destroyed by the clash between what is presented as Western materialism and the emphasis on spirituality in his own society. He cannot reconcile reason and faith. There is little room here for the indigenous African religious understandings found in the previous novels. Students learn about Muslim teachings in Kane's novel. Moreover, whereas all the novels we read present universal problems, Kane's is the most classical in that it questions the very meaning of human existence, a question that tends to be very meaningful to students in their teens and early twenties.

Since I allow one and one-half weeks for each novel in the course, *Ambiguous Adventure* is at times quite difficult for students. The next novel is also long; so I have found that this is a good place for a small break in the class. Students, for whom images have become a cardinal component of the learning process, can now be shown slides, videos, or films for a couple of classes as they begin reading Ousmane Sembène's *God's Bits of Wood* (1986).[4]

This book was chosen for the course because it is a fictional account of a historic event, the Dakar-Bamako Railroad strike of 1947–1948.[5] This strike is presented to us by Sembène as the first step in the battle for decolonization in that African workers are shown demanding respect from their foreign bosses. Racism on the part of the colonizers, labor-management relations, and the role of women in both the family and the strike are themes illustrated throughout the novel, offering excellent topics for class discussion. The way Sembène depicts these issues enables students to catch a glimpse of popular culture in two Senegalese and one Malian city during the immediate post–World War II period.

Ousmane Sembène, who is also a renowned film director, paints his narrative with a descriptive, panoramic brush, which can be somewhat confusing for students at first. It is helpful to supply them with a list of the characters mentioned in the novel, classified by their stance toward the strike. I also draw a chart indicating the progression of action taken alternately by labor and management during the strike.

Of particular interest for contemporary readers of this novel is the portrayal of women of different ages and social and educational status, particularly the way the strike propels them out of the family compound into public life and ultimately into decisive, independent action. The strike changes not only their self-image but also the way the men perceive them.

Sembène wrote *God's Bits of Wood* as a memorial to the struggle for independence. The remaining novels read for the course describe the disappointments of the postindependence period: dictatorship, poverty, and the difficulties encountered by women under these new regimes. I am not concerned here with the extent to which postindependence conditions are an aftermath of colonialism or, as some believe, are due to continuing Western imperialism. I merely help students to learn about conditions in the region today.

This exploration begins with *The Suns of Independence,* in which Kourouma (1981) gives us a fictional portrayal of the Ivory Coast, illustrating the effects of social change on the Ivorien individual. Kourouma is a supporter of independence at all levels, which can be seen in the way he adapts the French language to his own needs, using Malinké words, literal translations of indigenous idioms, and fractured syntax. (The translator for the English edition has carefully preserved Kourouma's very personal use of language.) Yet Kourouma also bemoans the abuses of the new African government. In order to demonstrate these themes, he chooses as hero of his novel Fama, a weak man unable to adapt.

Fama's is the tragedy of any proud man who cannot adjust to changed circumstances, but the tragedy is presented in terms characteristic of his culture. He is a prince reduced to begging by a new society that has deprived him of his hereditary status, has no place for him because he is illiterate in Western languages, and persecutes him because he is perceived as an enemy by the tyrannical new ruler. What is worse for him than all these other misfortunes is the fact that he has no children. This is still the ultimate calamity in Fama's society. Not having children means that a person will be no one's ancestor and is only mortal. Allah is considered to have abandoned such a person. I insist on the importance the culture attaches to leaving descendants and explain how this affects contemporary efforts to institute birth control in many parts of the African continent, not only in the Ivory Coast.

At Fama's side, occupying an important place in the novel, is his wife, Salimata. She has adjusted to the new social milieu and makes a modest living for both of them, cooking and selling her food in the marketplace. However, Salimata too is obsessed by the fact that she has no children. She assumes that this is because of her infertility, and in accordance with local practice she sees this physical problem as a divine punishment. Salimata prays to Allah; she lets herself be taken advantage of by unscrupulous marabous and "fetishists"—Muslim and indigenous religious practices are intertwined in the novel—but to no avail. The sterile one is actually revealed to be Fama!

As our readings have progressed through the course, female characters become increasingly visible. The next assigned novel, *So Long a Letter* (Bâ 1981), written in an epistolary-journal form, is by a woman and very explicitly about women. It was the earliest bestseller by a female author in francophone Africa. In it the heroine, Ramatoulaye, addresses her closest woman friend, who is far away. Ramatoulaye is at a critical time in her life. Writing is cathartic for her and provides some of the support her friend's presence would have given her. The story is about the difficulties and pain she, an educated woman, encounters in male-dominated, Senegalese Muslim society. The book is clearly a statement about a woman's rights and an attack against polygyny (Bruner 1993; James 1990). This short novel is about feelings and domestic struggles rather than public events, and it allows students an introspective pause prior to coming to grips with the difficulties posed by Chinua Achebe's *Anthills of the Savannah* (1988).

In this novel Achebe, for the first time in his career, gives a prominent voice to a female character, but his emphasis is on politics and questions of national identity. Whether in fact nationhood can be attained in countries artificially carved out in the nineteenth century by European powers to suit their own purposes remains a burning question in western and central Africa today. This novel was selected to show how an African writer presents the political problems that continue to plague the region, problems that are familiar to at least some North American students because they are often discussed in electronic and print media here.

Under the veil of fiction, Achebe describes life in Nigeria and the deleterious effects of a capricious dictatorship and its many abuses of power. Europeans are irrelevant in the novel; what matters is an examination of the past in order to discover where things went wrong and to find a formula for a government that is viable for the very different urban and rural populations of the country.

Achebe tries to define nationhood in the novel and wonders whether it can be achieved in a region with hundreds of different ethnic groupings, many of which speak mutually unintelligible languages. Yet his faith in the people, in particular in the workers and students, prompts him to suggest that a new sense of community might yet be created. He closes his tragic tale on a note of hope with a description of the naming ceremonies for a baby boy, symbolic of renewal and continuing possibilities for Nigerian people.

This is a most interestingly structured novel, but it can be difficult for students to comprehend. Scenes become meaningful only some time after they have been described, and readers see events through the eyes of three, sometimes four, quite different main characters, all of whom illustrate aspects of Achebe's own concerns. The difficult structure of *Anthills of the Savannah* requires a good deal of intervention on the part of the instructor.

Throughout the course, at the start of every new novel, students receive a list of questions meant to help them avoid misunderstanding, focus on the elements of particular interest for this class, and select a subject for the paper they must write after each novel has been discussed. Such a study aid is particularly indispensable for *Anthills*. It is also very helpful to establish connections between class readings and current events in Nigeria and other parts of the continent. Dailies and magazines are sometimes useful for this; email and the Internet offer interesting possibilities for keeping students abreast of recent developments in Africa as well. The Internet has many Web pages devoted to nations in our area of study. These pages are of unequal value; some are in French and a majority are in English. I have found it more fruitful to ask students to subscribe to a couple of lists, which, of course, I also monitor during the term. These lists relate news, information, and commentary often sent by indigenes of African countries and are revealing of some of the viewpoints of people most directly concerned with local life and cultural practices in the countries being studied. Information gathered by these means provides suitable material for additional, in-class discussions and for term papers. In spring 1996, for instance, we concentrated on the Saro-Wiwa tragedy, human rights, population control, and female circumcision, using electronic as well as more conventional text-based research sources.

There are always some current events and subjects of debate that tie in with what the students have discussed in class, and they discover that what they have learned from their readings enables them to better understand current problems on the continent. This understanding may encourage them to remain interested in Africa. Thus African novels can provide North American students both a window into Africa's past and a sense of connection to and greater sympathy for its future. They are an indispensable tool in the classroom.

NOTES

1. Ngugi is Kenyan, but I have included this novel in the course because it fits in so well thematically.

2. See Basil Davidson, *Africa: A Voyage of Discovery,* 8 video cassettes. (Chicago: Home Vision), #8339092, I–IV. Excerpts are shown in class throughout the term.

3. See Ngugi Wa Thiong'o (1986), *Decolonizing the Mind,* and Irele (1990: 27–65). A special issue of *Peuples noirs peuples africains* (1987–1988) is also devoted to the use of the French language in former French colonies. Most articles are in French, a couple in English.

4. Sources for African films: Library of African Cinema, 149 Ninth Street, San Francisco, CA 94103; New Yorker Films, 16 West 61st Street, New York, NY 10023; Filmmakers Library, 124 East 40th Street, New York, NY 10016.

5. A video, *Chroniques francophones 2* (New York: FACSEA), shows the railroad in operation today and talks about its history. The video is in French. I give students an English synopsis of the script as a handout.

SUGGESTIONS FOR
FURTHER READINGS AND RESOURCES

Abrahams, Roger D. 1983. *African Folktales.* New York: Pantheon Books.

Achebe, Chinua. 1988. *Anthills of the Savannah.* New York: Doubleday.

Bâ, Mariama. 1981. *So Long a Letter,* trans. M. Bodé-Thomas. Portsmouth, N.H.: Heinemann.

Curtin, Philip D., Steven Feierman, Leonard Thompson, and Jan Vansina. 1994. *African History: From the Earliest Times to the End of Colonialism,* 2nd ed. New York: Icon.

Bohannan, Paul, and Philip Curtin. 1995. *Africa and Africans,* 4th ed. Prospect Heights, Ill.: Waveland Press.

Bruner, Charlotte H., ed. 1993. *African Women's Writing.* Portsmouth, N.H.: Heinemann.

Courlander, Harold. 1996. *A Treasury of African Folklore.* New York: Marlowe.

Gailey, Harry. 1979. *The History of Africa in Maps.* Chicago: Denoyyer-Geppert.

Iliffe, John. 1995. *Africa: The History of a Continent.* New York: Cambridge University Press.

Irele, Abriola. 1990. *The African Experience in Literature and Ideology.* Bloomington: Indiana University Press.

James, Adeola, ed. 1990. *In Their Own Voices.* Portsmouth N.H.: Heinemann.

Johnson, John W., Thomas A. Hale, and Stephen Belcher, eds. 1997. *Oral Epics from Africa.* Bloomington: Indiana University Press.

Kane, Cheikh Hamidou. 1972. *Ambiguous Adventure,* trans. Katherine Woods. Portsmouth, N.H.: Heinemann.

Kourouma, Ahmadou. 1981. *The Suns of Independence,* trans. A. Adams. New York: Africana.

Laye, Camara. 1954. *The Dark Child,* trans. Jane Kirkup and Ernest Jones. New York: Farrar, Straus and Giroux.

Mandela, Nelson. 1994. *The Long Road to Freedom.* Boston: Little, Brown.

Ngugi Wa Thiong'o. 1986. *Decolonizing the Mind.* Portsmouth, N.H.: Heinemann.

———. 1987. *Weep Not, Child.* Portsmouth, N.H.: Heinemann.

Oliver, Roland, and J. D. Lafarge. 1988. *A Short History of Africa,* 6th ed. London: Pelican Books.

Peuples noirs peuples africains. 1987–1988. 59–62 (special issue) (Sept.–Dec./ Jan.–Apr.).

Sembène, Ousmane. 1986. *God's Bits of Wood,* trans. Francis Price. Portsmouth, N.H.: Heinemann.

Shillington, Kevin. 1995. *History of Africa,* rev. ed. New York: St. Martin's Press.

WEB SITES

African Studies Center Online. http://www.sas.upenn.edu/~africa/.

Islamic Association for Palestine. http://www.iap.org.

News Resource. http://newo.com:80/news/africa.html.

Nigeria Today. http://nigeriatoday.com.

PART TWO

CONTROVERSIAL SUBJECTS AND CURRENT ISSUES

6

TEACHING THE
AFRICAN SLAVE
TRADE WITH DOCUMENTS

CURTIS A. KEIM

Teaching undergraduate survey courses is one of the most challenging and interesting tasks in the academy. Students (and teachers) quickly tire of basic lectures and textbooks, but the large number of students, their beginning level, and the need for rapid and broad coverage often make it difficult to conduct more interesting classes, particularly lively discussions and individual research. To attempt to solve this problem in my one-term African history survey, I often ask students to react to sets of documents. For example, when covering African geography, I provide students with a series of maps in class and ask them to work out principles to explain why the rain forest is in the middle of the continent and how wet and dry seasons vary according to one's location. When we talk about precolonial African states, my students read Niane's *Sundiata: An Epic of Old Mali* (1995) and portions of a contrasting verse version, al-Bakri (Murphy 1972), *Ibn Battuta* (Hamdun and King 1975), and a sixteenth-century description (Sousa 1971) of Mwanamutapa (in Zimbabwe) so they can begin to formulate a critical approach to African epics and leadership principles, based on primary sources. I often use similar small sets of sources for other topics such as human evolution, village life, Bantu expansion, the Scramble for Africa, and independence struggles. There must be dozens of further topics that would be interesting and feasible with this kind of approach, such as Egypt and the Greeks, Shaka, the Great Trek, Mau Mau, missionaries, and development projects.

If I choose the documents and questions well, students remain interested and learn how historians work. The challenge is finding original sources suitable for this kind of teaching because published collections of documents tend to be either too specialized or too general. I have learned that the documents need to be short and their points relatively clear. They should also come in sets so that they reflect on each other. And they should raise significant problems as well as illustrate the facts I am teaching.

The slave trade documents I use provide an example of how such sets can function in the classroom. This set consists of materials related to life along the lower Gambia River in the late eighteenth century. I first started collecting these sources in the early 1980s after several of my Africanist colleagues, both African and North American, mentioned that Alex Haley's *Roots* (1967) was not an accurate portrayal of life in the old Gambian town of Juffure. On a number of occasions Haley has been taken to task and to court over elements of *Roots,* and we know now that for all his book reflects the terrible emotional reality of slavery and the slave trade, historical events were often invented or disregarded (see Britt 1993; Nobile 1993; Ottaway 1977; and Wright 1981 for perspectives on Haley). Haley portrayed his ancestor Kunta Kinte as having been kidnapped by white slavers from an idyllic and totally African Juffure. But if this was inaccurate, I wondered what the story of Juffure would have been like had Haley used the original sources as a historian would. So I began to collect accounts of life on the Gambia River from published travel narratives and from scholars such as Donald Wright (1981) and Philip Curtin (1975), who had done oral research in the Gambia or had searched the relevant archives.

Those wishing to use the documents discussed in this chapter can locate most of them in North American libraries.[1] The most complete accounts are selections from travel narratives by Francis Moore (1736) and Mungo Park (1799), who visited the Gambia River in the 1730s and 1790s respectively. Modern scholars Philip Curtin (1975), Winifred Galloway (1978), J. M. Gray (1966), and Donald Wright (1979) include maps, charts, chronologies, and documents in their studies. Two of my documents are inaccessible to all but the most persistent. One (Anonymous 1776), from the French National Archives in bad French (translated for students), is a highly prejudiced account of the lower river. The other (Littleton 1789) is the testimony before the House of Parliament of William Littleton, a man who had been a slave trader on the Gambia River in the 1760s and 1770s. An excerpt of his testimony is included in note 1. Teachers will also need to provide a brief glossary to explain a few unfamiliar words and because some documents use older place names such as Jillifree for Juffure or Barra for Niumi.

My list could probably be improved with further research and perhaps with suggestions from readers of this chapter. Whatever the limitations, however, the sources get at many major points about the Gambia River trade. They show that the river was part of a complex trading system in which Europeans and Africans cooperated. African slavers called *slatees* purchased war captives far inland on the upper Niger River and brought them in caravans to the coast. These *slatees* had a number of economic choices to make as they approached the coast. They could choose either the Senegal River, where the French dominated, or the Gambia River, where the British held sway. On the Gambia they could either sell upriver for a quick but low sum or travel to the mouth, where they had the choice of selling immediately or waiting with a local host for a good price. Even at the mouth of the Gambia River *slatees* had a choice of customers: the British, local African brokers, or a small French post.

The documents show that Africans at all levels of society were deeply involved in the trade. Coastal kingdoms such as Niumi got their principal revenue from the trade; trading towns were controlled by African *alcades* who were appointees of the kings; and local residents produced food, salt, donkeys, hides, gold, beeswax, and other goods to sell to the traders. Most supplies of slaves came from Africans, and Philip Curtin (1975) believes his data indicate that most slaves were originally captured in the interior as a result of local "political" disputes and not as an "economic" response to demand on the coast. Yet some people were also enslaved purely for profit, as is seen in the way coastal African justice was corrupted in order to make enslavement for petty crimes easy.

One of the more interesting aspects of the documents is that they show the balance of power between Africans and Europeans on the coast. Both depended on the trade and on each other. Europeans not only desired slaves; they were virtual hostages of Africans, since they could survive for only short periods without local help. The British lived on James Island, a tidewater rock guarding the mouth of the river that had no fresh water or gardens. Africans could use the French as allies, periodically attack the British, or withhold provisions, but they could do so only for a short time because the British were ultimately stronger than the French and because profits from tolls and trade funded the royal court.

Over time the interaction between Europeans and Africans also produced a group of African and Eurafrican women traders known as *senhoras*. European men sometimes married African women on the coast for companionship and trade advantages, and some of these women became traders in their own right because of their intelligence and the high European mortality rate—which meant their husbands frequently died and left them with a stock of goods. The *senhoras* therefore could achieve wealth and high status in both the African and European communities.

When I first began to teach with these documents, I introduced them with Haley's description of how he discovered his ancestor Kunta Kinte and with his description of the kidnapping (see Haley 1967 and Schoumatoff 1995). Now I rarely mention Haley because the issues surrounding the veracity of *Roots* seem to divert students from the African issues that I consider more important. The assignment now varies but usually asks students for a general description of what was going on. For example, in a recent term I gave the following assignment: "You are a historian who has been asked to write a short article for nonspecialists (about 600–800 words, typed or printed) on what was going on in the late eighteenth century on the Gambia River. A small collection of primary sources on the topic is on reserve in the library. You may also use the lectures and the assigned textbook reading on the slave trade." The textbook reading I use is something I wrote, but there are a number of other suitable introductory readings.

If we have plenty of time, it is possible to have students read the documents, then talk about them in class before they write the paper. Papers are much better this way, as the assignment requires students to consider the nature of the sources. Most often, however, the schedule is pressing us onward, and an introductory lecture on the slave trade and a general reading are all that precede the assignment. Thus the papers are primarily a device to be sure that students have read the sources and have done preliminary synthesis and analysis.

On the day the papers are due, we have a full discussion of the documents and the issues they raise. I begin by asking volunteers to summarize their "what was going on?" papers while I make a list of terms and points on the board (e.g., *slatees, alcades, senhoras,* kings, British vs. French). Then I turn to the sources themselves and discuss those that many students puzzle over, such as the list of items traded for slaves (which can inform us about African preferences for goods), the chart of values and prices of slaves over time (which Curtin uses to defend his "political" model of the trade), or the maps.

Next I ask about the quality of all the sources, and students consider questions such as who the authors are, when they wrote, whether we can trust them, what to do with contradictions, what points of view we lack, and what we cannot know. Invariably these considerations bring students into conflict with each other because, as historians themselves do, they see the sources differently. Soon we are discussing specific passages and why one source might be better than another. If we can, we draw up some principles about how to use the sources. Most important, I make sure that students understand that Africans did not get to write these sources and that the situation on the Gambia River has both similarities and differences with the trade in other parts of Africa.

I do not try to conclude that one student or source is right and another wrong, because not only are the sources ambiguous on some points but the students often come to the discussion with deeply held beliefs that interfere with their seeing either the ambiguity or the implications of certain passages. Some students, for example, will assert that the sources must be lying when they state that white men rarely if ever kidnapped Africans for fear of ruining trade relationships with them. Generally there is quite a bit of emotion in the statement because they want to know who should take blame for the trade rather than how the trade was carried on. The question of blame is important, but I would rather deal with it head on and a bit later than get caught up in an argument over whether kidnapping was common. I merely note that evidence from all along the African coast suggests that few Europeans risked alienating their African trading partners by kidnapping. As long as students stick with discussing the sources I let them have their say—so they can understand the problems historians themselves face—without my entering their debate over whether one source or another is true or false.

Inevitably we do come to the question of blame, either because the students raise the issue or because I do. In my classes at Moravian College, where I often have an entire class of white students (Moravian is overwhelmingly white, and all students are required to take one course in a non-Western culture), the question sometimes comes up as an expression of relief that whites are not as bad as they have been portrayed—because Africans participated in the trade, too—or students might express anger at those who fail to teach or admit this or wonder at how "they" could do this to "their own people." At Lehigh University, where I sometimes teach as an adjunct professor, my classes are more likely to be multicultural and multiracial. African American students are likely to raise the question of whether Europeans are not really to blame for the whole trade even if Africans participated. Emotions can get strained and students can see how so-called historical problems frequently reflect current ones.

Now the challenge is to move students from "good guys–bad guys," "right and wrong," "them and us" views of history to a fuller understanding of our common humanity and our own ambiguous involvements in human affairs. I can sometimes help the discussion along (i.e., appeal to reasoned argument) by asking students to compare the effects of the slave trade on European and African societies, which usually helps show that both societies gained and lost but that Africans gained much less and lost much more than Europeans. I also note that the trade must have had a great deal to do with forces outside of Africa because Europeans and Americans were able to stop it when they adopted industrial-age economics and ethics (which present their own set of problems). Africans who attempted to end the trade would have certainly failed.

Sometimes it helps students if I ask them to consider the similar questions surrounding the present-day drug trade between the United States and countries to the south. Who is involved? Who should get the blame? What are the effects on societies? Who are the victims? Ironically, the equation is changed here, for we tend to blame the suppliers—the producers and drug lords in other countries and our own—some of whom would be African in the case of the slave trade. In fact, however, the drug trade occurs not because some races, countries, or individuals are good and others are bad but because humans operate with mixed motives. We live in a time when opportunities to produce and sell drugs offer irresistible temptations and benefits for many people, both in the North and the South. The comparison with the slave trade, which had its own temptations and benefits, becomes obvious.

I recently posted a message about these documents on a scholarly Internet listserv and described the emotions that many students feel when they learn the extent of the involvement of Africans in the slave trade. Two responses seem relevant here by way of conclusion. One colleague argued that the Gambia River documents should not be taught to students because *Roots,* not the documents, catches the emotional reality of the slave trade and documents should focus on African resistance. Another asserted that we have neglected African involvement in the trade for the black-and-white picture given by *Roots* and that we need documents such as these to understand the humanity of the situation. I agree with the latter view but note that teachers who do not sympathetically take into account the former will be in trouble. If, for example, teachers present any documents as representative of the entire African end of the Atlantic slave trade rather than as a case study, they will seriously misrepresent African history.

Those who want to explore the various effects of the slave trade in Africa might begin with *The Atlantic Slave Trade,* a book of documents and articles edited by David Northrup (1994). This collection is also useful in classes where time allows a more extensive consideration of the slave trade. Those searching for an effective example of the terrible effects of the trade might read Northrup's selection from Joseph Miller's *Way of Death* (1988). Another useful source is *The Atlantic Slave Trade: Effects on Economies, Societies, and Peoples in Africa, the Americas, and Europe,* a collection of scholarship on the subject edited by Joseph Inikori and Stanley Engerman (1992).

We should remember that any group of Africanist historians will disagree with each other on how to interpret documents. But the uncertainty and our groping attempts to reduce ambiguity with facts and interpretations are what makes history so engaging and important. If we provide students with the raw materials of history—that is, the sources—they enter into historical debates over the meanings of facts, and they learn how to make credible arguments. If, however, we merely present facts and interpretations in traditional lecture-textbook style, students miss much of what history offers. I am concerned that my students learn facts and interpretations, but I am even more concerned that they see that history is about our corporate construction of reality. Facts rarely speak for themselves. They gain meaning through the dialogue that we call history. In working with the documents students learn to enter the dialogue about meaning that is so important to those of us who study Africa.

ACKNOWLEDGMENTS

Many thanks to Bill Scott, Karen Keim, and the editors for their critical readings of this chapter.

NOTES

1. Following are the student handouts. Maps: Curtin (1975: 97); Gray (1966: end map); Moore (1736), mouth of the Gambia River from the map accompanying the book. Charts: Curtin (1975: 172, 331). Chronology: Galloway (1978). Glossary: Alcade/Alkkade/Alcaid, Albreda, Barra/Bar/Barrah, factory, Fort James, Juffure/Jillifree/Gillyfree, Niumi/Nomi, St. Domingo. Translation: of Anonymous (1776). Summary: my three-paragraph summary of Gray (1966). Document: Littleton (1789). Excerpts: Park (1799: 4, 25–26); Moore (1738: 42–43, 46, 54–59, 127–128); for the excerpt from Littleton (1789), see below.

Excerpt from the testimony of Captain William Littleton:

> *Have you been at Gambia?* Yes.
> *In what capacity did you go?* As Mate.
> *In what Year?* In 1762.
> *How long did you continue there?* Eleven Years—trading there as a Merchant.
> *In the course of your trade did you go up the river Gambia?* Yes.
> *Was you acquainted with the Language of the country?* Sufficiently so to do my business with the natives.
> *Are you acquainted with their manners and customs?* Tolerably so— as much as a man could be who resided chiefly on board his vessel.
> *Is Slavery known in that Country as a general condition?* Yes.
> *Do the Freemen keep many Slaves?* Some do.
> *How are the Slaves obtained, which are sold to the Europeans?* By various modes—a great proportion of them from the Black traders, who are Mahometans, and traverse the interior part of the Country to get Slaves.
> *Do you know of any wars being carried on for the purpose of obtaining Slaves to sell to the Europeans?* I never heard of any carried on for that purpose. The wars have always originated from their own dissentions.
> *Are wars beneficial, or otherwise, to the Slave trade carried on by the Europeans?* Wars in the vicinity of the trading ports are always injurious to the trade in articles of every kind; and I have been told by the Black Merchants that they have gone 3 or 400 miles to avoid those countries where wars existed.

Do you know of the practice of kidnapping slaves, or that they are taken by fraud or violence, by Blacks or Whites? I never heard that a Whiteman ever kidnapped a Slave; if he did, it would put a total end to that man's trading—I never heard of such a thing—I speak of the river Gambia only, I don't know what is done on the other parts of the Coast—I never heard that of any of the natives in that part where I resided and did business.—If they made any attempt of that kind, they would be sold themselves.

Have you ever heard of any parties going out armed at night to take Slaves? Never, but against their enemies, with whom they were at open war.

SUGGESTIONS FOR
FURTHER READING AND RESOURCES

Anonymous. 1776. "Détails sur l'Etablissement des Français dans la Rivière de Gambie et sur le Caractère de Quelques Rois de Ce Pays." Archives Nationales de France, C612.

Britt, Donna. 1993. "Rooting Up Haley's Legacy." *Washington Post* (March 2): B1, B4.

Curtin, Philip. 1975. "The Lower Gambia About 1750." In *Economic Change in Precolonial Africa.* Madison: University of Wisconsin Press.

Galloway, Winifred. 1978. "Chronology of James Island." In *A Nutshell History of James Island,* 2nd ed. Banjul: Vice-President's Office, Oral History and Antiquities Division.

Gray, J. M. 1966. *A History of the Gambia.* London: Frank Cass.

Haley, Alex. 1967. *Roots.* New York: Doubleday.

———. 1972. "My Furthest-Back Person—'The African.'" *New York Times,* section 6 (July 16): 12–16.

Hamdun, Said, and Noël King. 1975. *Ibn Battuta in Black Africa.* London: Rex Collings.

Inikori, Joseph E., and Stanley L. Engerman, eds. 1992. *The Atlantic Slave Trade: Effects on Economies, Societies, and Peoples in Africa, the Americas, and Europe.* Durham and London: Duke University Press.

Keim, Curtis A. 1996. "Africa and Europe Before 1900." In *Africa,* 3rd ed., ed. Phyllis M. Martin and Patrick O'Meara. Bloomington: Indiana University Press, 115–133.

Littleton, William. 1789. "The State of the African Slave Trade." Testimony of Captain William Littleton to the Committee of the Whole House of Parliament. Public Record Office, ZHC 1/82, June 18.

Miller, Joseph C. 1988. *Way of Death: Merchant Capitalism and the Angloan Slave Trade, 1730–1830.* Madison: University of Wisconsin Press.

Moore, Francis. 1736. *Travels in the Inland Parts of Africa.* London: Edward Cave.

Murphy, E. Jefferson. 1972. *History of African Civilization.* New York: Dell, 110–111.

Naine, Djibril Tamsir. 1995. *Sundiata: An Epic of Old Mali,* trans. by G. D. Pickett. New York: Longman African Classics, Addison-Wesley.

Nobile, Philip. 1993. "Uncovering Roots." *Village Voice* 38, 8: 31–38.

Northrup, David, ed. 1994. *The Atlantic Slave Trade.* Lexington, Mass.: D. C. Heath.

Ottaway, Mark. 1977. "Tangled Roots." *Sunday Times* (London) (April 10): 17, 21.

Park, Mungo. 1799. *Travels in the Interior Districts of Africa.* London: Blumer.

Schoumatoff, Alex. 1995 (1985). *The Mountain of Names: A History of the Human Family.* New York: Kodansha International, 220–224.

Sousa, Manuel de Faria E. 1971. "The Kingdom of the Mwanamutapa." In *African History: Text and Readings,* ed. Robert O. Collins. New York: Random House, 396–398.

Wright, Donald. 1979. "Eurafrican Women of Juffure." In "Niumi, The History of a Western Mandinka State Through the Eighteenth Century." Ph.D. diss., Indiana University, Bloomington.

———. 1981. "Uprooting Kunta Kinte: On the Perils of Relying on Encyclopedic Informants." *History in Africa* 8: 205–217.

7

TEACHING STUDENTS ABOUT ETHNICITY IN AFRICA

BILL BRAVMAN

One day, an American driving across the savannah of southeastern Kenya saw two young Maasai men gesturing hopefully for a ride. The American picked them up and, after a few pleasantries, asked them where they were going. "Just here," one said, pointing to a gas station the truck was fast approaching. "We work here."

They had covered about half a mile, and the American looked confused. "You *are* Maasai?" he ventured. When they agreed that they were, he added tentatively, "I thought Maasai walk very long distances." The young men looked at each other, and one turned to the American. "It is nicer to ride," he said, then invited the American (myself, fresh out of college in 1983) to join them for a soda at the gas station.

If you ask your students, "What is an African ethnic group?" their answers will probably reflect the common knowledge they (and we) grew up with: They are groups of people united by ancient ties of blood and culture. In this conventional wisdom, ethnic ties are a primordial force of nature—ethnic groups have long pasts and rich cultures—but when students are pushed to identify the sources of those ties and customs, most ultimately hold that they are rooted in an antediluvian biological commonality. How ubiquitous is this view? References to someone's ethnicity as her blood remain commonplace far beyond the classroom.

I often ask my students to explain the difference between an African ethnic group and an African tribe. Most say that "tribe" is a pejorative term, and some add that it emphasizes primitivism and barbarism, but students' views of African ethnicity usually repackage many of the stereotypes about tribes in a less offensive manner. Many Westerners, students included, see African ethnic groups as either living according to ancient ways or in continuing thrall to those ways despite a veneer of modernity. Modernity, according to this conventional wisdom, bemuses or threatens ethnically bounded Africans or (when ethnicity gets linked to African violence, as in 1990s Rwanda) simply recontextualizes primordial blood feuds.[1]

However, scholars studying ethnicity in Africa have known for decades that Western conventional wisdom on the subject is both wrong and misleading. Virtually all researchers now agree that African ethnic groups do not stem from ancient biology but instead developed shared identities through social interactions that date to particular historical eras. Scholars of Africa still argue about the timing and causes of ethnicizations, as well as over terms by which to decide when groups become "ethnic," but such debates take place within a general consensus on the historical character of ethnicity. Africanists have reached other points of consensus as well, all of which run against the grain of Western common knowledge. Some ethnic affiliations are indeed quite old, but many arose in the nineteenth and even the twentieth centuries. We know, too, that not only have African ethnic groups adapted to the modern world, many ethnic identifications have flourished most fully in modern contexts: Zulu ethnicity, for instance, has been most thoroughly articulated and mobilized in the twentieth century. Further confounding the biologized common view of ethnicity, abundant scholarship has shown that ethnic groups are often extremely porous: "Outsiders" have often joined or left particular ethnic affiliations, and people have often strategically blurred their identities across different ethnic affiliations.

Finally, it is clear that African ethnic cultures change—and quite a bit—over time, usually without weakening peoples' identification with them. This is evident in everyday life (where young Maasai men hitchhike short distances to work at gas stations) and in wider social spheres (Zulu ethnicity is now mobilized as much through a political party as through its 180-year-old kingship). This also holds true in what countless movies, old documentaries, and *National Geographic*s have romanticized to Westerners as a particularly timeless, "tribal" realm: rituals and formal performance.

To provide teachers with tools for explaining the current thinking about ethnicity in Africa, I discuss in this chapter how I teach the topic in a small-class setting using a well-known ethnic group, the Maasai. I then draw on the history of a less well-known group, the Taita, to show how I lecture about ethnicity in a large introductory class where less reading and interaction are possible. In both settings I begin by addressing preconceived notions about ethnicity in Africa as a prelude to reshaping them. The Maasai and Taita cases also emphasize an important point about contemporary Africa: Even though African ethnic groups are historical rather than biological, many Africans have internalized their ethnicities as fundamental and critically important to their identities. This puts African ethnicity on par with, say, American national identity. After all, the United States is only a few hundred years old and most citizens' ancestors arrived in the country more recently still; yet many of its people all-but-unconsciously consider Americanness and an American "national character" central to their identity.

SMALL-CLASS TEACHING: MAASAI ETHNICITY

In almost any Western classroom, students asked to name an African ethnic group will mention the Maasai. Certain pervasive images have made the Maasai the archetype for Western imaginings of African ethnic peoples: Tall and noble of profile, the fierce warriors with ochered hair roam the plains with spears while the women, bedecked in elaborate beadwork, remain in thornbush-fenced circular compounds. Older men and women, bareheaded and wearing only loose shifts of cloth, seem to have the wisdom of the ages etched on their bodies. Maasai have long been seen by Westerners as haughtily pure of descent, consummately pastoral, and uncompromisingly traditional: They resist neighbors, modernity, and Westernization, sticking instead to their ancient, self-isolating ways of life.

When one examines the history of the Maasai, though, the findings do not match those images. I often broach this subject in small classes by juxtaposing an in-class examination of one of the many coffee-table books on Maasai with other images and subsequent reading as well as discussion of recent scholarship (Beckwith 1980; Ritts 1994; and others). Coffee-table photography of the Maasai typically has a quasi-anthropological style of catching life in the act, as well as high production values. It thus projects an authoritativeness often not questioned at first by students. When asked what they can discern about the Maasai from the pictures, they observe what is projected: a world where people's dress, rituals, and everyday activities seem closely knit together by tradition, a society utterly removed from Western ways and modernity.

But students can also quickly pierce the apparent transparency of such photos. When asked whether the pictures show us natural moments or are staged and framed, students soon notice how carefully (com)posed they often are. Then Pandora's box is open. I present students my own photos showing that Maasai usually wear some combination of local and Western items, that their homesteads normally have a similar mixture of objects, that there are pickup trucks among the cattle. They see the two young men working at the gas station, a picture of the vice president of Kenya (a Maasai with an economics Ph.D. from MIT), and, finally, a group of

Maasai in "traditional" dress doing "traditional" dances for a group of European tourists at a hotel. With a bit of research, the lecturer can find other published photographs that will accomplish the same debunking function for students.

Once it is established that Maasai do not really live in a time capsule from the distant past, I find students more receptive to and understanding of the idea that neither are the Maasai ethnically ancient nor are they pure of descent. Following the in-class exercise, I assign readings from *Being Maasai* (Spear and Waller 1993). The readings summarize the gradual migration, in the first millennium C.E., of eastern Nilotic speakers into the western Kenyan plains from what is now southern Sudan. The eastern Nilotic speakers interacted and intermixed with other groups moving into the region: southern Nilotic speakers, southern and eastern Cushitic speakers, Bantu speakers, and already-present hunting-gathering peoples. These groups intermingled biologically, linguistically, economically, and culturally in the Rift Valley and surrounding highlands, so that although groups each fell under a predominant linguistic ancestry, none were purely descended from any one line of migrants. Through the circulation of people, techniques, and languages, communities in the plains by the seventeenth century had become, in one scholar's words, social phenomena, not direct inheritors of primordial affiliations of blood and culture. The Maasai took shape only as a distinct ethnic group in the eighteenth and early nineteenth centuries after a millennium or so of cultural intermixings.

The readings also emphasize that the Maasai do not descend from an ancient, unalloyed line of herders. Before the 1700s, nearly all the communities in the Rift Valley and nearby highlands combined agriculture and pastoralism—including the eastern Nilotic-speaking groups whose descendants became the Maasai. In the eighteenth and nineteenth centuries, a combination of factors allowed those groups to emphasize herding, cease farming, and drive cultivation (and cultivators) from the plains. They increasingly used iron weapons, filled their herds with breeds of cattle well suited to semiarid conditions, developed institutions that gave their communities increased social and religious cohesiveness, and benefited from droughts and famines that induced farmers to retreat to highlands with more consistent rain. It was in that context that a subset of eastern Nilotic speakers—Maa-language speakers—consolidated into the Maasai and came to idealize a purer form of pastoralism.

As Maasai culture coalesced, it valued livestock keeping as the noblest form of activity and livestock as the highest form of wealth. Farmers and farming were denigrated. Still, the idea that they stood above others never prevented Maasai from interacting with neighbors. Various chapters in *Being Maasai* show that they have maintained close connections with surrounding agricultural and hunting-and-gathering societies and continue to intermix culturally and biologically with them as well. People not born Maasai have been able—even encouraged—to join Maasai communities. Other groups have blurred distinctions between their own and Maasai ways, sometimes presenting themselves as virtually Maasai. The text makes clear that through interactions with other people, and with the wider world over succeeding centuries, Maasai culture has not been timelessly traditional but has constantly transformed itself.

In class discussion of the readings, we combine the text and a reconsideration of the photographs to reflect on the fact that despite the coffee-table books, Maasai culture has shown itself to be decidedly innovative and adaptable. In *Being Maasai,* Waller notes that Westerners have been predicting for a century that the Maasai, as such rigid traditionalists, would soon dissolve before the sociocultural onslaught of modernity. The second class discussion thus concerns the fact that the Maasai are still very much with us and that their practices and ethnic identity are far more flexible than are outsiders' images of them, despite such books as Amin and Willetts (1990) that continue to present the Maasai as unchanging. When students are reexamining the photographs, I often tell them that some Maasai are *post*modern enough to have turned their ethnicity into a modern capitalist resource by commanding wages from safari companies and tourist hotels all across East Africa (as well as from professional photographers) to present themselves to Western eyes as traditional.

LARGE CLASSES: TAITA ETHNICITY

Though discussion is harder in a large class setting, students asked about the characteristics of an African ethnic group still tend to emphasize common origin, social cohesiveness, and traditionalism. In large classes, I like to begin with those responses, then talk about Taita ethnicity. Taita ethnicity confounds many student expectations, for it jelled as an identity only in the early 1900s, and its characteristics have changed considerably since then. Nonetheless, it gained thorough cultural acceptance by the 1920s and has since been fully internalized as a social identity. My lecture on the Taita turns on how an ethnic identity gets established and on the fact that its content remains fluid even though the identifying ethnic name is generally stable.

The Taita example also underlines that the process of ethnic formation and change derives not only from historical forces of group cohesion but also from intragroup struggles over proper behavior and proper belief. The Taita example thus allows me to discuss the fact that African (and other!) ethnic groups generally defy the conventional wisdom that they are conflict-free. They often have internal conflicts, and these conflicts can be an important driving force in the remaking of the content of an ethnic identity over time. For class reading, I often assign an essay by Shula Marks (1989) that underlines the latter point in a different ethnic context. For further information, see Bravman (forthcoming).

The Taita live in the Taita Hills of southern Kenya, a small cluster of mountains 100 miles inland from the East African coast. In my lecture I explain that, like many other African ethnic groups, their origins are diffuse. Ancestors of the modern Taita first came into the Hills from nearly every direction on the map and continued to arrive in waves and trickles for centuries thereafter. In the 1600s, four sizable groups of immigrants established independent communities in different parts of the Hills, in the process absorbing the small number of people already there. The four gradually spread out into a larger number of small, autonomous communities. Later immigrants came from still other locales and directions and were absorbed into established communities.

I often check in with my students at this point by asking if this sounds like an ethnic group to them. Most say no, it is too uncohesive, and I give them evidence that supports their view: Local groups in pre–twentieth-century Taita tended to distrust, remain aloof from, and raid one another. The local communities of Taita did not coalesce into a larger polity or interwoven society but instead kept up connections with the distant places from which they had come. Still, during the seventeenth to nineteenth centuries, some sociocultural similarities began to develop in the region through local communities' tentative interactions. Here I mention intra-Hills migrations, itinerations by ritual specialists, blood brotherhoods that allowed people to build ongoing ties across community boundaries, and occasional rituals to which people from elsewhere in the Hills were welcome. By such means and over the course of centuries, people in this small region gradually developed linguistic, social, and cultural similarities. Still, Taita's communities had almost no everyday interconnections by the late 1800s; in times of crisis they still attacked one another and turned to far-flung ancestral connections for support.

I then explain that Taita identity was one of many African ethnicities that emerged or came into sharp focus only with the onset of colonialism (at this juncture I always add that many ethnic identities long predated colonialism and often assign a bit of *Being Maasai* to reinforce the point). In Taita, colonial conquest and rule set in train profound political, economic, and cultural changes across the Hills. Amid the tremendous flux, older men began to rework Taita's sociocultural similarities into a claim of Taita ethnic commonality. In a good year, a student raises a hand to ask why old men did such a thing. The answer is that in the early 1900s, they recognized that colonial change was dissolving their authority over their sons, daughters-in-law, and local communities. The rise of a cash-earning migrant-laborer class, the emergence of local Christianity, and the colonial imposition of young chiefs with broad powers were combining to reduce older men's predominance. Older men responded by asserting the existence of Taita ethnicity—and, critically, laying down their view of proper Taita ways. In so doing, they were attempting to fashion a new basis for social cohesion and setting up a new framework that might let them rebuild their social power. My students grasp this readily when asked to consider a parallel, such as whether there are norms of how a "good" Hispanic girl is supposed to behave and to think about where that idea of "goodness" comes from.

I also discuss the historical underpinnings and contemporary circumstances that helped people assimilate this new Taita identity quickly. Like many other identities, it gained broad acceptance in large part by recycling and broadening the meanings of older community-based practices, which added new weight to the region's long-standing similarities. In the 1910s–1920s, it also resonated with dramatically increased intra-Hills interactions facilitated by colonialism. Taita ethnicity provided people with an effective language for dealing with the colonial state as well, coinciding as it did with British officials' mental templates of African societies as inherently tribal. Thus people's belief in their Taita ethnicity solidified and continues to remain solid today.

Finally, I explain that despite broad acceptance of Taita ethnicity, just how to be Taita has never been cast in stone: Ethnicity did not freeze Taita society into following what older men deemed proper Taita ways. Indeed, younger men and women overturned older men's turn-of-the-century ideas about how society should be ordered—sometimes more than once. To give but two brief examples, in the 1900s an initial handful of Christians struggled to keep from being considered outcasts because of their threateningly non-Taita beliefs. By 1960 they had not only affirmed the security of their Taita identity, they had become numerically predominant. In the 1910s, proper Taita men and women remained under the firm social and economic control of a living parent. By the 1950s, the young had used their wage-earning abilities to lever themselves considerable autonomy and had forced substantial changes in intergenerational power relations. But Taita ethnicity was not vitiated by struggles and changes; it was continually remade and revitalized by them. Succeeding generations have not merely survived Taita's adaptations of Christianity, market capitalism, and the nation-state system, they have thrived.

IN CONCLUSION:
WHY DOES AFRICAN ETHNICITY MATTER?

Conventional wisdoms die hard, and the Western one about African ethnicity is deeply ingrained. The alternative model of African ethnicity sketched out in this chapter lacks the popular romanticism and elegant simplicity of the common-knowledge view and thus can compound the difficulty of teaching against the grain of this view—especially in survey classes. In some African circles, too, the argument that ethnic identities may be relatively recent constructions is culturally and politically anathema. For instance, in a 1993 speech for Shaka Day—a modern Zulu holiday celebrating the group's long cultural heritage—KwaZulu chief minister Mangosuthu Buthelezi denounced Shula Marks's (1989) argument that Zulu ethnic mobilization got a dramatic boost from mission-educated African elites in the early twentieth century.

However, the conventional wisdom on African ethnicity is not benign in its Western romanticism or in its African cultural politics. In African contexts, it feeds into an essentializing of ethnic difference that can have polarizing social and political consequences. In the West, it perpetuates a (sometimes unconscious) condescension, for whether it derides African primitiveness or celebrates African nobility, it elides into an evolutionist narrative of Africans caught in a prior stage of social development. This narrative perpetuates the false juxtaposition between ever-laggard or unchanging Africans and the forever fast-changing West. It therein sets up African ethnic groups and practices as dysfunctional: They either coarsen modern institutions through cronyism and blood feuds or are delicate hothouse flowers that cannot adapt to modernity, only wither and die before it. The former view is a staple of Western news reporting; the latter was recently revisited in a *Time Magazine* (September 1, 1996) article, "Vanishing Africa."

Most Western university students reject harsh stereotypes about Africans, but many do not recognize how often those images are rooted in the romantic, conventional wisdom about African ethnicity to which they may yet subscribe. Highlighting this relationship can be useful in teaching about African ethnicity, for it brings the stakes to the forefront for students and gets them to appreciate the importance of rethinking the subject. More broadly, juxtaposing scholarly knowledge about African ethnicity with conventional wisdom can encourage students to examine how other common understandings about Africa are produced and reproduced, and ultimately to approach those "understandings" more critically as well.

NOTES

1. Movies such as *The Gods Must Be Crazy* underline those stereotyped views. So do TV documentaries on Africa, which usually show Africans in a stereotypically tribal way, often as a backdrop to animals. Children get such images from cartoons, such as the opening trailer for *Johnny Quest.*

SUGGESTIONS FOR
FURTHER READING AND RESOURCES

Ambler, Charles. 1988. *Kenyan Communities in the Age of Imperialism: The Central Region in the Late Nineteenth Century.* New Haven and London: Yale University Press.

Amin, Mohammed, and D. Willetts. 1990. *The Last of the Masai.* Nairobi: Westlands Sundries.

Atkinson, Ronald. 1992. *The Roots of Ethnicity: The Origins of the Acholi of Uganda Before 1800.* Philadelphia: University of Pennsylvania Press.

Barth, Frederik. 1969. "Introduction." In *Ethnic Groups and Boundaries,* ed. F. Barth. Boston: Little, Brown.

Beckwith, Carol. 1980. *Maasai* (with text by Telipit ole Saitoti). New York: H. N. Abrams.

Bravman, Bill. forthcoming. *Communities and Their Transformations: Making Ethnic Ways in Taita, Kenya, 1800–1950.* Portsmouth, N.H.: Heinemann.

Erlmann, Veit. 1991. "'Horses in the Race Course': The Domestication of *Ingoma* Dance." In *African Stars.* Chicago and London: University of Chicago Press.

Geertz, Clifford. 1973. "The Integrative Revolution: Primordial Sentiments and Civil Politics in the New States." In *The Interpretation of Cultures.* New York: Basic Books.

Hamilton, Carolyn, and John Wright. 1990. "The Making of *AmaLala*: Ethnicity, Ideology, and Relations of Subordination in a Precolonial Context." *Southern African Historical Journal* 22.

Kratz, Corinne. 1981. "Are the Okiek Really Maasai? or Kikuyu? or Kipsigis?" *Cahiers d'Etudes Africaines* 79, 3: 355–368.

Lonsdale, John. 1992. "The Moral Economy of Mau Mau: Wealth, Poverty, and Civic Virtue in Kikuyu Political Thought." In *Unhappy Valley: Conflict in Kenya and Africa, Book Two: Violence and Ethnicity,* ed. Bruce Berman and John Lonsdale. London: James Currey; Nairobi: Heinemann Kenya; and Athens: Ohio University Press.

Marks, Shula. 1989. "Patriotism, Patriarchy, and Purity: Natal and the Politics of Zulu Ethnic Consciousness." In *The Creation of Tribalism in Southern Africa,* ed. Leroy Vail. London: James Currey.

Morrell, Robert, ed. 1996. *Political Economy and Identities in KwaZulu-Natal: Historical and Social Perspectives.* Durban: Indicator Press.

Ritts, Herb. 1994. *Africa.* Boston: Little, Brown.

Spear, Thomas, and Richard Waller, eds. 1993. *Being Maasai: Ethnicity and Identity in East Africa.* Athens: Ohio University Press.

Thompson, Richard. 1990. *Theories of Ethnicity: A Critical Appraisal.* New York and London: Greenwood Press.

Vail, Leroy. 1989. "Introduction." In *The Creation of Tribalism in Southern Africa,* ed. Leroy Vail. London: James Currey.

8

CONFRONTING STEREOTYPES ABOUT HIV/AIDS AND AFRICANS

KEARSLEY STEWART

The HIV/AIDS epidemic in Africa emerged in the mid-1980s in eastern Africa, particularly in Uganda, Rwanda, and Zaire. It is now an urgent public health issue in most parts of Africa, most recently developing in southern Africa and especially in Zimbabwe, Botswana, and South Africa. Although the spread of the virus in Africa has slowed in some regions, HIV/AIDS in Africa will continue to be a "current events" topic well into the next century. But for the nonspecialist who wishes to lead a class discussion or devote a week of meetings to the topic, assembling useful and up-to-date materials can be overwhelming. The state of the literature on HIV/AIDS is paradoxical. Although vast, the great majority is published in specialized journals using highly technical jargon, and articles in popular magazines or newspapers may oversimplify a complex issue or reinforce old stereotypes about African promiscuity or prostitution. This chapter outlines an introductory lecture, discusses a student project working with health statistics and demographic models, presents materials suitable for organizing an in-class debate or role-playing exercise, reviews videos, and suggests questions for classroom discussion. These activities will increase student awareness of HIV/AIDS on four levels: objective (facts), affective (attitudes), analytic (skills), and behavioral (individual action).

TEACHING MODULE 1: BASIC INFORMATION

Student interest in HIV/AIDS is usually keen, and some students may know an HIV-positive person or have lost a friend or family member to AIDS. In

1996, the Centers for Disease Control and Prevention (CDC) announced that AIDS had become the leading cause of death for *all* young Americans aged 20–44. Despite this chilling statistic, American students generally have only a limited understanding of the virus and its etiology. Before discussing HIV/AIDS in Africa, you should consider devoting at least one classroom session to establishing a comfortable atmosphere for the students, defining terms, reviewing basic information about HIV/AIDS, and soliciting and answering student questions. If your students do not develop a basic understanding of some of the most important biological, epidemiological, and cultural issues related to the disease, they will not be able to understand fully why the epidemic is so intense in some parts of Africa and why they themselves may be at risk of HIV transmission.

Sensationalized coverage by the popular media likely informs students about HIV/AIDS in Africa. Rather than dismiss these articles or concerns as unacademic, it is important to ask the class to reflect on the indiscriminate use of shocking statistics and stereotypes about African sexual behavior. For example, epidemiologists and molecular biologists do not clearly understand the origins of HIV/AIDS. The lack of a scientific explanation increases the currency of such alternative theories as a CIA plot, sex with green monkeys, or contaminated polio inoculations in Zaire. Assign Garrett (1994) or Weiss (1994) for a broad perspective on this issue. Popular media coverage can promote a fear of contagion spread by foreigners and create an us-versus-them equation that keeps the disease at a safe distance from our daily lives. This fear reinforces stereotypes about Africa as a chronically diseased place and obscures the historical link between local and global economies and the high prevalence of infectious disease in Africa. Have your students compare early newsstories on the disease in Africa (Nordland, Wilkinson, and Marshall 1986) with more recent coverage (McKinley 1996) or analyze the modern version of travel writing in Africa along the "AIDS highway" (Conover 1993; Murphy 1993; Shoumatoft 1988).

1. Begin the class with an AIDS memorial on the blackboard. List names of famous persons or personal friends you know who are living with the disease or have died from it. Encourage the students to write names on the board also.

2. Set the ground rules for the discussion by creating an atmosphere of honesty and tolerance. Allow all questions even if you cannot answer them. If students are shy about speaking in class, pass out notecards before the class and then discuss the questions anonymously. Ask them to write down common myths and misconceptions as well. Anticipate that this may be an emotional topic for some students; reassure them that you will not pressure anyone to participate if he or she is uncomfortable.

3. Invite a speaker from your university, perhaps a student advocate from the campus health center, a nurse from the communicable disease section of your local public health department, a volunteer at an AIDS organization, or an HIV-positive person. This strategy works well if you cannot present your own lecture or feel unable to handle the students' questions directly.

4. Prepare handouts that list sources for local anonymous, free HIV testing, volunteer opportunities with churches or hospital outreach programs, contact names for the Red Cross, access to free condoms.

5. If you devote a week to the topic, have the students keep a journal of personal thoughts and emotions they chose not to share with the class. Also give them specific questions to discuss in their journal: "Discuss your reaction to . . ." "Have you changed your own behavior? How?" "Have you educated others about HIV/AIDS?"

6. Your introductory lecture should touch on the following topics:

   a. Define HIV virus and AIDS disease and distinguish the two; briefly explain the immune system; discuss how the virus enters the body and uses RNA to replicate itself, antibodies, window period difference between HIV-1 and HIV-2, other viral subtypes.

   b. Outline how the virus is transmitted.

   c. Discuss stages of the disease and progression to illness and death.

   d. Review testing options and implications of positive *and* negative test results; discuss new home testing options.

   e. Briefly touch on other sexually transmitted diseases (STDs) and remind students that currently their age group in the United States suffers from the highest levels of STDs since the 1940s.

   f. Review current treatments available and cost; discuss the ethics of vaccine trials.

   g. Cover prevention: how to protect oneself, proper condom use, and reasons for condom failure.

   h. Brainstorm with the students about the difference between biological/physical aspects of the virus (opportunistic infections, incubation period) and the social/cultural and economic/psychological issues of the disease (stigma, discrimination, association with poverty).

TEACHING MODULE 2: WORKING WITH STATISTICS AND DEMOGRAPHIC MODELING

Once the students gain a perspective on popular media presentations about HIV/AIDS, they can critically analyze the data behind the stories. It is not necessary to be a specialist in either epidemiology or statistical modeling to make the students aware of the complicated nature of these data and calculations. Public health statistics about Africa are not as statistically reliable and valid as data from the United States or Europe because of the enormous logistical difficulties of collecting health data in Africa. Estimates of the number of HIV-positive Africans are derived from complex mathematical models that *begin* with incomplete public health data and then apply generalized rates of virus transmission to predict the future course of the epidemic. The World Health Organization and various ministries of health in Africa depend on these data to make important funding and policy decisions about primary and sexual health care issues such as testing, vaccine trials, or treatments. Although there is no doubt that the HIV/AIDS epidemic is a serious public health problem in many African nations, malaria and TB account for far more adult deaths than AIDS. Dehydration kills more infants than childhood AIDS. Can African nations continue to concentrate precious health care resources on HIV/AIDS? Understanding these statistics can help students consider important ethical questions about policymaking procedures and the distribution of scarce health care resources.

1. Unless you are familiar with population studies, start with Anderson and May (1992), Bongaarts (1996), and Mertens and Low-Beer (1996) for a basic orientation to the issues. For example, projections of HIV infection rates and future AIDS mortality in Africa can differ significantly (Bongaarts 1996: 37).

2. The U.S. Department of State Interagency Working Group produced a model of the AIDS epidemic in an "average" sub-Saharan country to assist policymakers in planning for future health needs (Way and Stanecki 1991). The model was not designed to predict actual numbers of HIV infection or AIDS mortality but was intended to sensitize policymakers to the complex public health and cultural issues that shape the epidemic. Use the model to help your students read demographic tables; learn population-studies terms such as "crude birth and death rate"; understand the impact of HIV/AIDS on fertility, life expectancy, and population growth; distinguish new cases of infection (incidence) from overall rates of prevalence; and grasp the difficulty of modeling the impact of such cultural factors as rural/urban migration and divorce and sexual lifestyle behaviors on the epidemic.

   a. Organize the class into study groups according to sections in the Way and Stanecki paper—demography, epidemiology, intervention, and executive summary. Have each group discuss its data. In addition, make sure students can explain the major demographic impacts predicted by an increased incidence of HIV/

AIDS for infants, children, adolescents, adults, urban, rural. Have each group find at least one supporting scholarly article that demonstrates its aspect of the hypothetical model. Supplement this exercise with "real" epidemiological data from the U.S. Bureau of the Census HIV/AIDS Surveillance Data Base (see "Web Sites" for more information).

b. Challenge students to explore the general assumptions of this hypothetical model regarding, for example, sexual behavior, rates of STD, fertility, urban/rural migration patterns, condom use, blood screening. How do these assumptions reveal potential weaknesses in the "real" models they found in their literature search?

c. Ask them to brainstorm about the implications of HIV/AIDS on the quality of life of Africans. For example, what does it mean for urban productivity that HIV/AIDS mortality is high or for rural agriculture (remember, women often dominate food production, whereas men often dominate cash crops)? How does HIV/AIDS change family structures? What are the potential psychological results of the epidemic? What is its impact on the health care system?

d. If you were a minister of health, how would you prepare for the future? How do you stretch your country's health care resources? Do you accept all offers of foreign aid or do you choose some programs over others (UN Children's Fund [UNICEF], Cooperation for Assistance and Relief Everywhere [CARE], Oxford Committee for Famine Relief [Oxfam], Medecins sans Frontières, U.S. State Department)? What is the potential cost-benefit comparison of HIV/AIDS behavioral intervention programs versus TB or malaria programs? How do you assess the efficacy of local "cures" for HIV/AIDS? What should be the role of traditional healers in HIV/AIDS prevention or providing home care for AIDS patients?

3. For a more advanced exercise, have students compare the methods of predicting sub-Saharan AIDS mortality for 2000–2005 by Bongaarts (1996), UN (1995), and Way and Stanecki (1991).

TEACHING MODULE 3:
UNDERSTANDING THE TERMS OF THE DEBATE

Complications from research bias extend beyond statistical issues to include the cultural biases of the scientists themselves. It is increasingly evident that much of the HIV/AIDS era social scientific research on

African sexual behaviors reveals how European and American gender and racial biases created the concept of African AIDS. These scholars first sought to explain why the dominant mode of transmission of HIV/AIDS in Africa was heterosexual and why it did not mimic the pattern of homosexual transmission found in the United States and Europe. Research focused on supposed African promiscuity rather than the cofactors now known to promote HIV/AIDS transmission in Africa—malnutrition, civil war, and the presence of other sexually transmitted and infectious diseases. As a result many HIV/AIDS programs focus on changing female rather than male behavior despite the fact that most African women in long-term relationships are exposed to HIV infection by their own partners. European and American researchers often failed to collaborate with African scholars and ignored the independent findings of these potential colleagues.

Organizing formal classroom debates can help students develop a critical awareness of how these shortcomings in the scientific community interfere with slowing the epidemic as well as how they shape our own ideas about Africans and HIV/AIDS. I suggest the following two debate topics because they are easy to research, the positions are clearly defined, and the issues are guaranteed to generate student interest. Refer to the resources section further on for published materials.

Resolution 1. There is sufficient and compelling evidence to support Caldwell's model—rather than Ahlberg's—of two distinct and internally coherent models of African and Eurasian sexuality.

Resolution 2. The June 17, 1994, decision by the U.S. National Institutes of Health to suspend phase 3 HIV vaccine trials in the United States and the October 1994 decision by the World Health Organization to approve phase 3 trials in Africa were correct and ethical.

1. Assign a moderator, divide the class into teams, and give them time to research their topic. I allow my students to read a script if they are nervous about speaking in front of the class. For a fifty-minute class I assign three students to each debate team and each student gives a five-minute presentation focusing on different issues. For example, the vaccine subtopics could be biology of HIV, ethics/informed consent/confidentiality, statistical and sampling problems, costs of vaccine development, cultural issues. Subtopics for the Ahlberg-Caldwell debate might include quality of sources, (a)historical versus anthropological methods, the role of Christianity, problems of sexual behavior research.

2. Classroom debate format is as follows. Debate team 1 defends the resolution with three five-minute presentations. Debate team 2 then attacks

the resolution with three five-minute presentations. Debate team 1 gives a rebuttal for three minutes, then debate team 2 gives rebuttal for three minutes. The winning team is decided by a vote of the student audience.

TEACHING MODULE 4:
VIDEO, DISCUSSION, AND ROLE PLAYING

The final step is to introduce material that will allow students to explore their own gendered and raced ideas about Africans. Videos and films that feature Africans discussing the impact of the epidemic on their communities expose the student to a common human perspective about the complications and contradictions of the disease. For example, once students realize that Africans confront many of the same ethical issues as Americans (e.g., Should an HIV-positive woman conceive? What can one do if a partner will not agree to condoms? Should employers be told that employees are HIV positive?), they learn that stereotypes about African sexuality explain less and less about the epidemic.

A list of professionally produced films about HIV/AIDS in Africa is in the resources section. All are available in English, easily obtained through mail order, reasonably priced, and selected to offer a variety of viewpoints about the epidemic. If you decide to screen video materials in your classroom, I strongly recommend that you show at least two. Each piece is powerful in its own way; each is flawed as well. If you screen only one, you lose the chance to demonstrate to your students the heterogeneity of the individual African experience of HIV/AIDS as well as the diversity of media representations of the disease. For example, if you show one of the long films, *AIDS in Africa* or *Side by Side,* also show one or two of the shorter videos. Then focus on a similar theme, for example, each video's presentation of women, religion, community-based care, impact on the family, or emotional/psychological issues.

If you show only one film or no film at all, have the students present minidramas or role-playing exercises based on the characters and dialogue in the film or in printed materials (Berer and Ray 1993; Murphy 1993; Mwale and Burnard 1992; Obbo 1993; Schoepf 1988). First-person accounts of life as an HIV-positive person poignantly demonstrate more similarities than differences between Africa and the United States. The testimony of contemporary male and female Africans who are coping with rapidly changing gender roles complicates our clichés about timeless patriarchies and powerless women. This is not to argue, of course, that African women are now fully empowered to protect their own sexual health or that they can easily negotiate condom use with their partners. But in those areas of Africa hit hardest by HIV/AIDS, expectations between men and women about sexual behavior are in flux, and Africans themselves, both men and women, are searching for ways to halt the epidemic.

Some general discussion questions:

1. What are the various messages and approaches of each video? Does each present factual information or challenge stereotypes? Does the film discuss community-based organizations or government interventions? Is the format educational, entertainment, documentary, or drama? Who is the intended audience? Do you detect a relationship between the message and the producer of the video?

2. What are the different kinds of knowledge or experiences of HIV/AIDS presented in these videos? How do the filmmakers juxtapose different "professional" explanations of HIV/AIDS (scientific, biomedical, public health, religious, social science) with "personal" explanations of HIV/AIDS (grassroots/community, individual people with AIDS, "person in the street")? Are certain positions favored over others? What is the impact of testimony from, for example, the director of the World Health Organization (WHO) Global Program on AIDS in comparison with the many unnamed, unidentified people with HIV/AIDS?

3. What are the contrasting political, ethical, cultural, economic, gender, and religious issues relating to condom use?

4. Which women seem better able to reduce their own risk of exposure to the HIV virus? When and why are others less able to control that risk?

5. Why would strategies for counseling HIV-positive persons differ in the United States and Africa, especially concerning advice to young mothers-to-be?

6. A common theme throughout the videos is the strength of the "traditional" African extended family to care for people in need. How has HIV/AIDS challenged that pattern of home-based caregiving?

7. Some of these videos, especially *The Faces of AIDS* and the Strategies for Hope series, are intended as teaching videos for use in Africa. Film is a powerful medium of expression in Africa. What is your assessment of these films as communicators of AIDS information? Do they break down stereotypes of HIV-positive persons, or do they reinforce some widespread images of modes of transmission (African promiscuity) or Africa as a place of only apocalyptic events (e.g., the war imagery and language in *AIDS in Africa*)?

SUGGESTIONS FOR
FURTHER READING AND RESOURCES

PRINTED MATERIAL—TEACHING MODULES 1 AND 4

Benditt, J., ed. 1993. "AIDS: The Unanswered Questions." *Science* 260: 1253–1293. Concise, accessible discussion of the scientific and social issues related to HIV/AIDS. Profiles of individual scientists. Excellent color graphics suitable for duplication onto transparencies. Check more recent issues for other graphics.

Berer, M., and S. Ray. 1993. *Women and HIV/AIDS: An International Resource Book.* London: Pandora Press. Very simply written, suitable for high school students and college undergraduates. Presents basic information about HIV/AIDS, focuses on implications of epidemic for women. Includes many first-person accounts by HIV-positive women all over the world.

Cohen, P. T., M. A. Sande, and P. A. Volberding, eds. 1994. *The AIDS Knowledge Base: A Textbook on HIV Disease,* 2nd ed. Boston: Little, Brown. Excellent, clear coverage of basic issues. Chapters include basic science, epidemiology, clinical, legal, prevention, ethics.

Conover, T. 1993."Trucking Through the AIDS Belt." *New Yorker* (August 16): 56–75.

Essex, M., ed. 1994. *AIDS in Africa.* New York: Raven Press. One of the only volumes devoted entirely to HIV/AIDS in Africa, this is the authoritative resource for many aspects of the African epidemic and is written by leading public health and social scientists.

Garrett, L. 1994. *The Coming Plague: Newly Emerging Diseases in a World out of Balance.* New York: Farrar, Straus and Giroux. See especially pp. 281–389. Garrett's 100-page chapter on the origin of AIDS has a breathless, pulp mystery–novel air about it but in fact is well researched and draws together many aspects of the epidemic—from the tussle between Gallo and Montagnier over who "discovered" the infectious agent in HIV to a visit to a rural clinic in northwestern Tanzania.

Mann, J. M., D.J.M. Tarantola, and T. W. Netter, eds. 1992. *AIDS in the World: A Global Report.* Cambridge: Harvard University Press.

———. 1996. *AIDS in the World II: Global Dimensions, Social Roots, and Responses.* New York: Oxford University Press.

These two volumes are a good place to start for a global perspective on HIV/AIDS. Succinctly written, they include plenty of excellent graphics suitable for classroom instruction. The texts cover the basics as well as special topics such as the role of circumcision in HIV transmission, HIV and prison populations, and the future of the epidemic.

McKinley, J. C., Jr. 1996. "An African Struggle Against AIDS: A Ray of Light Is Seen in Uganda." *New York Times,* International Section (April 7): 1–6.

Murphy, D. 1993. *The Ukimwi Road: From Kenya to Zimbabwe.* London: John Murray. Chapter 6 (pp. 119–140), "Feminism Rampant: Fort Portal to Kyotera," offers an unusual view on the intersection of gender and ethnic tensions.

Mwale, G., and P. Burnard. 1992. *Women and AIDS in Rural Africa: Rural Women's Views of AIDS in Zambia.* Aldershot, U.K.: Avebury/Ashgate. Testimony by Zambian women about their intimate lives and personal experiences with HIV/AIDS is interspersed with social scientific analysis about the epidemic.

This is an excellent tool for discussing interview and survey methodologies as well as for providing authentic material for in-class role playing.

Nordland, R., R. Wilkinson, and R. Marshall. 1986. "Africa in the Plague Years." *Newsweek* 108, 21 (November 24): 44–47.

Obbo, C. 1993. "HIV Transmission: Men Are the Solution." *Population and Environment* 14, 3: 211–243.

Schoepf, B. G. 1988. "Women, AIDS, and Economic Crisis in Central Africa." *Canadian Journal of African Studies* 22, 3: 625–644.

Shoumatoft, A. 1988. "In Search of the Source of AIDS." *Vanity Fair* 51, 7 (July): 96–117.

Weiss, R. 1994. "Of Myths and Mischief." *Discover* (December): 36–42.

PRINTED MATERIAL—TEACHING MODULE 2

Anderson, R. M., and R. M. May. 1992. "Understanding the AIDS Pandemic." *Scientific American* (May): 58–66.

Bongaarts, J. 1996. "Global Trends in AIDS Mortality." *Population and Development Review* 22, 1: 21–45.

Mertens, T. E., and D. Low-Beer. 1996. "HIV and AIDS: Where Is the Epidemic Going?" *Bulletin of the World Health Organization* 74, 2: 121–129.

United Nations. Department for Economic and Social Information and Policy Analysis, Population Division. 1995. *World Population Prospects: The 1994 Revision*. New York: UN. Check for most up-to-date edition. In this edition, see especially pages 7–15 and 40–94.

Way, P. O., and K. Stanecki. 1991. "Demographic Impact of an AIDS Epidemic on an African Country: Application of the IWG AIDS Model." Center for International Research Staff Paper 58 (February). Available on microfiche through the American Statistical Index ASI-91-2326-18.57 or U.S. Congressional Information Service MFC J 83.A45.

PRINTED MATERIAL—TEACHING MODULE 3

Ahlberg, B. M. 1994. "Is There a Distinct African Sexuality? A Critical Response to Caldwell." *Africa* 64, 2: 220–242. This is the most important critique of Caldwell et al. 1989.

American Anthropological Association Task Force on AIDS. 1993. "Anthropological Issues in the Design and Implementation of HIV/AIDS Vaccine Trials: A Position Paper." Unpublished manuscript available from the American Anthropological Association (703) 528-1902.

Caldwell, J. C., P. Caldwell, and I. O. Orubuloye. 1992. "The Family and Sexual Networking in Sub-Saharan Africa: Historical Regional Differences and Present-Day Implications." *Population Studies* 46: 385–410. Here the authors respond to some of their critics.

Caldwell, J. C., P. Caldwell, and P. Quiggin. 1989. "The Social Context of AIDS in Sub-Saharan Africa." *Population and Development Review* 15, 2: 185–234. This is the original presentation of the "African sexual system" model.

Christakis, N. A. 1988. "The Ethical Design of an AIDS Vaccine Trial in Africa." *Hastings Center Report* 18, 3: 31–37.

Cohen, J. 1994. "The HIV Vaccine Paradox." *Science* 264, 5162: 1072–1074.

Dixon, D. O., W. N. Rida, P. E. Fast, and D. F. Hoth. 1993. "HIV Vaccine Trials:

Some Design Issues Including Sample Size Calculation." *Journal of Acquired Immune Deficiency Syndromes* 6, 5: 485–496.

Green, J. 1995. "Who Put the Lid on gp120?" *New York Times Magazine* (March 26): 51–82.

Heald, S. 1995. "The Power of Sex: Some Reflections on the Caldwells' 'African Sexuality' Thesis." *Africa* 65, 4: 489–505. An attempt at a "balanced" critique of Caldwell et al.

Hoth, D. F. 1993. "Issues in the Development of a Prophylactic HIV Vaccine." *Annals of the New York Academy of Sciences* 685: 777–783.

LeBlanc, M.-N., D. Meintel, and V. Piche. 1991. "The African Sexual System: Comment on Caldwell et al." *Population and Development Review* 17, 3: 497–505.

Lurie, P., M. Bishaw, M. A. Chesney, M. Cooke, M.E.L. Fernandes, N. Hearst, E. Katongole-Mbidde, S. Koetsawang, C. P. Lindan, J. Mandel, M. Mhloyi, and T. J. Coates. 1994. "Ethical, Behavioral, and Social Aspects of HIV Vaccine Trials in Developing Countries." *Journal of the American Medical Association* 271, 4: 295–301.

Moore, J., and R. Anderson. 1994. "The WHO and Why of HIV Vaccine Trials." *Nature* 372: 313–314.

Nowak, R. 1995. "Staging Ethical AIDS Trials in Africa." *Science* 269, 8: 1332–1335.

Schoofs, M. 1995. "We Could Have an AIDS Vaccine, So Why Don't We?" *Village Voice* (September 12): 20–26.

FILMS—TEACHING MODULE 4

AIDS in Africa. 1990. 52 minutes. National Film Board of Canada for the Montreal International AIDS Conference. Filmmakers Library, 124 East 40th Street, New York, NY 10016, (800) 555-9815, (212) 808-4980, fax (212) 808-4983. Purchase $445, rental $75, shipping $10. This film covers Burundi, Ivory Coast, Malawi, Rwanda, South Africa, Uganda, Zaire. It assumes no previous knowledge of Africa or HIV/AIDS. Opens with the delegates to the 1989 Montreal AIDS conference and continues with a discussion of the epidemiology of AIDS in Africa and the myth that HIV/AIDS originated in central Africa. Interviews a Canadian missionary in Ituri Forest in Zaire; Samuel Okware, the Uganda minister of health; and the remarkable Noerine Kaleeba, director of one of the most successful community-based AIDS organizations in Africa. It shows alternative theater using puppets in South Africa and talks with Mr. Jimmy Katumba, a popular Ugandan actor. This long film does a good job exploring the relationship between underdevelopment and disease, but watch out for occasional lapses into familiar metaphors about apocalyptic Africa.

AIDS in Africa: Living with a Time Bomb. 1991. 33 minutes. Films for the Humanities and Sciences. PO Box 2053, Princeton, NJ 08543-2053, (800) 257-5126, fax (609) 275-3767. Purchase $149, rental $75, shipping $6–$9. This film covers Kenya. A standard approach to the topic—statistics, colorful graphics of the virus, and talking-head interviews with professional African social scientists. However, the film offers an unusual discussion of some of the psychological aspects of living with HIV/AIDS, for example, counseling techniques, suicide, deciding to be tested, and tensions between men and women.

Born in Africa. 1990. 90 minutes. WGBH Boston (PBS). Development Through

Self-Reliance (DSR), 6679P Santa Barbara Road, Elkridge, MD 21075, (410) 579-4508, fax (410) 579-8412, www.catalog.com/DSR. Purchase $69, rental $20, shipping $8. Otherwise, try AIDS Action Committee. Educational Materials Distribution Center, 131 Clarendon Street, Boston, MA 02116, (617) 450-1234. Free rental, pay shipping costs only. This film covers Uganda. Philly Bongoley Lutaaya was a pop superstar in eastern Africa in the 1980s. This is the powerful story of his struggle with HIV/AIDS early in the epidemic, when the stigma of going public was still devastating. Despite this and the toll on his health, Philly toured rural and urban Uganda in an effort to educate people about HIV/AIDS.

The Faces of AIDS. 1991. 20 minutes. Family Health International, AIDSTECH/ AIDSCAP, funded by USAID. DSR, Inc. (see address above). Purchase $40, rental $20, shipping $8. This film covers Cameroon and Zimbabwe. Intended as a teaching tool for Africans, this award-winning video focuses on the effect of HIV/AIDS on the family. Africans speak directly about how HIV/AIDS affects their personal lives. Also discusses the emotional devastation of isolation and stigma and the problems facing AIDS orphans. Students should see similarities in HIV/AIDS stigmata between the United States and Africa. Highly recommended.

It's Not Easy. 1991. 48 minutes. Media for Development Trust (Zimbabwe), USAID/Kampala. DSR, Inc. (see address above). Purchase $69, rental $20, shipping $8. The film covers Uganda. This award-winning, scripted dramatic story follows the fortunes of Suna, a young businessman, as he discovers that he has infected his wife and their infant son with HIV. Some of his neighbors, coworkers, and friends reject him; others support him. Good production values, didactic at times.

Side by Side: Women Against AIDS in Zimbabwe. 1993. 47 minutes. Peter Davis, director. Danida, Oxfam, CIDA funded. Villon Films–Harvey McKinnon Production. Harvey McKinnon & Associates, 2211 West 4th Avenue, Suite 218, Vancouver, BC V6K 4S2, (604) 732-4351. Purchase only, $150; shipping $6. One of the best; covers Zimbabwe. The film intersperses Dr. Sunanda Ray (coauthor of *Women and HIV/AIDS*) leading focus group discussions with documentation of the charismatic Mrs. Anatolia Mushaya taking her safer-sex message literally on the road. A powerful segment films women performing an AIDS play in a rural beer hall and the hostile reaction of the male customers. A lot of candid discussion by Africans on condoms and the dilemma of promoting health education without access to radio or television. Compare the effectiveness of this film about what women are *doing* with other videos that focus on AIDS information only.

Strategies for Hope Series. A: *TASO: Living Positively with AIDS*. 1990. 25 minutes. B: *The Orphan Generation*. 1990. 40 minutes. C: *AIDS Counseling: The TASO Experience*. 1990. 30 minutes. Small World Production and the Television Trust for the Environment, UK. TALC, PO Box 49, St. Albans, Hertfordshire AL1 4AX, UK, (727) 853-869, fax (727) 846-852. Purchase £45 (includes shipping). This film covers Uganda. Without sentimentality describes the daily operations of one of the most successful community-based AIDS care organizations in Africa. Shows Ugandans directly confronting the epidemic and making remarkable progress with few resources.

Une Conversation. 1991. 20 minutes, subtitles in English. Harvard AIDS Institute. DSR, Inc. (see address above). Purchase $40, rental $20, shipping $8. This film covers Senegal with footage from the eve of the Sixth International Conference on AIDS in Africa. Juxtaposes a Muslim cleric's view on the teaching of the

Koran about homosexuality with other, less strident positions. Unusual street interviews with commercial sex workers (CSWs), frank discussion about condoms with both CSWs and their clients, and stark dialogue from a recently widowed HIV-positive woman.

TELEPHONE RESOURCES

The CDC operates a telephone hotline for brief answers to any questions related to HIV/AIDS: (800) 342-2437. You can bring CDC expertise into your school with "Classroom Calls"—all you need is a speaker phone. Designed for middle and high schools. Available in English and Spanish.

National AIDS Clearinghouse offers a list of research and teaching resources, some distributed free of charge: multimedia materials (slides, videos), articles, reports, brochures, and classroom posters. (800) 458-5231.

WEB SITES

The World Wide Web is an excellent place to get the latest information on HIV/AIDS.

AIDS Outreach Center. http://www.aoc.org/resource.htm. This site offers a list of international resources on HIV/AIDS as well as links to many other sites.

CDC National AIDS Clearinghouse. http://www.cdcnac.org (or go directly to its databases at http://www.cdcnac.org/database.html). Includes a searchable database of more than 19,000 HIV/AIDS-related organizations.

Centers for Disease Control and Prevention. http://www.cdc.gov. Includes a database of article abstracts from the *AIDS Daily Summary, Morbidity and Mortality Weekly Report, HIV/AIDS Surveillance Report,* and many other features, including links to other sites.

Joint United Nations Programme on HIV/AIDS. http://www.unaids.org/. This is an excellent source for global HIV/AIDS statistics, conferences, and basic information on HIV/AIDS.

HIV InSite. http://HIVinsite.ucsf.edu or by email at prevention@sfaids.ucsf.edu. An innovative, interactive site that provides comprehensive cross-disciplinary information on clinical, prevention, social, and ethical issues in an easy-to-access format.

Twelfth World AIDS Conference. http://www.aids98.ch/ or email: info@aids98.ch. Held in Geneva, Switzerland, June 28–July 3, 1998, the abstracts on the latest research and other information related to the largest biennial conference on AIDS can be found here.

U.S. Bureau of the Census HIV/AIDS Surveillance Data Base. http://www.census.gov/ipc/www/hivaidsn.html or request diskettes directly by email: kstaneck@census.gov. This is a unique central repository of HIV seroprevalence studies conducted in developing countries. Much of the material is unpublished and unavailable elsewhere.

World Health Organization.. http://www.who.ch/ gopher://gopher.who.ch:70/1 telnet://gopher.who.ch:231 (login:gopher). The latest statistics and much more.

9

CONTEXTS, CONTROVERSIES, DILEMMAS: TEACHING CIRCUMCISION

CORINNE A. KRATZ

Circumcision has never been a planned topic in my course syllabi or the central concern of my research, writing, or museum work. Nonetheless, students and others regularly ask me about the recent debates surrounding circumcision practices, particularly what is often called "female circumcision" and practiced in Africa, the Middle East, and Southeast Asia. In this chapter I outline the basic approach I adopt when people seek such guidance and information—whether in classes, at public lectures, or in interviews.[1]

In my experience, classroom discussion can be an important safe space where students can explore the full range of questions and issues involved in current debates, consider the arguments and counterarguments advanced, and form their own opinions. Students usually appreciate the chance for such discussion. They often seem quite relieved to be able to admit their uncertainties and questions and are eager for information that represents the range of positions and will help them understand the debates. To create a classroom setting that encourages open discussion, I find it essential to present circumcision as a controversy, as a dilemma, and as a variable practice embedded in a range of cultural and historical contexts. Discussion about circumcision practices thus carries broader lessons about how to approach other controversies: by identifying the different positions and interests in play, weighing competing arguments, analyzing their rhetorics, and taking account of the history of the issues and positions at stake. These same analytical skills can be used to understand debates concerning issues of social justice, abortion rights, human rights, or other matters. The discussions also help students learn to consider sources carefully and develop their own independent, critical judgment. I will sketch some important aspects of teaching recent circumcision controversies in this way; included in the sketch are questions and examples that might be incorporated into discussions with students.

CONTEXTS FOR UNDERSTANDING

Widespread and vociferous controversies today center on female genital operations; such debates are not new, and they have not always been about female body modifications. Since the early 1990s, international debates about female circumcision have again become increasingly heated, highly politicized, and polarized. Greater media coverage in the 1990s and publicity over legal cases concerning African immigrants have brought the debates to a wider public,[2] but this recent resurgence of anticircumcision activity began in the 1970s, buoyed by the UN Decade of Women (1975–1985).[3] It continues much longer traditions of missionary and colonial opposition and African activism. Earlier campaigns in Kenya, for instance, were framed as judgments about local customs that violated Christian behavior and were shaped by church interests and politics in the mother country as well.

To understand today's debates, students will find it helpful to think about them in relation to several contexts. Most central are the sociocultural contexts of the practices at issue and the history and contexts of current controversies themselves. An effective way to highlight the issues and perspectives involved is to teach about these contexts comparatively, to ask students either to relate two kinds of situations and practices or to explore similarities and differences among several controversies (e.g., debates about male and female genital operations, debates that occur at different historical periods, or debates that might concern different practices but are presented in similar ways—such as *sati* in India).

As discussed further on, the term "female circumcision" includes a very wide range of specific practices. It may not be possible to teach about each of these, but students could consider several specific examples using anthropological or historical studies as primary teaching materials. Case studies demonstrate that female genital operations are related to basic understandings about gender roles and relations, age, authority, and many other important social relations. They cannot be understood in isolation. Men and women alike are involved, and female operations are almost always associated with a counterpart operation for males. Examining cultural practices in context also means identifying the different actors, perspectives, and meanings involved. Students should recognize that trying to understand unfamiliar practices does not necessarily mean supporting them.

However, if they want to oppose or help alter practices that they consider problematic, they must work *with* the people involved, as equal peers. Such understanding is critical to effective engagement.

To place contemporary controversies in context, students should learn about their history and the different arenas where debates occur. Their relations to feminist movements in various times and places, to colonial administration and missionary campaigns, to Islamic religious movements, and other issues that have been associated with such debates are all important topics that could be addressed. Arenas of debate have shifted over the years as different constituencies become involved. One of the best documented historical examples is the 1920–1930s circumcision controversy that took place in central Kenya during the colonial era. This debate encompassed British politics (with pressure from feminist parliamentarians and anticolonial activists), the colonial administration in Kenya, local Kenyan communities, and rivalries among Christian denominations with missions in Kenya. The debate became connected to anticolonial movements and the defense of cultural tradition, relations of authority between men and women and between women of different generations, the formation of independent schools, and even the introduction of maternity clinics. (See Murray 1974, 1976; Pederson 1991; Lonsdale 1992: 388–397; Davison et al. 1989; Thomas 1996, forthcoming.)

In tracing the shape of today's debates, I find it useful to distinguish three interacting arenas:

1. *Home countries* are countries in Africa, the Middle East, and Southeast Asia where circumcising practices have traditional standing. There may be a variety of traditions and practices that include genital modification within each home country and—if they are debated—a number of different positions within each community.

2. The *United States and Europe* are the second arena to consider. These countries also have a history of genital operations for both boys and girls. The histories are related to changing understandings of health, class, ethnicity, gender, and sexuality. In the U.K., for instance, male circumcision had become a middle-class fashion by the 1920s (Lonsdale 1992: 388). In Nazi Germany, it was taken as a mark of Jewish identity. In the United States today, white men are more likely to be circumcised than African Americans or Hispanics; higher education levels are also related to higher circumcision rates (Laumann, Masi, and Zuckerman 1997: 1053–1054). Clitoridectomy was a recognized medical treatment for women in these countries from at least the 1850s through the 1950s. It was used to treat insomnia, sterility, and masturbation, which was seen then as an ailment (Morgan and Steinem 1983; Pederson 1991). Concern about female genital operations within these countries is now related particularly to immigrants

from home countries, the first arena discussed. The operations have become the subject of recent laws in the United States, the U.K., and several other European countries, though legal definitions and restrictions vary.

3. The third arena is that of *international campaigns*. Though this arena is obviously related to the other two, it is useful to ask students to think about how international campaigns differ from debates within the other arenas, how international bodies and action groups establish their legitimacy to intervene in other countries, and how the international arena redefines issues central to particular communities and nations.

The social, cultural, and historical contexts of debates about female and male genital operations could be discussed with students for each of these arenas. In practice, this kind of orientation is often presented in conjunction with class discussion about the controversies themselves.

CIRCUMCISION CONTROVERSIES

Controversies can be confusing. Heated arguments based on strong convictions are rarely presented in ways that make clear the different assumptions, perspectives, and interests fueling contention. When controversies cross cultural and national boundaries, they can be very complicated indeed. To begin discussion about current circumcision debates, students need to know the grounds of controversy: Who is involved, what it is about, and what is at issue. Ask students to identify the many kinds of people and organizations involved. The range may be surprising; it begins to demonstrate that circumcision controversies concern a wide variety of actors and cross a number of social and legal arenas, from family and household relations to international tribunals.[4] Discussion of these varied positions also shows that the debates cannot be characterized in simple terms; it is inaccurate and misleading to describe them merely as contests between women and men or Africans and outsiders.

Identifying the diverse actors involved may be fairly easy. If students read or are provided with a variety of newsstories, many will be mentioned. Once discussion turns to what the controversies are about, however, it is important to make students aware of how selective inclusion and particular ways of presenting information are themselves part of the debate, rhetorically shaping issues and arguments. Circumcision controversies thus exemplify a larger lesson: the importance of critical judgment in reading sources, no matter how straightforward and descriptive they may seem. Definitions, descriptions, and names for female genital operations provide apt examples of the political shaping, debate, and rhetoric involved.

The names used reflect the history and divisions of the debates.

"Female circumcision" was the most common term for decades, the English phrase ordinarily used in the debates about British colonial attempts to outlaw female genital operations in Kenya in the 1920s–1930s. This term maintains the parallel and link between male and female genital operations, a correspondence that is often central to the way their practitioners understand them. In many contexts, ritual meanings and patterns unite the two and a single word refers to both operations in many local languages. The more partisan phrase "female genital mutilation" seems to have been coined and popularized in the 1970s. "Mutilation" is a term that judges and condemns as it labels rather than a descriptive term. Its adoption was part of an escalating anticircumcision campaign that used more sensationalistic terms and gory images. As this usage became more common, it was shortened to an acronym, FGM. At the same time, the term "female circumcision" was criticized as inaccurate for suggesting "erroneous" similarities to male circumcision and thus condoning what was, to those who preferred the FGM term, a brutal custom. The increasingly heated and polarized debate thus became encapsulated in its very terms. On a more neutral ground, a number of alternative terms have come into use recently: genital surgery, genital operations, genital modification, and body modification. The last is a broad term that points to similarities among such practices as male and female genital surgery, genital and other body piercing, and other cosmetic surgery. Differences and similarities among some of these practices might be explored with students.

Whether called female circumcision, female genital mutilation (FGM), genital cutting, genital operation, or genital or body modification, the topic at the center of controversy is an abstract category defined and shaped by that very debate. The category is created by extracting and combining fragments from many different cultural practices found in dozens of countries. The fragments all concern genital modification but may share little else. They are isolated, taken out of their social and cultural contexts, and combined into a new abstract category (e.g., "female circumcision").

Scientific, medical language is an important tool in this process. The clinical emphasis makes the general category seem like an objective and universal way to talk about women's bodies, but it also narrows the range of information that is defined as relevant to the debate. For instance, physically different operations are combined and treated as the same thing, though they vary considerably in extent and effects. Three operations are usually distinguished: clitoridectomy, excision, and infibulation (or, in an alternative set of terms: sunna circumcision, excision or clitoridectomy, infibulation). Parker (1995: 514) notes that there is considerable variation in what is actually done in the first two. Obiora (1997: 288) distinguishes a symbolic pricking as a fourth variety. There are also differences in the age of those concerned, ranging from a few days old (among the Yoruba in

Nigeria, like male circumcision in the United States and Europe) to six to eight years old (in much of Mali and Sudan) to early teens (in various communities in Kenya and Sierra Leone). In most cases the physical operation is one moment in a larger ceremony, but the rest of the ceremony is often ignored by those protesting the practice. In every case the specific practice is embedded in broader cultural understandings of identity, morality, adulthood, motherhood, authority, the body, and other important topics. For Kikuyu in Kenya, for instance, circumcision was the foundation of "moral self-mastery" (Lonsdale 1992) for women and men alike. Particular cases could be explored to help students understand such meanings and connections, as well as variations in the operations.

The terms used in circumcision controversies paint different pictures of actors involved as well. A number of African women and others have objected to the word "mutilation," for instance, because it misrepresents the actions of parents and families. It suggests that they intend harm to their children, likening what they might see as a cultural triumph "carried out for the noblest of reasons, the best of intentions, and in good faith" (Iweriebor 1996) to child abuse. (See also Apena 1996: 7; Obiora 1997: 289–290; Peters 1997: 482–483; Verdier 1992: 3; Dawit 1997.) Accounts often demonize women who perform the operations as well. In recent French legal cases, for instance, practitioners were portrayed as avaricious and predatory and received the harshest rulings.

The most common example of such misrepresentation concerns the way African or "third world" women in general are represented as a single, unified group. Students might look at such portrayals in news media, in informational publicity material produced by action groups, in scholarly writing, or in novels.[5] Thinking back to the range of actors involved, they might ask how differences based on nationality, class, ethnicity, religion, education, or age are accommodated in this generalized figure and whether this view affects the debates. The assumption of a general character for "African women" is usually formed by homogenizing divergent circumstances; it posits women as a preexistent, coherent group with shared interests and desires. This assumption requires removing and isolating the concept of "woman" from any specific cultural context or socially constructed notion of gender.

The "average" third world woman who emerges is thus contrasted to elite women, though the contrast is often implicit. This average woman lives in a village, carries heavy loads, bears many children, and "leads an essentially truncated life based on her feminine gender (read: sexually constrained) and being 'third world' (read: ignorant, poor, uneducated, tradition-bound, religious, domesticated, family oriented, victimized, etc.)" (Mohanty 1988: 65). These women are portrayed as powerless, constrained by a tradition defined by men, unable to think clearly, and having only problems and needs, not choices. Their oppression joins them into one group—spanning several continents and myriad religious, political, economic, and social situations—though they do not yet recognize it. What defines and unites them is shared victimization through "female circumcision." (For critiques of this representation of African women primarily as victims, see Apena 1996: 7; Obiora 1997: 303, 327–328; and Ogundipe-Leslie 1994.)

The premise underlying this view is that only women who have no choice, agency, or consciousness—precisely the third-world-women image created—would submit to such practices. Because they are unable to act for themselves, others must deliver them through international action. This is a rhetorical argument that advances a particular interpretation of circumcision practices, justifies the intervention of a range of people, and dismisses the beliefs and wishes of those involved as "false consciousness." Critics have called this view a "missionary mentality," "external messiah syndrome," and paternalistic.

The contrast to the generalized "third world women" are other, elite women, presented as self-conscious, active, choice-making agents. These elite women are not exclusively Western but also include women born in the third world who have joined the campaign against female genital modification. Yet African activists consistently protest that their work is rarely recognized when controversies are described. Nor is the role of activist men. Students can explore the rhetoric and structure of these controversies further by looking at how different kinds of men are portrayed or by considering parallel cases in contemporary campaigns against male genital operations, abortion, or welfare.

These different images of third world women and other actors in circumcision controversies are often bound up with notions of "progress" and other values as defined in Western contexts. But conflicting values are the very crux of controversy. Diverse social and political positions inform the perspectives of those involved, but they are also grounded in different cultural frameworks, competing definitions of the practices at issue, and what seem to be irreconcilable values. When students consider what is at stake in debates about female genital modification, they should be encouraged to formulate more than one position on each issue and to identify the priorities and cultural values associated with each. Discussion of what is at stake might include a number of issues, including the following.

HUMAN RIGHTS

Circumcision debates presented in human rights terms often emphasize the integrity and inviolability of the human body, sometimes using as analogies torture and child abuse. As noted previously, this view falsely attributes evil intent to parents and relatives. Human rights as a concept is itself under considerable debate. Should social and economic rights be included? Whose values will be enshrined as universal when there are fundamental disagreements (An-Na'im 1992; An-Na'im and Deng 1990)? How might the language of human rights accommodate the diverse people, practices, and circumstances involved?

SELF-DETERMINATION

This human rights approach does not fit easily with another common way of framing circumcision debates—in terms of self-determination. Self-determination can be defined in relation to individuals, families, or communities, each with rather different implications. Upholding family autonomy, community values, or religious freedom would seem to support continuing traditional practices understood as central to personal and community identity. Does such support include male and female initiation ceremonies? How does individual self-determination apply in the intricate contexts of family and community relations? How do questions of self-determination apply to children of different ages?

Examples of different body modifications can be used to focus discussion on the different kinds and contexts of "choice" involved. Operations for breast reduction or enhancement, multiple ear piercings, and body piercings (including genital piercings) are modifications often presented by their American or European practitioners as ways to take control of one's body. These self-definitions are very much like local definitions of female genital operations in initiation, also seen as a sign of self-control, maturity, and both social and personal change. (For African cases, see MacCormack 1979: 32–33; Boddy 1997, 1989: 55, 57–58, 74; Kratz 1994; Obiora 1997: 330; Lonsdale 1992: 388ff; Davison et al. 1989: 40–42.) In both cases, the practices are linked to understandings of the body, aesthetics, sexuality, and gender relations, but the understandings are rather different, as are their social and institutional settings.

HEALTH ISSUES

Opponents of female genital operations seem to be on firmer ground here. Any surgical operation holds risk of infection and complications, and genital modifications are no exception. Infibulation, the most severe operation, may well be related to complications in childbirth as well, though clinical studies are contradictory (Obiora 1997: 292; Parker 1995: 514–516). There are intense debates among African activists about whether a medicalized, minor form of female genital modification should be promoted as an interim substitute for more severe operations. In considering health issues, students might discuss the health effects claimed for male genital operations as well.

SEXUALITY

Claims about sexuality have been central to debates about female circumcision, but the evidence and issues involved are among the most murky and disputed. In discussing sexuality and circumcision practices, it is important to distinguish questions of sexual desire, sexual activity, and sexual pleasure. Sexual desire and sexual activity may not diminish with female genital operations, but these are less pivotal in the debates.[6] The central concern has been whether circumcised women experience sexual pleasure. Evidence about sexual feeling and pleasure is variable, hard to define, and hard to come by. Despite adamant assertions by opponents that these women could not possibly feel pleasure or reach orgasm, studies suggest that this effect is not so clear and that the answer certainly varies with the kind of operation. (See Parker 1995: 514; Ogbu 1997: 414–415; Obiora 1997: 308–310; Koso-Thomas 1987: 37–42. On the absence of sexual pleasure as part of the Kenya colonialist debate, see Pederson 1991: 669–671.) A number of African women also counter these assertions. Some go further to question the very definition of sexuality prevalent in the debates. They see this emphasis on sexual pleasure as primarily reflecting Western concepts of sexuality. Even in Europe and the United States, this pleasure-oriented definition of sexuality became prominent only in recent decades. In this view, recent international debates about female genital operations have taken a form that resonates particularly with recent Western concerns and anxieties (Parker 1995; Pederson 1991: 669–671).

The paradoxical nature of questions of sexuality can also be brought into relief for students through comparison. Historically, classical theologians and philosophers made parallel claims about men; they promoted male circumcision because it reduces male sexual passion (Boyarin 1992: 486–487; Lyons 1981: 503–504). Though circumcised men today might not agree, similar assumptions still inform medical research. A study publicized on National Public Radio in 1997 found that circumcised men are more "sexually adventurous" but explained this as compensation for loss of sexual feeling (Laumann, Masi, and Zuckerman 1997). "Adventurousness" was defined according to behavioral range and frequencies, suggesting that sexual interest, desire, and activity were actually greater with circumcision. These gender reversals can help students think critically about all these claims and recognize that understandings of sexuality are neither universal nor unchanging.

Questions of sexuality have also figured in opponents' efforts to explain female genital modifications. These opponents commonly assert that male desire to control female sexuality is the origin and explanation for all such practices. This universal conspiracy theory, however, is not presented in a way that is well reasoned or responsive to what is known. There is no evidence or discussion of how this practice occurred in so many places at the same time, how this theory would account for the variety of circumcising practices, why women also staunchly defend them, or how the theory relates to explanations offered by practitioners.

Yet students may well ask why the practice continues. I have talked with many people who seek a "logical" explanation or rationale for traditions of female genital modification. When I summarize what Okiek in Kenya might say in response—that initiation is necessary for children to become adults—North Americans have a hard time understanding and accepting such a "reason." What for Okiek are logically satisfying, deeply felt, and natural understandings do not have for North Americans the same intuitive sense and resonance. It is equally hard to answer Okiek questions about North Americans, whom they sometimes encounter as tourists: Why do the women paint their mouths to look like they drink blood? Why do they walk about without clothing (e.g., in bathing suits); don't they feel shame? Why are girls not initiated—how can they live their entire lives as children?

There are no simple, single explanations to such questions, for they pinpoint the nexus where fundamental perceptions and lived understandings of aesthetics, morality, society, and personhood come together with questions of authority, class, power, gender, and history. Returning to a particular case and its multiple contexts, actors, and complexities is one way to impress on students that these are not isolated issues. (Boddy 1982, 1989; Kratz 1994; and MacCormack 1979 could be used as case studies in this way.) But the very opaqueness of this nexus might also open the way for students to discuss recalcitrant problems and issues of cultural translation, celebrated closer to home in the T-shirt slogan "It's a _____ thing; you wouldn't understand." In this respect, teaching about recent circumcision controversies can draw student attention to the limits and dilemmas of cultural relativism and moral judgments. How are such judgments, choices, and even laws to be made in plural societies (which ultimately means all societies)? Can incommensurable values be accommodated? As Sir Isaiah Berlin noted, "A certain humility in these matters is very necessary" (1991: 18).

CULTURAL AND MORAL VALUES: DILEMMAS OF RELATIVISM

Many students will agree that cultural difference and diversity should be recognized, respected, and accommodated. Cultural relativism has fairly wide currency in the United States as a general way to approach cultural difference, though it coexists with popular notions of cultural evolution and civilizational hierarchy.[7] The relativist view that each society's practices and values are valid and understandable in the particular context of their lives may be easiest to hold, however, when applied to distant people or to practices that seem strange but harmless. What happens when people with incompatible practices and values live closely together, when culturally justified practices seem to be physically harmful, or when an overarching national legal system must deal with radically different values? Does cultural relativism imply moral relativism as well? There are no easy answers to these questions, but students might discuss or debate some of the issues involved.

The controversies over genital operations present such dilemmas and flashpoints. The songs, dances, costumes, and other beliefs that are usually associated with ceremonial performances and that give them meaning are readily accepted as part of "tradition," as markers of particular forms of ethnic or religious identity. Scarification or tattooing might also be recognized and appreciated as part of a different aesthetic or religion, so what is different about genital operations? Why are they seen as an exception that raises this moral dilemma? What other practices pose similar dilemmas?

In the late 1980s through the 1990s, legal cases dealing with African immigrants in the United States and Europe have raised these issues in particularly clear and urgent ways. Discussing some of these cases—particularly examining court procedure and sections of testimony—could be a way for students to again consider the different actors and interests involved, this time in situations even closer to home. Many questions might be raised for discussion:

- Legislation is written in general terms, intended as applicable to the broadest range of cases. However, laws are interpreted through individual cases and precedents. Should a case about, for instance, Somali immigrants (who practice infibulation for young girls) serve as precedent for families from Sierra Leone (where initiated individuals are older, the operation is less severe, and family relations are quite different)?
- Whose legal rights should be protected and when? Parents' rights to raise their children in accordance with their beliefs and traditions? What if parents disagree? The rights of the girls affected? What if they *choose* to undergo the operation? What if they are minors?
- When female genital operations are outlawed, who is legally responsible and liable for prosecution? At different times and places, the accused have included fathers, mothers, initiates, and surgeons. What constructions of actors, intentions, and meanings are involved in each of these scenarios?

- When court proceedings involve immigrants, how are issues of adequate translation and adequate legal representation handled? These were important problems in the way some mid-1990s French cases were handled.
- Are judges, juries, lawyers, and those concerned with civil liberties informed about the communities and cultural values involved? For instance, a lawyer in one case argued that the girls affected would have psychological problems when they realized they were not like other women, but the "other women" assumed in this statement were not women of the immigrant community. In fact, most women in that ethnic community had had the operation, making this lawyer's argument one that would more appropriately support the operation (cf. Matias 1996: 4).
- How do gendered differences in immigrant experiences influence knowledge about relevant laws and services and the ways people participate in legal proceedings?

Such questions lead students from general discussion of cultural translation and moral dilemmas to considering some of their practical implications. By working through specific contexts, controversies, and dilemmas, students can understand and engage with more general controversies that are puzzling and sometimes troubling in their passions and complexities.

NOTES

1. Some people raise these questions with me because I have written about initiation ceremonies in Kenya (Kratz 1994). In the Okiek communities where I have worked, as in many other settings, initiation into adulthood includes circumcision for boys and excision for girls. Okiek initiation continues for several months and includes much more as well: moral teaching, family and community engagement, new social relationships, and important cultural meanings and values. Although the operations are a central initiation trial and create a permanent physical mark of adulthood, initiation cannot be reduced to circumcision or excision alone.

2. For instance, several 1990s immigration cases and asylum claims in the United States have been based on arguments about the persecution of women through genital operations. Lydia Oluloro, a Nigerian woman, fought deportation on the grounds that she was protecting her daughters from the procedure. Her case was profiled in newspapers and on television in a segment of *Sixty Minutes* in 1994. A woman from Togo, Fauziya Kasinga, was also granted asylum in 1996. Highly publicized cases in France in the 1990s prosecuted immigrant parents and ritual surgeons who continued the practice in their new country (Verdier 1992; Winter 1994). Interested students could develop a class project or research paper that traced changing patterns in media coverage of debates about both male and female circumcision.

3. Previous efforts to have the topic taken up by the World Health Organization in the late 1950s were not effective. In the 1970s a number of publications and publicizing efforts converged successfully to promote international attention, including articles in African publications in the mid-1970s, a Swiss press conference held before the WHO Assembly in 1977, and Fran Hoskens's publications in the United States (McClean and Graham 1985: 8). The Inter-African Committee on Traditional Practices affecting the Health of Women and Children was formed in Geneva in 1977. A 1979 WHO seminar in Khartoum was part of the beginning of regular discussion of female genital operations by international bodies and at regular conferences.

4. For each "home country" (i.e., countries in Africa, the Middle East, and Southeast Asia, where circumcising practices have traditional standing), students might consider the positions of national governments and politicians; local NGOs and national action groups; international action groups; churches; religious and ethnic communities whose circumcising practices may differ and whose histories of education and involvement with government also differ. Within each circumcising community, differences of gender, age, education, religion, and wealth also influence positions. For example, a Christian mother, her non-Christian husband, his educated brother, and their school-child daughter might disagree about whether the girl should participate with her friends in initiation ceremonies during a school holiday. Peters (1997: 484–486) discusses the different positions within the Togolese family and community in the asylum case of Fauziya Kasinga. See Gruenbaum (1996: 463-470) and the film *Bintou in Paris* (Pimsleur and Johnson 1996) for other examples.

5. A number of scholarly papers discuss the problems with these generalized images and show how they are constructed; Mohanty (1988) and Stephens (1989) are a good starting place. Alice Walker's books *Possessing the Secret of Joy* and *Warrior Marks* are commonly used as novelistic examples. Her representations of African women have been discussed by a number of scholars; Obiora (1997: 323–328) and Mugo (1997) are examples focused on Walker's books' relation to controversies about female genital modification.

6. See Apena (1996: 8); Kratz (1994: 345–346); Lyons (1981: 507, 510); Obiora (1997: 298). Matias (1996: 3) and Ogbu (1997: 414) cite examples where they are seen as enhancing sexuality. Again, the type of operation is critical. Infibulation is more often discussed as reducing desire (Boddy 1989: 54), though Obiora (1997: 310) cites a study in the Sudan with the opposite conclusion. And regarding sexual pleasure, according to Gruenbaum, also writing about the Sudan, some infibulated women do have orgasms, perhaps because "many midwives, fearing hemorrhage, leave much of the clitoral (erectile) tissue intact beneath the infibulation when they perform the surgeries" (1996: 462). She notes, though, that other infibulated women report finding sex unsatisfying.

7. A Social Sciences Research Council conference on the legal and cultural dimensions of pluralism provided the occasion and stimulation for my thinking in this section; it was organized under the aegis of the Committee on Culture, Health, and Human Development in April 1997 (see Shweder et al. 1997). Most introductory anthropology textbooks discuss cultural relativism and problems of ethical or moral relativism. The Berlin (1991) essay cited in the text includes an elegant and clear discussion of problems with the notion of cultural relativism and the difference between relativism and pluralism. It includes a number of examples that could be used in class discussions based on the sources in the following section.

SUGGESTIONS FOR
FURTHER READING AND RESOURCES

This list includes sources for teaching comparative and historical cases; they were identified separately in the notes.

PRINTED MATERIAL

An-Na'im, Abdullahi, ed. 1992. *Human Rights in Cross-Cultural Perspectives: A Quest for Consensus.* Philadelphia: University of Pennsylvania Press.

An-Na'im, Abdullahi, and Francis Deng, eds. 1990. *Human Rights in Africa: Cross-Cultural Perspectives.* Washington, D.C.: Brookings Institution.

Apena, Adeline. 1996. "Female Circumcision in Africa and the Problem of Cross-Cultural Perspectives." *Africa Update* 3, 2: 7–8 (see below for Web version).

Berlin, Isaiah. 1991. *The Crooked Timber of Humanity.* New York: Alfred A. Knopf.

Boddy, Janice. 1982. "Womb as Oasis: The Symbolic Context of Pharaonic Circumcision in Rural Northern Sudan." *American Ethnologist* 9: 682–698.

———. 1989. *Wombs and Alien Spirits.* Madison: University of Wisconsin Press.

———. 1997. "Clitoridectomy and Infibulation." In *Encyclopedia of Africa South of the Sahara,* ed. John Middleton. New York: Charles Scribner's Sons.

Boyarin, Daniel. 1992. "'This We Know to Be Carnal Israel': Circumcision and the Erotic Life of God and Israel." *Critical Inquiry* 18, 3: 474–505.

Daly, Mary. 1990 (1978). "African Genital Mutilation: The Unspeakable Atrocities." In *Gyn/ecology.* Boston: Beacon Press.

Davison, Jean, with the women of Mutira. 1989. *Voices from Mutira: Lives of Rural Gikuyu Women.* Boulder: Lynne Rienner.

Dawit, Seble. 1997. "Letter from a Female Circumcision Activist." *Colloquium: The On-line Magazine of the Case Western Reserve Law Review* (November 1997): lawwww.cwru.edu/cwrulaw/publications/colloquium/dawitfea.html.

Gruenbaum, Ellen. 1996. "The Cultural Debate over Female Circumcision: The Sudanese Are Arguing This One Out for Themselves." *Medical Anthropology Quarterly* 10, 4: 455–475.

Gunning, Isabelle. 1997. "Uneasy Alliances and Solid Sisterhood." *Case Western Reserve Law Review* 47, 2: 445–460.

Hoskens, Fran. 1979. *The Hoskens Report.* Lexington, Mass.: Women's International Network News.

Iwieriebor, Ifeyinwa. 1996. "Brief Reflections on Clitoridectomy." *Africa Update* 3, 2: 2 (see below for Web version).

Kenyatta, Jomo. 1965 (1936). *Facing Mount Kenya.* New York: Vintage Books.

Koso-Thomas, Olayinka. 1987. *The Circumcision of Women: A Strategy for Eradication.* London: Zed Books.

Kratz, Corinne. 1994. *Affecting Performance: Meaning, Movement, and Experience in Okiek Women's Initiation.* Washington, D.C.: Smithsonian Institution Press.

Laumann, E. O., C. M. Masi, and E. W. Zuckerman. 1997. "Circumcision in the United States: Prevalence, Prophylactic Effects, and Sexual Practice." *Journal of the American Medical Association* 277, 13: 1052–1057.

Lonsdale, John. 1992. "Wealth, Poverty, and Civic Virtue in Kikuyu Political Thought." In *Unhappy Valley: Conflict in Kenya and Africa,* ed. B. Berman and J. Lonsdale. London: James Currey.

Lyons, Harriet. 1981. "Anthropologists, Moralities, and Relativities: The Problem of Genital Mutilations." *Canadian Review of Sociology and Anthropology* 18, 4: 499–518.

MacCormack, Carol. 1979. "Sande: The Public Face of a Secret Society." In *The New Religions of Africa,* ed. Bennetta Jules-Rosette. Norwood, N.J.: Ablex.

Mascia-Lees, Frances, and Patricia Sharpe, eds. 1992. *Tattoo, Torture, Mutilation, and Adornment.* Albany: SUNY Press.

Matias, Aisha Samad. 1996. "Female Circumcision in Africa." *Africa Update* 3, 2: 3–6 (see below for Web version).

McLean, Scilla, and Stella Efua Graham. 1985. "Female Circumcision, Excision, and Infibulation." Minority Rights Group Report 47. London: Minority Rights Group.

Mohanty, Chandra. 1988. "Under Western Eyes: Feminist Scholarship and Colonial Discourses." *Feminist Review* 30: 61–88.

Morgan, Robin, and Gloria Steinem. 1983. "The International Crime of Genital Mutilation." In *Outrageous Acts and Everyday Rebellions,* ed. Gloria Steinem (originally a 1979 article in *Ms.* magazine).

Morsy, Soheir. 1991. "Safeguarding Women's Bodies: The White Man's Burden Medicalized." *Medical Anthropology Quarterly* (n.s.) 5: 19–23.

Moses, Meredith. 1997. "Watching the Watchdog: Female Circumcision in the *New York Times.*" Student paper, Emory University.

Mugo, Micere. 1997. "Elitist Anti-Circumcision Discourse as Mutilating and Anti-Feminist." *Case Western Reserve Law Review* 47, 2: 461–480.

Murray, Jocelyn. 1974. "The Kikuyu Female Circumcision Controversy, with Special Reference to the Church Missionary Society's 'Sphere of Influence.'" Ph.D. diss., University of California, Los Angeles.

———. 1976. "The Church Missionary Society and the 'Female Circumcision' Issue in Kenya, 1929–1932." *Journal of Religion in Africa* 8, 2: 92–104.

Obiora, L. Amede. 1997. "Bridges and Barricades: Rethinking Polemics and Intransigence in the Campaign Against Female Circumcision." *Case Western Reserve Law Review* 47, 2: 275–378.

Ogbu, M. A. 1997. "Comment on Obiora's 'Bridges and Barricades.'" *Case Western Reserve Law Review* 47, 2: 411–422.

Ogundipe-Leslie, Molara. 1994. *Recreating Ourselves: African Women and Critical Transformations.* Trenton, N.J.: Africa World Press.

Parker, Melissa. 1995. "Rethinking Female Circumcision." *Africa* 65, 4: 506–524.

Pederson, Susan. 1991. "National Bodies, Unspeakable Acts: The Sexual Politics of Colonial Policy-making." *Journal of Modern History* 63: 647–680.

Peters, Pauline. 1997. "Another Bridge to Cross: Between 'Outside' and 'Inside.'" *Case Western Reserve Law Review* 47, 2: 481–490.

Shweder, Richard, Hazel Markus, Martha Minow, and Frank Kessel. 1997. "The Free Exercise of Culture: Ethnic Customs, Assimilation, and American Law." *Items* 51, 4: 61–67.

Stephens, Julie. 1989. "Feminist Fictions: A Critique of the Category 'Non-Western Woman' in Feminist Writings on India." In *Subaltern Studies VI,* ed. R. Guha. New York: Oxford University Press.

Thomas, Lynn. 1996. "'Ngaitana (I will circumcise myself)': The Gender and Generational Politics of the 1956 Ban on Clitoridectomy in Meru, Kenya." *Gender and History* 8, 3: 338–363.

———. forthcoming. "Imperial Concerns and 'Women's Affairs': State Efforts to Regulate Clitoridectomy and Eradicate Abortion in Meru, Kenya, c. 1920–1950." *Journal of African History.*

Verdier, Raymond. 1992. "The *Exiseuse* in Criminal Court: The Trial of Soko Aramata Keita." *Passages* 3: 1–3.
Winter, Bronwyn. 1994. "Women, the Law, and Cultural Relativism in France: The Case of Excision." *Signs* 19, 4: 939–974.

FILMS

Dedman, Penny. 1990. *Rites*. Produced for Channel 4 UK, 52 minutes. New York: Filmmakers Library.
Gladsjo, Leslie Asako. 1991. *Stigmata: The Transfigured Body*. Documentary film. San Francisco: L. A. Gladsjo (PO Box 411144, San Francisco, CA 94141).
Pimsleur, Julia, and Kirsten Johnson. 1996. *Bintou in Paris*. Supported by CAMS (Commission for the Abolition of Sexual Mutilation of Women), 17 minutes. Watertown, Mass.: Documentary Educational Resources.

WEB SITES

Africa Update. Articles by Apena, Iweriebor, and Matias. http://h-net.msu.edu/~africa/sources/clitoridectomy.html.
National Organization of Circumcision Information Resource Centers (NOCIRC). http://www.nocirc.org/.

10

Student Projects for Learning About Gender and Development

Jane L. Parpart

Courses on gender and development in Africa can become little more than a litany of woes that undervalue the rich and varied history of the continent and reinforce stereotypes of a chaotic, underdeveloped Africa. Over the years, I have discovered that student-designed development projects help to overcome this tendency. The project proposal requires students to identify a problem that affects women and men differently in a specific African country, that is, a problem of gender inequity, and to design a project that will at least begin to address this inequity within a specified time period and budget. Identifying a gendered developmental problem requires considerable knowledge about a particular country as well as some understanding of the way that problem might be addressed. The need to consider how to tackle a development problem thus pushes students to think more broadly about gender and development in Africa, particularly about the limitations of as well as the possibilities for change.

Students respond enthusiastically to the project assignment because it challenges them to tackle theory and practice simultaneously, to become familiar with conditions in a specific country, and to think creatively about social transformation and the role of Western "experts" in the development process. For example, the vitality and complexity of West African market women's work life often attracts student interest. The need to identify a project pushes them to read studies such as Claire Robertson's (1990) *Sharing the Same Bowl* and Bessie House-Midamba and Felix Ekechi's (1994) *African Market Women and Economic Power*. These studies reveal some of the problems facing African women traders, but they also highlight the rich organizational life of the marketplace. As a result, students have to consider how their projects will relate to these indigenous organizations. Class projects such as credit schemes and crèches have been set up in consultation and cooperation with these organizations.

Situating projects within local contexts is particularly relevant for students addressing practices that are deeply embedded in African cultural systems. For example, many students become interested in reducing female genital mutilation (FGM), a set of practices that occur in a number of African countries. They soon realize that a purely medical approach is not sufficient when dealing with such a culturally sensitive and emotional issue. As a result, student proposals have largely focused on development theater and educational programs, often designed by members of the community, rather than on the provision of clinics, other medical facilities, and external biomedical professionals. Projects on AIDS in Africa have often taken a similar tack as students realized that changing sexual practices required more than simply handing out condoms and information about the disease. Projects focused on improving women's access to education, especially higher education, have had to struggle with attitudes that assume women's and girls' education should take second place to that for males. Even projects focusing on economic or legal matters, such as assistance with income-generating skills or legal problems, have had to develop strategies for changing attitudes and finding local allies. Thus although the project proposals can vary widely in their topical focus, they all challenge students to learn more about the lives of women and men in Africa while also thinking creatively about the possibilities, and limitations, of social transformation through development interventions.

I have learned through experience that three elements of organization and course structure are critical to the success of this approach. First, lectures and associated reading assignments must introduce the rich and varied conditions of women's and men's lives in the many societies of Africa. At the same time, the focus on development as well as gender requires some familiarity with the way scholars and development practitioners have sought to understand and "solve" gendered developmental problems on the continent. I have also discovered that breaking students into small groups (preferably about ten to twelve people) for discussions and debates facilitates this type of learning, and role-playing exercises help to introduce students to the complexities of project design and implementation. This chapter deals briefly with each of these three modes of instructional approach before discussing the specific project assignment in greater detail.

Reading assignments and lectures in the course are organized within a structure designed to let students learn from each other's research. Each student is initially required to pick a particular country, which will be the basis for his or her research paper and development project. A broad overview lecture at the beginning of the course is designed to help students decide what country would best fit their interests. I focus on those countries with the richest data on gender issues, notably Zambia, Nigeria, Senegal, South Africa, Kenya, and Ghana, although the availability of CD-ROM searches has made research on other African countries much easier than ever before. The Hay and Stichter (1995) volume is particularly helpful here. Before turning to substantive themes in the course, I spend some time introducing the major conceptual approaches to women, gender, and development. The aim is to help students recognize the link between theory and practice—for example, that a focus on women will lead to women-only projects, whereas a focus on gender requires consideration of both women and men, their relationships, and their relative positions in society. This understanding provides a framework for more closely considering themes such as the gendered nature of rural and urban life, education, health, culture, family life, politics, and the environment. Because the students are trying to identify an issue that can become the basis for a development project, they have to do more than simply collect information. They have to think through how a particular issue could be addressed in a development project, including the approach they want to take. I encourage comparative analysis by asking students to report on their own country as well as the general reading. Thus during the week on gender and health, the students who have chosen Nigeria are expected to contribute data to the class as a whole on Nigerian health issues. This approach enhances comparative understanding and pushes students into an early start on their development proposal.

I have discovered that breaking students into small groups for discussion and debates is an important tool for teaching this material. Small-group work places responsibility for learning on the students, gets them involved, and encourages lively discussions both in the groups and the class as a whole. I find this approach particularly useful for teaching theory. I used to bore students with long lectures on various theoretical debates but soon realized this detracted from the essential point, namely that concepts shape the "solutions" we think are both necessary and possible. Having students revisit one development case (culled from *Two Halves Make a Whole* [CCIC and MATCH 1992] or *The Oxfam Gender Manual* [Williams 1994] or other appropriate sources), from three different theoretical perspectives, hammers this point home. I sometimes discuss, as an example, the introduction of a well into a West African village. When students examine the case from a women in development (WID) perspective, they focus on women's use of the well, whereas a gender and development (GAD) approach pays attention to the way women and men use the well and how the well affects their relationships with one another (use Rathgeber 1990; Kabeer 1994; and Sen and Grown 1988 as sources for this exercise). The alternative-development approach is more interested in empowerment and participation at the local level (see Marchand and Parpart 1995; Kabeer 1994). After each theoretical perspective is introduced, students break into small groups to analyze the case and make suggestions for its improvements from the perspective under discussion. This exercise throws students on their own resources, forces them to work together to solve a problem, and even frustrates them together. When the class reconvenes, each group is anxious to hear the other groups and compare their answers. In order to reduce classroom domination by a few verbal students, the group rapporteur must be different each time. One group reports in full; the others only add new points, thus avoiding repetition and keeping the conversation lively. I also encourage a general discussion after the report back on each question. The wrap-up summary by the teacher brings all the various strands together. It should touch all the important bases but relate directly to the class discussion.

By the time students have revisited the case three times, they begin to see that different approaches to the same problem affect both understanding and "solutions" to development problems. They can then bring this understanding to the substantive discussions in the weeks to come. I often use small-group work during the substantive weeks as well as when discussing the general article in order to challenge students to come up with some generalizations from their comparative data.

Because the students have to design their own development project, I also introduce some rudimentary material on projects and project design, especially for those who have no previous knowledge of development practice and planning. I find role playing an effective teaching device in this case. The aim is to demonstrate the intersection between planning and the complex, often competing interest groups and institutions in even the smallest communities. For example, a project to improve women's literacy in a village can seem like a simple undertaking, but the role-playing exercise soon reveals its complexity. The students are assigned different roles and identities in the community, such as the husbands of potential literacy students, their brothers, female relatives, children, and community leaders. I try to cluster several students in each role so they can work together. The students break into groups by roles and have about twenty minutes to work out a position regarding the proposed project. When the class comes together as a whole, I appoint a moderator who organizes the discussion. She or he calls on each group to state its opinion of the project, reminding students to always speak in first person to increase a sense of identity with the group. I find this exercise clarifies the many competing interest groups that can undermine or facilitate a project. In the literacy project, for example, students soon discover that husbands are worried about wives neglecting their children and domestic work. Some of the older women are hostile because they think the newly literate women will take over the community and undermine the senior women's authority base. Other groups are supportive. Thus a project that seemed an obvious, simple good for the whole community emerges as a source of conflict and discussion. After the role-playing exercise, I divide the class into several groups and ask them to redesign the project, taking into consideration what they have discovered through the exercise. When they reconvene, they present their revamped projects. The exercise helps students to think strategically and collectively about designing development projects that can meet challenges from competing interest groups and preexisting cultural practices. The writings of Caroline Moser (1993) and Sue Ellen Charlton (1984) on gender planning provide a useful background for the discussion, and students should have read some of this material before the exercise begins.

Since the development-project proposal is the core around which the course is built, I discuss it at various points throughout the course. When the class first meets, I hand out a description of the proposal and explain what is expected. At this point, I am particularly concerned to reassure students who have no background in development that they will get the needed assistance to design a proposal. I also try to inspire them by pointing out that the project proposal is an opportunity to be creative, to choose whatever issue they think needs addressing, and to try their hand at actually designing and thinking through the implementation of a development project. I offer a number of illustrations of projects that have been done in the past, reassuring them that many of them were done by students with little expertise in development planning and policies. I try to include examples that might interest the class and to address topical issues such as the environment, FGM, AIDS, and economic development. This overview has to be done in a lively and compelling fashion to keep student interest and minimize anxiety. I also hand out the assignment description and explain it thoroughly. The project paper has three sections. The first two are more self-evident, as they are based on research and are basically similar to most research papers for undergraduates. The project proposal itself is the third section.

The first section is a general description of the country they have chosen. I want students to be clear about the basic attributes of the country they are focusing on, so they have to summarize the geography, politics and government, economy, and the social and economic indicators for the country. They can use the UN Development Program's (UNDP) human development reports as a basis for many of the statistics, as well as other general resources. I include a guide to relevant journals, monographs, collections, and reference books and often set up a library research tour for the class. I also encourage students to ask reference librarians for help when needed. I cap this section at three to four pages, as otherwise it tends to grow too large and overwhelms the second, more important research section of the paper. The country section is meant to lay the groundwork for the next two sections rather than to be a central focus for the entire project. It is an essential background for thinking about gender in the country under consideration.

The second section focuses more specifically and intensively on gender and women in the country being discussed. This section is an in-depth analysis of the way three major topics affect the lives of women and men in the country under discussion. I offer students a list of themes, such as the political and legal status of women and men, access to health care and contraceptives, gendered relationships to the environment, degree of control over property and one's production of goods, major economic activities, participation in women's or more broadly based community associations, roles in public life, female-headed households, and access to education. I also encourage students to think of other topics, but they have to receive permission from me before they can proceed on any topic strictly of their own choice. I often give students permission to narrow down the topic when sufficient literature is available. For example, there is a great deal of material on gender and Yoruba agriculture, so I am happy to let a student focus on that rather than discuss agriculture in Nigeria as a whole. I try to encourage students to draw their project from one of the three research foci in their second section. A student writing on Yoruba agriculture as one of her themes in the second section, for example, would benefit from constructing a project based on that research. Indeed, students have set up projects on credit and legal assistance to help Yoruba women obtain ownership of land, relying on the writings of Simi Afonja and others for guidance. In this way, research and the project inform each other. This section of the paper is the longest (at least fifteen pages with five for each theme) and should be fully documented with at least four sources per subsection. I encourage students to use the articles they read during the course as the basis for their research for this section. This focus helps them to see that the entire semester's work builds toward the research and the project proposal. The students are also encouraged to think about the theoretical perspectives of the authors they read so that they can evaluate the authors' assumptions and potential biases.

The development project constitutes the third section of the proposal. Although the project proposal is introduced on the first day, it is important to keep returning to it throughout the course. The time spent revisiting a development case from three different theoretical perspectives, for instance, permits the instructor to discuss a number of different approaches to project design and planning. The role-playing exercise puts much of this learning into practice, especially in regard to implementation. As we go through the various substantive discussions, I find that students begin to discover potential development projects. For example, during the week on education one student was shocked to learn that the average literacy rate for women in Senegal was well below 50 percent. As a result, she became interested in the topic and eventually set up a project to increase female literacy in that country. I encourage students to keep an open mind while doing their initial research, as they may change their ideas for a project as they learn more about a particular subject. One student entered the class determined to carry out an inclusive gender project with both men and women in Nigeria, but after reading about northern Nigerian society with its strict separation of the sexes, he realized that a woman-only project would make more sense in this social context. In order to keep the project in the forefront during the weeks spent discussing theory and substantive themes, I ask a few students each week to discuss the project they are currently considering. I also discuss potential project topics when they fit into class discussions. This takes only a small amount of time, but it keeps students from putting off their project and helps them learn from each other as well. I also encourage students to meet with me during office hours so we can discuss possible project ideas and the research resources that would help them develop their projects.

The guideline handed out on the first day of class provides a detailed list of subjects to be covered in the project proposal. It has to begin with a statement of the problem to be addressed, followed by a rationale for the project. Thus the exemplary student interested in improving the literacy rates of women in Senegal first explains the project and its goals, then discusses why this is an important issue for gender equity in Senegal. The rationale requires a page or so describing the general problem, including the cultural, economic, and political contexts that affect the issue being addressed. The proposal itself focuses on the particularities of the project, explaining the exact location, population, and subjects who will be involved. To continue with my exemplary student interested in Senegalese women's literacy, she drew on the work of various scholars and soon realized that she should place her project in a number of villages in the peanut-growing area of Senegal. Sometimes a student is lucky and has local knowledge he or she can use, but more usually a project locale has to be discovered through research. The level of detail available naturally limits the degree of specificity possible, but I encourage students to be as concrete as they are able.

After describing the locale and target population, each proposal should spell out as clearly as possible the specific context in which the project will operate, especially the cultural, economic, and political structures and practices that may affect the project. The gender assumptions and practices in the area, and the way they may affect the project, should also be discussed. This information will play a central role in the implementation phase, which has to be written out in considerable detail. For example, an understanding of the gendered assumptions and practices in Muslim Senegal affected the literacy project. Students had to work out how to deal with the problems of working with women in a Muslim environment without abandoning the goal of gender equity. Thus the implementation stage had to clarify what kind of persons would be sent to the region from North America, what training they would require, and how long they would stay. The proposal also explained what groups these development practitioners would link up with locally, how they would establish contact, and how collaboration would be achieved.

The implementation has to cover the entire life of the project—usually five years—and must discuss how to deal with potential problems as well as how to make the project sustainable after the money ends and the foreign "experts" disappear. The proposal has to include at least an approximate budget and an explanation for budgetary expenses. The potential sources for funding should also be provided. Therefore, as much as possible within the undergraduate class context, the project proposal should be like those that major development funding agencies receive on a regular basis.

Because a development project requires innovation and can be rather daunting, especially for those with little knowledge of development planning, it helps if students have a chance to present their projects to the class as a whole. They have ten to fifteen minutes for their presentation, which makes them formulate the key elements of their project more clearly and concisely. After the presentation, the project is discussed by the class. I encourage critical comments and hard questions, but always given in a spirit of cooperation and collegiality. The students then have some time to integrate this feedback into their final proposal. This effort may require further research or simply some clarification, but it gives students an opportunity to rethink and revise their proposals (and the research sections as well) before handing them in. I usually leave two or three class sessions for these presentations and find them very useful for everyone concerned.

Gender and development is a challenging and exciting subject to teach in the classroom. Although this topic has the potential to become mired in the negative statistics and jargon so common in the development literature, the approach outlined works against this tendency. Designing and implementing a project addressing gender inequities requires students to think about gender and the category of development itself in a more complex manner. The need to identify potential allies, discover competing interest groups, and find entry points for the transformation of gender relations in a particular society forces students to adopt a more fluid, multifaceted approach to the topics under consideration. The deeply entrenched nature of gender assumptions and relations cannot be denied, either at home or abroad, but in confronting social transformation in development projects, students learn to think imaginatively about social change in a more global context. Whereas the course deliberately undermines easy assumptions about the capacity of Western "experts" to alter gender relations, the need to design a project pushes students toward a more realistic assessment of the possibilities for undermining gender inequities while reminding students that gender equality continues to be an important goal, both in Africa and elsewhere.

SUGGESTIONS FOR
FURTHER READING AND RESOURCES

Afonja, Simi. 1986. "Land Control: A Critical Factor in Yoruba Gender Stratification." In *Women and Class in Africa,* ed. Claire Robertson and Iris Berger. New York: Holmes and Meier.

Bryceson, Deborah. 1995. *Women Wielding the Hoe: Lessons from Rural Africa for Feminist Theory and Development Practice.* Oxford: Berg.

Callaway, Barbara, and Lucy Creevy, eds. 1994. *The Heritage of Islam: Women and Religion and Politics in West Africa.* Boulder: Lynne Rienner.

Canadian Council for International Cooperation (CCIC) and MATCH International Center. 1992. *Two Halves Make a Whole.* Ottawa: CCIC.

Charlton, Sue Ellen. 1984. *Women in Third World Development.* Boulder: Westview Press.

Gladwin, Christina, ed. 1991. *Structural Adjustment and African Women Farmers.* Gainesville: University of Florida Press.

Hansen, Karen, ed. 1992. *African Encounters with Domesticity.* New Brunswick, N.J.: Rutgers University Press.

Hay, Margaret Jean, and Sharon Stichter. 1995. *African Women South of the Sahara,* 2nd ed. Harlow: Longman.

House-Midamba, Bessie, and Felix Ekechi, eds. 1994. *African Market Women and Economic Power.* Westport, Conn.: Greenwood Press.

Kabeer, Naila. 1994. *Reversed Realities: Gender Hierarchies in Development Thought.* London: Verso Press.

Koso-Thomas, Olayinka. 1987. *The Circumcision of Women: A Strategy for Eradication.* London: Zed Books.

Marchand, Marianne, and Jane Parpart, eds. 1995. *Feminism/Postmodernism/ Development.* London: Routledge.

Meena, Ruth, ed. 1992. *Gender in Southern Africa.* Harare: SAPES Books.

Moser, Caroline. 1993. *Gender Planning and Development: Theory, Practice, and Training.* London: Routledge.

Oxfam. 1995. *The Gender and Development Handbook.* Oxford: Oxford University Press.

Parpart, Jane, and Kathleen Staudt, eds. 1988. *Women and the State in Africa.* Boulder: Lynne Rienner.

Rathgeber, Eva. 1990. "WID, WAD, GAD: Trends in Research and Practice." *Journal of Developing Areas* 24: 489–502.

Robertson, Claire. 1990. *Sharing the Same Bowl: A Socio-economic History of Women and Class in Accra, Ghana.* Ann Arbor: University of Michigan Press.

Sen, Gita, and Caren Grown. 1988. *Development, Crises, and Alternative Visions: Third World Women's Perspectives.* London: Earthscan.

Snyder, Margaret, and Mary Tadesse. 1995. *African Women and Development.* London: Zed Press.

Turshen, Meredith, ed. 1991. *Women and Health in Africa.* Trenton, N.J.: Africa World Press.

United Nations Development Programme (UNDP). Annual. *Human Development Report.* New York: Oxford University Press.

Williams, Suzanne, with Janet Seed and Adelina Mwau. 1994. *The Oxfam Gender Manual.* Oxford, UK: Oxfam Publishing.

11

TEACHING AFRICAN PEACEKEEPING, PEACEMAKING, AND PEACEBUILDING

SANDRA J. MACLEAN, KATHERINE ORR, AND TIMOTHY M. SHAW

It is unfortunate but appropriate that a volume on teaching contemporary African studies should include a chapter on keeping, making, and building peace. In recent years, measures to deal with complex emergencies and postconflict reconstruction—from humanitarian interventions to exit options—have become disturbingly common concerns for policymakers and analysts involved with Africa. Although the proliferation and immediacy of emergency events and the search for humane solutions have stressed and frustrated both material and intellectual resources in national and international communities, considerable effort and some progress is being made in the analysis and treatment of such situations, especially in Africa. As a result, it is becoming increasingly evident that the root causes of any crisis, the management of the acute phase, and the possibilities for sustainable peace and security are dependent on a nexus of interrelated political, economic, and social factors. Furthermore, whereas holders of formal political or administrative offices may play the most visible roles in the activities surrounding the events, various nonstate actors (for example, nongovernmental organizations [NGOs], multinational corporations [MNCs], factional military leaders, organized-crime groups) are now recognized as critical participants in the causal circumstances or the remedial strategies involving the so-called humanitarian-military coalition.

For teachers of African studies, the challenge is to find creative ways to identify the various actors in particular cases and to show how the relationships among the economic, the political, and the social at various levels (local, national, regional, and transnational) and forms (formal or informal) of interaction may contribute to the development and treatment of crisis situations. One method for teaching these issues employs interactive training modules such as those that have been used successfully by the Lester B. Pearson Canadian International Peacekeeping Training Centre (PPC) at Cornwallis in Nova Scotia, Canada, for briefing international operants on the various aspects of crisis management and conflict resolution. Although the modules are used to train actively engaged peacekeeping professionals (particularly those in the military but also government and NGO personnel), they are adaptable for use in teaching university or high school students about the factors surrounding working for peace in contemporary Africa: from confidence-building measures and early warning to reconstruction and reconciliation. Also, although the modules are designed to be used in a concentrated, time-limited format, they can be modified for classroom teaching over several days or weeks.

REVISED CONCEPTS OF PEACEKEEPING AND SECURITY

Until very recently, and certainly during the Cold War, peacekeeping was considered to be a highly technical exercise engaging specifically trained military personnel serving under a UN mandate. Although such conditions still apply, recent peacekeeping missions have highlighted the range and complexity of issues and participants involved in attempting to resolve conflict situations and to build or rebuild social and political structures in order to prevent the recurrence of problems. Certainly, recent "emergencies" in Ethiopia, Somalia, Angola, Mozambique, Rwanda, Burundi, and Zaire (the Democratic Republic of Congo) have demonstrated that not only national leadership but regional and international political intervention can be relevant in this context.

Expanded views on peacekeeping are related to revised concepts of security. In particular, there is growing recognition that security relates directly to human development. Indeed, some analysts and institutions have come to conceive of security as part of the more inclusive notion of "human security." For example, we are told that "the concept of human development is much broader than the conventional theories of economic development" or even of political development (UNDP 1995: 11). In short, the "new" security agenda in which peace operations are devised and carried out is seen to involve much more than the protection of national integrity or interests. Instead, it also involves "the four major elements in the concept of human development . . . productivity, equity, sustainability and empowerment" (UNDP 1995: 12).

Presently, then, teaching about security-related functions such as peacekeeping in Africa requires an understanding that there has been a "sea-change in the way security itself is perceived." As Gary Buckley observes, there are several ways in which this realization is transforming approaches to teaching the subject. First, the end of the Cold War has shifted the focus on conflict studies toward nonnuclear, even nonmilitary, concerns; second, the "problem-oriented" approach is being replaced by those that involve wider theoretical concerns; third, greater attention is being paid to history; fourth, the importance of the regional dimension is being emphasized; fifth, the intersection between international political economy and international security is taken more seriously; and sixth, there is now a greater concern with international as well as national security (Buckley 1993: 5–7).

Recent events in Africa, perhaps more than any other region, highlight the importance of this broadened and more nuanced approach to security and peacekeeping studies. In particular, there is a need to focus on the relationship between the centrality of Africa in recent peacekeeping missions and growing "peripheralization" of many of its countries in the global economy.[1] Negative social consequences following increases in unemployment, high costs of living, and cuts to social programs include growing migration, disease, and crime rates; declining ecological conditions; food insecurity; and, often, exacerbated gender inequalities. As well, although a more positive consequence of the withdrawal of the state has been increased space for civil society, pressures for democratization by NGOs, human rights groups, and others are often met with intensified counteraction by authoritarian states (cf. Kenya). Often states in democratic transition are faced with ethnic and regional tensions and conflicts that were more or less successfully suppressed under previously centralized, authoritarian regimes. In sum, the processes that contribute to the heightened need for African peacekeeping are of a dialectical nature, and the roles that national, transitional, and regional civil societies play in processes of democratization and social and political reconstruction may be as important as those played by formal politicians in national, regional, and UN institutions.

PREPARING A TEACHING MODULE ON AFRICAN PEACEKEEPING

The teaching-module approach used by the Pearson Peacekeeping Centre (PPC) has proved to be an effective method for presenting the range of issues and actors involved in peacekeeping, peacemaking, and peacebuilding generally and is applicable to the present African situation. Consisting of small-group preparation of answers to set questions followed by general discussion, it allows the diversity of participants and issues surrounding the subject of peacekeeping in Africa to be introduced within a fairly limited time frame. This approach requires active involvement from the participants, thus furthering interactive learning. It is also a method that lends itself to adjustment, depending on the experience and knowledge base of the students, and to extension by including other methodologies such as simulation and role playing. Finally, it has the potential (ideally, and depending on the source material used) for students to extrapolate from their own interactive involvement in the module to the broader interrelatedness of local/global, North/South, security/development issues.

The general procedure for PPC modules is that they follow lectures and readings that serve as a general overview of the subject and provide specific information for use in the "syndicate discussions" (small-group sessions). A great deal of preparation is required of the students prior to the group sessions. Each group must choose a spokesperson to present its answers to the class. The questions are assigned, and students must prepare their answers during the evening prior to the discussion. The preparation of each answer in the PPC module, including assigned readings, requires approximately two hours. Students are encouraged to make their presentations interesting, using visual aids whenever possible and drawing on their own professional experience (many PPC students are in the midcareer stage). Wider reading is also encouraged as a prelude to preparing answers and participating in the discussion that follows each presentation.

A module that is used by PPC for teaching about the politicians and diplomats involved in peacekeeping provides some examples relevant to Africa.[2] Three cases are concerned with theoretical issues: The first is related to the revised nature of peacekeeping within changing political economies; the second, to the notion that in general, the North and South may have alternative, even opposing, views on peacekeeping because of their respective positions in the global political economy; and the third, to the role of civil societies in determining the outcomes of peacekeeping operations. Two other questions apply to more practical, "on-the-ground" concerns that have plagued recent peacekeeping missions. One involves the issue of "legitimate authority"; that is, in a crisis situation where government systems may have collapsed, how should peacekeeping operants determine which political force to support? The other is concerned with the control that politicians and diplomats may exert over peacekeepers to prevent them from becoming or being perceived as an army of occupation in strife-torn countries.

Each case is structured around a preamble that establishes the issue to be addressed and a question that will focus the participants' discussion. For example, a quote from "third world" scholar Asoka Bandarage is used in the preamble that sets up the first case. It suggests that "peacekeeping requires a transformation of human consciousness from domination to partnership, and its practical application to the realms of politics and economics" (Bandarage 1994: 39). The remainder of the preamble relates this quote to the proposition that Bandarage's "transformation" requires rethinking the extent and nature of the state's authority, making a general reevaluation of present systems of governance and regulation (especially of the market), and recognizing the "blurring" of the definitions and the roles of politicians and diplomats.

The question asks whether participants agree with the analysis presented and asks them to show how the analysis has relevance for those involved in peacekeeping. After each group has presented its answer, there is time for discussion among the groups. The PPC module includes a series of points for deliberation that the instructor can use to promote further discussion. Many of these points refer to other articles that participants have been advised to read, thus providing a cohesive framework in which the various readings may be analyzed and debated.

ADAPTING THE MODULE FRAMEWORK

The setup for subsequent cases in the example module is similar, although in those involving practical issues, assertions by participants in actual peacekeeping operations rather than academics are used as the focal points for the questions and discussion. In other classrooms, different introductory measures or props might be substituted. For example, videos or segments of television news reports might be used to highlight a particular issue for discussion.[3] Furthermore, depending on the size of the class, the time available, the particular issue at hand, and the expected knowledge base of the students—at the PPC many participants have already worked in peacekeeping organizations at least once—all working groups in the module might answer the same question, different questions related to the same issue, or questions concerning separate issues associated with peacekeeping in Africa.

Obviously, to be most effective, students must read the assigned material in advance of the class period. Yet as any teacher knows, motivating students (and occasionally even mature, professional participants) to come to class prepared can be a major challenge. This problem does not necessarily speak to an inherent weakness in the approach, since there are various possible solutions. One possibility—granted, based on a negative incentive—is to incorporate graded, written assignments based on the readings. An alternative, and perhaps more encouraging option, is to have students find newsstories or interviews that support or contradict a particular viewpoint in the readings. Although it would be especially useful if students could find source material from African media or from participants—refugees, peacekeeping soldiers, NGO personnel—who have been involved as recipients or operants in peacekeeping missions, such material is not readily available to students in the North. However, with the increasing availability of the Internet to students and the growing numbers of Web sites and information networks on African issues,[4] more immediate and intimate connections with African sources are possible.

In short, there are a variety of techniques and tools by which instructors can adapt this teaching-module approach to classes on working for peace in Africa. Moreover, beyond its adaptability, this teaching method lends itself well to including other approaches to learning. Simulations and role playing are good examples. For example, following discussions on the multiplicity of issues and actors involved in the subject, as well as the lessons learned from previous peacekeeping "successes" and "failures," it would be appropriate to have students discuss the problems involved in putting a peacekeeping and -making mission in place in a hypothetical crisis situation. Conversely, students might assume the roles of various relevant actors from among UN agencies, national governments, combatants' headquarters, military establishments, mercenaries, multinational corporations, local communities, refugee communities, NGOs, and regional organizations. (Since "coalitions" vary between cases and periods, it would be of value to let students discuss and decide what groups would take part in coalitions in any particular case.)

CONCLUSIONS

As individuals respond differently to various teaching methodologies, it makes sense that effective approaches would utilize a variety of audiovisual tools and techniques. Moreover, as one important objective of high school and early university education is to develop students' competency in expression, it also makes sense to incorporate projects that provide opportunities for encouraging improvements in speaking and writing skills. The teaching-module approach as described is flexible enough to address each of these pedagogical concerns. And equally important for teaching on Africa, it is an efficient and effective method for indicating and understanding the diversity, complexity, and interrelatedness of the forces, actors, issues, and attributes that contribute to the current state of political economies and cultural issues in contemporary Africa.

The emerging discourses surrounding African peacekeeping, peacemaking, and peacebuilding can be understood only in the context of this complicated nexus and consequently require a teaching approach that can readily investigate and incorporate a broad spectrum of ideas and ideologies. The interactive teaching-module approach described is an innovative, participatory, and flexible method that can adapt not only to the needs of instructors and students but to the rapidly changing subject of security and peacekeeping needs and responsibilities in Africa at the end of the twentieth century.

NOTES

1. Timothy M. Shaw argues that the neoliberal reforms, especially structural adjustment programs (SAPs) insisted upon by the international financial institutions (IFIs), the International Monetary Fund (IMF), and the World Bank play a large role in "generat[ing] the conditions which call for multifaceted peacekeeping coalitions." See Shaw, "Beyond Post-Conflict Peacebuilding: What Links to Sustainable Development and Human Security," *International Peacekeeping* 32, 2 (Summer 1996): 36–48. See also Shaw with Clement Adibe, "Africa and Global Developments in the Twenty-first Century," *International Journal* 51, 1 (Winter, 1995–1996): 1–26.

2. However, it should be noted that problems of working for peace in Africa are exacerbated by the degree of economic marginalization and institutional collapse of many countries and the complexity of both formal and informal regional relationships.

3. There are a number of good videos available from local libraries, NGOs, UN agencies, the International Red Cross, and other groups that deal with peacekeeping in Africa. The National Film Board (NFB) of Canada has produced a number of excellent titles, including the recent five-part Rwanda series on the genocide in Rwanda, and *Rape: A Crime of War* (the NFB's Web site is http://www.nfb.ca).

4. Following are some useful Web sites:

Canadian Association of United Nations Peacekeeping, http://pk.kos.net/cavunp.html
International Committee of the Red Cross, http://www.icrc.org
International Federation of Red Cross and Red Crescent Societies, http://www.ifrc.org
International Peace Academy, http://www.ipacademy.inter.net
Lester B. Pearson Canadian International Peacekeeping Training Centre, http://www.cdnpeacekeeping.ns.ca/
Medecins sans Frontières (Doctors Without Borders), http://www.dwb.org
Relief and Rehabilitation Network, http://www.oneworld.org/odi/rrn/index.html
ReliefWeb, http://www.reliefweb.int
United Nations Department of Peacekeeping Operations, http://www.un.org/depts/dpko
United Nations Peace Academy, http://www.un.org/depts/dpko/training/ipa.htm
WorldAid98 (ICVA), http://www.worldaid.org

Information is also available on home pages with news about Africa (e.g., Africa News Online: http//www.africanews.org) or on home country pages such as Somalia, Mozambique, Rwanda, Zaire, Burundi. The latter are often set up by expatriates from these countries who are now living in North America or Europe. The material offered varies in quality, credibility, and usefulness, but the authors may have direct links to people in or from those countries and the information may include interesting items: personal accounts, photos, and so on from the "other side" of peacekeeping. In general, Internet sources should be used with caution and skepticism, as some sites are biased and have little accountability. Others contain useful information that is often unavailable elsewhere.

SUGGESTIONS FOR FURTHER READING AND RESOURCES

GENERAL

Bandarage, Asoka. 1994. "Global Peace and Security in the Post–Cold War Era: A 'Third World' Perspective." In *Peace and World Security Studies: A Curriculum Guide,* 6th ed., ed. Michael T. Klare. Boulder: Lynne Rienner.

Bercovitch, Jacob, and Jeffrey Rubin, eds. 1992. *Mediation in International Relations: Multiple Approaches to Conflict Management.* New York: St. Martin's Press.

Berdal, Mats R. 1993. *Whither UN Peacekeeping?* Adelphi Paper 81. London: International Institute of Strategic Studies.

Black, D. R., and S. J. Rolston, eds. 1995. *Peacemaking and Preventative Diplomacy in the New World (Dis)Order: Proceedings of a Colloquium.* Halifax, N.S.: Centre for Foreign Policy Studies.

Bloomfield, Lincoln P., and Allen Moulten. 1997. *Managing International Conflict: From Theory to Policy—A Teaching Tool Using CASCON.* New York: St. Martin's Press.

Boulden, Jane. 1991. "Building on the Past: Future Directions for Peacekeeping." *Behind the Headlines* 48, 4: 1–17.

Boutros-Ghali, Boutros. 1992. *An Agenda for Peace: Preventive Diplomacy, Peacemaking and Peace-Keeping—Report of the Secretary-General Pursuant to the Statement Adopted by the Summit Meeting of the Security Council on 31 January 1992.* New York: United Nations.

Buckley, Gary B. 1993. "Rethinking the Teaching of Security Policy in a Post–Cold War Environment." *International Studies Notes* 18, 3 (Fall): 5–7.

Cox, David. 1993. *Exploring an Agenda for Peace: Issues Arising from the Report of the Secretary-General.* Ottawa: Canadian Centre for Global Security.

Crocker, Chester A., Fen Osler Hampson, and Pamela Aall, eds. 1996. *Managing Global Chaos: Sources of and Responses to International Conflict.* Washington, D.C.: U.S. Institute of Peace Press.

Damrosch, Lori Fisler, ed. 1993. *Enforcing Restraint: Collective Intervention in Internal Conflicts.* New York: Council on Foreign Relations Press.

Daniel, Donald C.F., and Bradd C. Hayes, eds. 1995. *Beyond Traditional Peacekeeping.* New York: St. Martin's Press.

Department of National Defence. 1997. *Civil-Military Cooperation in Peace, Emergencies, Crisis, and War.* Ottawa: DND.

Durch, William J., ed. 1993. *The Evolution of United Nations Peacekeeping: Case Studies and Comparative Analysis.* New York: St. Martin's Press.

Goodpaster, Andrew J. 1996. *When Diplomacy Is Not Enough: Managing Multina-*

tional Military Interventions. Washington, D.C.: Carnegie Corporation of New York.

Hill, Stephen M. 1996. *Peacekeeping and the United Nations.* Aldershot: Dartmouth Press.

Karns, Margaret P., and Karen A. Mingst. 1994. "Maintaining International Peace and Security: UN Peacekeeping and Peacemaking." In *World Security: Challenges for a New Century,* 2nd ed., ed. Michael T. Klare and Daniel C. Thomas. New York: St. Martin's Press.

LaRose-Edwards, Paul, Jack Dangerfield, and Randy Weeks. 1997. *Non-Traditional Military Training for Canadian Peacekeepers: A Study Prepared for the Commission of Inquiry into the Deployment of Canadian Forces to Somalia.* Ottawa: Public Works and Government Services Canada.

Morrison, A., James Kiras, and Stephanie Blair, eds. 1995. *The New Peacekeeping Partnership.* Clementsport, N.S.: Canadian Peacekeeping Press.

Murphy, Sean. 1996. *Humanitarian Intervention: The United Nations in an Evolving World Order.* Philadelphia: University of Pennsylvania Press.

Pugh, Michael, ed. 1997. *The UN, Peace, and Force.* London: Frank Cass.

Ramsbotham, David. 1995. *The Changing Nature of Intervention: The Role of United Nations Peacekeeping.* London: Research Institute for the Study of Conflict and Terrorism.

Ratner, Stephen R. 1995. *The New United Nations Peacekeeping: Building Peace in Lands of Conflict After the Cold War.* New York: St. Martin's Press.

United Nations. 1990. *Teaching About United Nations Peacekeeping.* New York: UN.

———. 1993. *Teaching About Peacekeeping and Peacemaking.* New York: UN.

———. 1994. *UN Peacekeeping Training: Basic Information for Junior Ranks Handbook.* New York: UN.

———. Various years. *United Nations Peacekeeping.* New York: UN.

United Nations Development Program (UNDP). 1995. *Human Development Report 1995.* New York: Oxford University Press.

Warner, Daniel, ed. 1995. *New Dimensions of Peacekeeping.* Boston: M. Nijhoff.

Weiss, Thomas G., David P. Forsythe, and Roger A. Coates. 1994. *The United Nations and Changing World Politics.* Boulder: Westview Press.

White, N. D. 1993. *Keeping the Peace: The UN and the Maintenance of International Peace and Security.* New York: St. Martin's Press.

Whitman, Jim, and David Pocock, eds. 1996. *After Rwanda: The Coordination of United Nations Humanitarian Assistance.* New York: St. Martin's Press.

AFRICA

Adebajo, Adekeye. 1995. "The UN's Unknown Effort." *Africa Report* 40: 60–63.

Albright, Madeleine K. 1994. "The Tragedy in Rwanda: International Cooperation to Find a Solution." *U.S. Department of State Dispatch* 5, 27: 438–439.

Alexander, McGill. 1995. *An African Rapid-Deployment Force for Peace Operations on the African Continent.* Fort Leavenworth: Foreign Military Studies Office.

Anglin, Douglas G. 1995. "The Life and Death of South Africa's National Peacekeeping Force." *Journal of Modern African Studies* 33: 21–52.

Anstee, Margaret J. 1993. "Angola: The Forgotten Tragedy—A Test Case for U.N. Peacekeeping." *International Relations* 11: 495–511.

Bolton, John R. 1994. "Wrong Turn in Somalia." *Foreign Affairs* 73: 56–66.

Bryden, Matthew. 1995. "Somalia: The Wages of Failure." *Current History* 94: 145–151.

Burkhalter, Holly J. 1994–1995. "The Question of Genocide: The Clinton Administration and Rwanda." *World Policy Journal* 11: 44–54.

Chopra, Jarat. 1994. "Breaking the Stalemate in Western Sahara." *International Peacekeeping* 1: 303–319.

Cilliers, Jakkie, and Greg Mills, eds. 1995. *Peacekeeping in Africa,* vol. 2. Halfway House, South Africa: Institute for Security Studies (ISS).

Dallaire, Romeo A., and Bruce Poulin. 1995. "UNAMIR [UN Assistance Mission for Rwanda]: Mission to Rwanda." *Joint Force Quarterly* 7: 66–71.

De Waal, Alex, and Rakiya Omaar. 1995. "The Genocide in Rwanda and the International Response." *Current History* 94: 156–161.

Diehl, Paul F., and Sonia R. Jurado. 1993. "United Nations Election Supervision in South Africa: Lessons from the Namibian Peacekeeping Experience." *Studies in Conflict and Terrorism* 16: 61–74.

Dorn, A. Walter, and David J.H. Bell. 1995. "Intelligence and Peacekeeping: The UN Operation in the Congo, 1960–64." *International Peacekeeping* 2: 11–33.

Durch, William J. 1993. "Building on Sand: UN Peacekeeping in the Western Sahara." *International Security* 17: 151–171.

Finnegan, William. 1995. "A World of Dust." *New Yorker* 71, 20 (March): 64–77.

Fleischman, Janet. 1993. "An Uncivil War." *Africa Report* (Liberia) 38: 56–59.

Gibbs, David N. 1993. "Dag Hammarskjöld, the United Nations, and the Congo Crisis of 1960–1: A Reinterpretation." *Journal of Modern African Studies* 31: 163–174.

Hirsch, John L., and Robert B. Oakley. 1995. *Somalia and Operation Restore Hope: Reflections on Peacemaking and Peacekeeping.* Washington, D.C.: U.S. Institute of Peace Press.

Huband, Mark. 1993. "The Politics of Violence." *Africa Report* 38: 13–19.

Leitenberg, Milton. 1994. "Rwanda, 1994: International Incompetence Produces Genocide." *Peacekeeping and International Relations* 23: 6–10.

Lloyd, Robert B. 1995. "Mozambique: The Terror of War, the Tensions of Peace." *Current History* 94: 152–155.

Lyons, Terrence, and Ahmed I. Samatar. 1995. *Somalia: State Collapse, Multilateral Intervention, and Strategies for Political Reconstruction.* Washington, D.C.: Brookings Institution.

Magyar, Karl P. 1996. *Surveying the Middle Ground: Conceptual Issues and Peacekeeping in Southern Africa.* ISS Occasional Paper 2. Halfway House, South Africa: ISS.

Makinda, Samuel M. 1993. "Somalia: From Humanitarian Intervention to Military Offensive?" *World Today* 49: 184–186.

Malan, Mark, William Nhara, and Pol Bergevin. 1997. *African Capabilities for Training for Peace Operations: Report for the Organization of African Unity.* Halfway House, South Africa: ISS for Organization of African Unity.

Marnika, Maurice. 1995a. "The Challenge for Peacemaking in Africa: Conflict Prevention and Conflict Resolution." *Peacekeeping and International Relations* 24: 5.

———. 1995b. "Rwanda and UNAMIR [UN Assistance Mission for Rwanda]—The Backlash to Ethnic Slaughter." *Peacekeeping and International Relations* 24: 14.

McCormick, Shawn H. 1995. "The Lessons of Intervention in Africa." *Current History* 94: 162–166.

Moreno, Rafael, and Juan J. Vega. 1994. "Lessons from Somalia." *Peacekeeping and International Relations* 23: 11–12.

Oladimeji, Olutunde A. 1993. "Behold, African Peacekeepers." *Proceedings: U.S. Naval Institute* 119: 64–66.

"Rwanda: Short Memories." 1995. *Economist* 335 (June 17): 42–47.

Shaw, Mark, and Jakkie Cilliers, eds. 1995. *South Africa and Peacekeeping in Africa*, vol. 1. Halfway House, South Africa: Institute for Defence Policy.

Shepherd, Anne. 1993a. "Keeping the Peace." *Africa Report* 38: 56–59.

———. 1993b. "Vetting the Vote." *Africa Report* 38: 22–25.

Smock, David R., ed. 1993. *Making War and Waging Peace: Foreign Intervention in Africa*. Washington, D.C.: U.S. Institute of Peace Press.

Thakur, Ramesh. 1994. "From Peacekeeping to Peace Enforcement: The UN Operation in Somalia." *Journal of Modern African Studies* 32: 387–410.

Thakur, Ramesh, and Carlyle A. Thayer, eds. 1995. *A Crisis of Expectations: UN Peacekeeping in the 1990s*. Boulder: Westview Press.

Weller, Marc, ed. 1994. *Regional Peace-Keeping and International Enforcement: The Liberian Crisis*. New York: Grotius.

Willett, Susan. 1995. "Ostriches, Wise Old Elephants, and Economic Reconstruction in Mozambique." *International Peacekeeping* 2: 34–55.

Wurst, Jim. 1994. "Mozambique Disarms." *Bulletin of the Atomic Scientists* 50: 36–39.

PART THREE

New Technology in the Classroom

12

ON THE COMPUTER AND IN THE KITCHEN: EXERCISES FOR TEACHING PEOPLE-ENVIRONMENT RELATIONS

TAMARA GILES-VERNICK

As I contemplate organizing a syllabus for a history course addressing people-environment relations, I often find that I lose myself in a fantasy: Twenty-five students and I board a bus in West Africa, and for the next three months, we ride, hike, and boat our way through the continent in an effort to understand how African people and environments have shaped one another. We frequent urban centers, savanna farms, fishing villages, hunting camps, and diamond, gold, and copper mines. We learn about Africa's environmental history by talking to academics, farmers, griots, miners, hunters, traders, politicians, and development experts. We sample gari (dried and pounded manioc, or cassava), teff, palm oil, mealie meal, millet, squashes, leaf sauces, forest buffalo, and goat. The fantasy, however, abruptly runs aground when I imagine trying to animate tired, feuding students with substantial parasite loads to visit our twentieth maize field. The students mutiny, commandeering the bus to drive them to the closest beach as I trudge dejectedly back to my hotel room.

Even though the fantasy dissolves into images of incessant complaining, exhaustion, and rebellion, it is enormously useful. The fantasy speaks to the importance and the challenges of conveying the highly dynamic and deeply spatial relations between African people and their environments. African environmental history demands that students know and engage themselves with the histories of African places and people. Hence, as I organize my courses, I try to keep that fantasy in mind to incorporate additional learning experiences that enable students to gain familiarity with the people, activities, and places of these histories.

Most students have had no instruction in African environmental history; the little they do know about Africa seems to come from *National Geographic* and the Discovery channel. For them, this environmental history brings to mind big game, old-growth forests, Africans living "in harmony with nature," and saintly conservationists who protect sweeping fragile landscapes from marauding African cultivators, hunters, miners, or multinational corporations. African environmental history requires students to shed these deeply held visions of Africans and their environments. Thus my fantasy provides me with a springboard for developing exercises in which students can gain insight into the histories of *National Geographic* and Discovery channel images. They can explore the complexity of past and contemporary struggles over access to and control over resources.

This chapter suggests how teachers of African environmental history and issues can make the unfamiliar places and activities of Africa's past more comprehensible to students. It also proposes ways in which teachers can encourage more sophisticated, complex understandings of people-environment relations. It begins by examining why Africanists should consider teaching environmental history, or at least to incorporate environmental issues into their courses. It then turns to some suggestions for familiarizing students with unfamiliar histories and places and for challenging stereotypical visions of and interventions in people-environment relations in Africa. Such strategies encourage students to learn by seeing, eating, and doing.

WHY TEACH ENVIRONMENTAL HISTORY?

Defining "environmental history" is not as straightforward as it seems, though I often begin my environmental courses by elaborating a definition and justifying a semester-long course on it. Rather than falling back on an uncritical acceptance of nature-culture dichotomies, I encourage students to perceive environmental history as Tim Ingold (1992) has articulated it: a history of people-environment relations in which both people and environments constitute one another over time. Hence, Ingold observes, the environment encompasses past human activities just as people embody their past environmental relations. African environmental history therefore engages students with activities, images, and policies surrounding people-environment relations.

Understanding these people-environment relations is important and interesting for several reasons, I tell my students. As the cradle of humankind, Africa provides an important case study for understanding how people have interacted with their environments over a very long time. Africa's substantial fluctuations in climate and its ecological changes over the past 10,000 years provide us with an opportunity for exploring how Africans have coped with such changes. Africa contains very large and varied vegetational zones that have an important impact on regional and global climates. And for centuries the continent has provided resources for developing global economies. Finally, African people-environment relations have been the subject of mythmaking that has been enormously influential in conservation and development policies. These reasons provide a reference point for students throughout the semester as we examine histories that are unfamiliar to them. They also serve to shake up students' stereotypical visions of African people either pillaging or being victimized by their environments.

LOCATING AND CONSUMING ENVIRONMENTAL HISTORY

Providing students with spatial and bodily understanding of African environmental history is important, for it familiarizes them in small but crucial ways with how Africans have interacted with their environments in the past. One cannot, for instance, expect students to understand the problems of soil erosion and laterization or the politics of soil conservation when very few of them have ever stepped into a field. Nor can they truly comprehend the significance of cassava in the history of the Congo basin if they do not know what the tuber looks like and how it grows. I have developed two strategies for addressing students' unfamiliarity with the places, materials, and practices of environmental use in African history: an electronic archive of African images and "kitchen exercises."

The electronic archive brings together a wide variety of photographs of people, activities, and landscapes within Africa. It provides the raw material for various teaching tools that work very well in environmental courses. I will first address the different uses of the electronic archive in course Web sites, in classrooms, and on computer networks and then discuss how we have created such an archive at the University of Virginia.

The electronic archive can store images that form the basis for a course Web site. The thought of creating a Web site may well strike terror in the hearts of some Africanists, but there are compelling reasons for taking the time to do so. Many students already use the Internet daily to search for research paper materials and to read their email. A course Web site makes additional course materials easily accessible to students with computers linked to the university computer system. Even more important, a Web site can provide the crucial visual illustrations that effectively engage students in the material. It can translate information that students overlook into vivid images that they can peruse and contemplate. And finally, a Web site provides a service to people beyond the confines of one's class or university, for it makes these illustrations more widely available to Internet users.

The Web site for one of my environmental history courses contains a syllabus and links to relevant Web sites dealing with Africa and its environmental policies, of which there are many. The University of Pennsylvania's annotated list of African environmental Web sites contains links to Web sites and online publications addressing such issues as desertification, forestry, locust infestations, irrigation, and global environmental change and development.

The Web site for my environmental history courses also shows photographs depicting locations and activities relevant to our weekly topics. Students can, for instance, see photos of irrigation practices, of urban centers such as Johannesburg and Ibadan, of fishing activities on the Sangha River in central Africa, or of millet and rice farmers in Mali. The photos enable students to envision the people, practices, and lands about which they read. Students maintain that the Web site allows them to peruse images more carefully than they would if I simply showed slides in class. I have also incorporated photographs available on the Web site into paper assignments so that students must confront the ways in which images of Africans and their environments can illuminate but also mislead.

Setting up this Web site is not as difficult as it might seem. I knew nothing about hypertext markup language (HTML) before creating my first Web site. But it was not difficult to learn even for one as technically challenged as I am. I used a brief university HTML guide to create the Web site and relied on the kind and knowledgeable computer consultants in the history department and multimedia resources center. There are also several books about using HTML to create Web sites, available at computer and software stores. Many college and university computer centers have creative and capable consultants who can help instructors make effective use of an electronic archive of scanned images by designing course Web sites.

Electronic archives can also be useful to those instructors who are not interested in creating a course Web site. These instructors can simply make the archive available to students who wish to view images of various locations, people, and activities. Each week, for instance, instructors could provide students with a set of relevant keywords (discussed further on). Students with Internet access could then search for and peruse these relevant images in the archive, gaining many of the same benefits as students in courses with Web sites.

Finally, the electronic archive can make it easier for teachers to show a variety of photographs in the classroom without having to rely on cumbersome slide projectors and on borrowing, organizing, or copying slides from colleagues. Some classrooms at the University of Virginia are connected to the university computer network and equipped with computers that can project photos just like slides. The advantage of an archive is that the instructor has access to more stored images than she or he would have with a set of slides.

Our archive is still in its infancy. Currently accessible only to history department members, the archive contains photos and slides that I and colleagues in the History and Environmental Sciences Departments have taken while in Africa. We do, however, intend to make the archive accessible to the rest of the university community and are working with the Environmental Sciences Department to develop an archive that will be compatible with our own.

The archive itself consists of images scanned by a work-study student with a color flatbed scanner and a slide scanner at a resolution of 72 dots per inch (dpi). This resolution works best for displaying images on screens; higher-resolution (300 dpi) scanning creates very large and cumbersome files but is necessary for printing out these images. The student then stored each image in three different file formats on a sizable account on the university's server. We store images in *.tif, *.gif, and *.jpg forms. Although the *.tif files are very large, they conserve as much information as possible about the original image. The *.gif files are substantially smaller and contain far less information and far fewer colors than the original image; their advantage is that they load on the viewer's screen relatively quickly. The *.jpg files compress information from the large *.tif files but use a much wider range of colors than do the small *.gif files. I use both *.gif and *.jpg files in my Web sites. Viewers first see the easily loaded *.gif images and then can click on these images to see a more detailed *.jpg file of the same image. When we have finished scanning all of the available images, we intend to copy them onto CD-ROMs, which safely store them.

Each image has a name, description, and set of keywords that enables any database user to call up sets of related images. The computer consultant for the History Department has designed a program that allows the user to type in a particular keyword, such as agriculture, southern Africa, gender, or hunting, and view all images related to that keyword.

Instructors do not need to have binders full of slides and photos or numerous colleagues who have visited Africa to create an electronic archive. In addition to borrowing photos and slides from colleagues, instructors can contact owners of related Web sites to acquire their images electronically or can scan images from books after securing copyright permission from publishers or photographers.

I use a second, decidedly low-tech strategy for helping students to understand something about African agricultural practices: "kitchen exercises." After putting students to sleep with lectures about the origins of agriculture and the wonders of cassava, I decided to put them to work in the library and in their kitchens. As part of a unit addressing the origins of agriculture, I divide students according to five food groups (palm oil, millet, teff, cassava, and yams). Each group conducts library research on the history and uses of one of these foods. The group also receives a sample of the food as well as two recipes detailing its preparation. When the class meets, the groups give their presentations and serve their prepared foods to the rest of the class. The exercise is a simple one, but I notice that students no longer roll their eyes when I spend several minutes reiterating the historical importance of particular food crops: They have tasted these foods and conducted independent research on them. Eating these foods—these contemporary embodiments of historical relationships between Africans and land—helps many students connect in small but meaningful ways to activities that Africans undertake.

Instructors wishing to use such foods in their courses should try to locate African, Caribbean, Latino, or Asian grocery stores in their towns or in nearby cities.

CONVEYING THE COMPLEXITIES OF ENVIRONMENTAL ISSUES

Environmental history challenges students to move beyond stereotypical and romanticized notions of African people-environment relations. Many students entering environmental courses express some sort of vague political desire to conserve the environment, but they are often unaware of the struggles in which African people, states, multilateral aid organizations, multinational corporations, and conservationists engage over whether, how, and where such conservation measures can be implemented. It can be a formidable task to convey the highly contentious and complex nature of historical and contemporary debates over conservation in Africa. I have found that using role-playing exercises frequently helps students to realize that their romanticized conceptions of conservation do not adequately capture the complexity of conservation and the ways in which it alters Africans' environmental as well as political, social, and economic relations. In a seminar on the history of conservation, I asked students to divide into five groups representing various interests participating in the Dzanga-Sangha park and reserve in southwestern Central African Republic. Students represented a French-owned logging company, the World Wildlife Fund, the Central African Republic state, and African peoples living in the region, including migrants who sought employment with the logging company. They would all participate in a roundtable discussion in which they negotiated whether and how the forest and game in southwestern Central African Republic would be conserved. In preparation for this discussion, each group reviewed a packet containing scholarly articles, popular press accounts, and World Wildlife Fund reports on the Dzanga-Sangha Special Reserve and the Dzanga-Ndoki Park. Each group met outside of class to elaborate the strategies by which it would protect its interests in the forest during the roundtable discussions.

These materials were fairly easy for me to provide, since I had conducted research on the histories of people-environment relations in this region and thus had collected substantial materials about conservation there. But other instructors can replicate this exercise either by gathering writings on this region or by collecting publications on African parks, which have been well documented by anthropologists and historians and continue to occupy the interests of contemporary conservationists. Library and Internet searches and contacts with major conservation organizations such as the World Wildlife Fund (known as Worldwide Fund for Nature in Europe) or Wildlife Conservation International should provide instructors with sufficient teaching materials for an effective roundtable discussion.

When the roundtable convened, students introduced their characters and explained their interests in the forest and their histories in the region. I instructed students to discuss why the region should be conserved. Since they had already studied the historical and current debates over the goals of conservation, they settled quickly into delineating their interests and different perspectives on the proper use of the forest. They then undertook the contentious task of hammering out agreements concerning the forms that conservation would take, the rules governing protected species or regions, the enforcers of those rules, and the development strategies that would be consistent with conservation goals. In the end, no one could agree on anything.

But this result did not signal that the exercise had failed. Indeed, as the students debated the World Wildlife Fund's case for creating a park and multiuse reserve, they replicated some of the very same dynamics of shifting alliances and conflicts that have beleaguered actual conservation efforts in southwestern Central African Republic. By the end of the roundtable discussion, students realized that the conservation efforts and solutions to conflict over access to protected resources that they had so easily recommended throughout the semester were not as easy to implement as they had thought. In effect, the exercise helped them to realize that their preconceived ideas about conservation were unduly romantic and reductionist and that there were no easy answers to conservation dilemmas.

CONCLUSION

Encouraging students to learn about African people-environment relations is, of course, no substitute for a three-month journey through the deserts, forests, savannas, and urban landscapes of Africa. But such exercises do help bridge the fantasy of this journey and the realities of teaching African environmental history in a classroom. These strategies introduce, however, an additional challenge for instructors: As students learn more about how Africans have coped with and shaped their environments, they also encounter the stereotype of ignorant outsiders brutally destabilizing Africans' relationships with their environments. I have found myself spending entire class periods exhorting students to rely less on this stereotype and to pay closer attention to the historical particularities of African and European knowledge of and interventions in African environments. But perhaps I need to indulge in a new set of fantasies to devise alternative methods of convincing them.

APPENDIX: SAMPLE ASSIGNMENT

Your group will be responsible for presenting a summary of the history of manioc (cassava; *Manihot esculenta*). What is manioc? How does it grow? Where does it grow? How do Africans eat it? Where did it come from and when? What are its advantages and disadvantages for African farmers?

In order for you and other students to taste manioc, I have provided you with a bag of gari (dried and pounded manioc) and a simple recipe. You may prepare this dish, or you can simply cook the gari in boiling water. (Proportions should be about one to one.)

Your presentation should last no more than twelve minutes. Feel free to be creative.

Sources you may wish to consult include William O. Jones, *Manioc in Africa* (Stanford University Press).

SUGGESTIONS FOR
FURTHER READING AND RESOURCES

DZANGA-SANGHA SPECIAL RESERVE
AND DZANGA-NDOKI PARK

Reading materials to prepare students to conduct roundtable discussions on the Dzanga-Sangha Special Reserve and the Dzanga-Ndoki Park in Central African Republic are available and listed below. World Wildlife Fund also has a wealth of documents and may be willing to copy them for interested instructors. Finally, instructors can find published sources concerning such well-known parks as Serengeti.

Carroll, Richard. 1986. "Status of the Lowland Gorilla and Other Wildlife in the Dzanga-Sangha Region of Southwestern Central African Republic." *Primate Conservation* 7: 38–44.

———. 1988. "Relative Density, Range Extension, and Conservation Potential of the Lowland Gorilla in the Dzanga-Sangha Region of Southwestern Central African Republic." *Mammalia* 52, 3: 309–323.

Chadwick, Douglas. 1995. "Ndoki: The Last Place on Earth." *National Geographic* 188, 1: 2–45.
Giles-Vernick, Tamara. 1996. "'A Dead People'? Migrants, Land, and History in the Rainforests of the Central African Republic." Ph.D. diss., Johns Hopkins University.
Linden, Eugene. 1992. "The Last Eden." *Time* (July 13): 42–48.
Noss, Andrew J. 1995. "Duikers, Cables, and Nets: A Cultural Ecology of Hunting in a Central African Rainforest." Ph.D. diss., University of Florida, Gainsville.

OTHER READINGS AND RESOURCES

Africa News Service. 1985. *Africa News Cookbook: African Cooking for Western Kitchens*. New York: Penguin.
Anderson, David, and Richard Grove, eds. 1987. *Conservation in Africa: People, Policies, and Practice*. Cambridge: Cambridge University Press.
Cronon, William. 1990. "Modes of Prophecy and Production: Placing Nature in History." *Journal of American History* 76, 4: 1122–1131.
Fairhead, James, and Melissa Leach. 1996. *Misreading the African Landscape: Society and Ecology in the Forest-Savanna Mosaic*. New York: Cambridge University Press.
Graham, Ian S. 1996. *HTML Sourcebook: A Complete Guide to HTML 3.0,* 2nd ed. New York: John Wiley.
Grant, Rosamund. 1995. *Taste of Africa: 70 Easy-to-Cook Recipes from an Undiscovered Cuisine*. New York: Smithmark.
Ingold, Tim. 1992. "Culture and the Perception of the Environment." In *Bush Base: Forest Farm: Culture, Environment, and Development*, ed. by Elisabeth Croll and David Parkin. London and New York: Routledge.
Leach, Melissa, and Robin Mearns, eds. 1996. *The Lie of the Land: Challenging Received Wisdom on the African Environment*. Portsmouth, N.H.: Heinemann.
Maddox, Gregory, James L. Giblin, and Isaria N. Kimambo, eds. 1996. *Custodians of the Land: Ecology and Culture in the History of Tanzania*. London: James Currey.
McIntosh, Susan Keech, and Roderick J. McIntosh. 1981. "West African Prehistory." *American Scientist* 69: 602–613.
Neumann, Roderick P. 1995. "Ways of Seeing Africa: Colonial Recasting of African Society and Landscape in Serengeti National Park." *Ecumene* 2, 2: 149–169.
Rampino, Michael R., et al., eds. 1987. *Climate: History, Periodicity, and Predictability*. New York: Van Nostrand Reinhold.
Wells, Michael, and Katrina Brandon, with Lee Hannah. 1992. *People and Parks: Linking Protected Area Management with Local Communities*. Washington, D.C.: World Bank, World Wildlife Fund, and U.S. Agency for International Development.

13

USING THE WORLD WIDE WEB TO TEACH ABOUT AFRICAN ART

BENJAMIN C. RAY

In the next century, technologically equipped classrooms and large collections of electronically produced images will be readily available. Advances in computer technology already provide enormous opportunities for innovative teaching that some instructors are only now beginning to discover. The educational value of computer technology in the humanities lies both in the informational resources of the Internet and the creative potential of the World Wide Web. The textual and visual capability of the Web not only fosters student-oriented teaching and collaborative learning in the classroom but also enables students to produce new informational resources for the Web, especially projects involving the use of images.

In 1996, I created a course at the University of Virginia titled African Art and the Virtual Museum, offered jointly by the Department of Religious Studies and the Department of Art. The course was designed to enable students to learn about African art and to demonstrate what they had learned by creating original Web-based exhibitions of African art. Two class meetings a week were devoted to illustrated lectures and student presentations; a third involved computer instruction, including a lab session offered for extra credit. Two museum visits provided a venue for lectures by curators at the National Museum of African Art and the Virginia Museum of Fine Arts.

The course utilized the digitized image resources of the Fowler Museum of Cultural History of the University of California at Berkeley, provided through the Museum Educational Site Licensing Project,[1] as well as images from the African art collections of the Bayly Museum of the University of Virginia and the Hampton University Museum of Hampton

University, Hampton, Virginia. Following a set of exhibition guidelines, students drew upon lectures, assigned readings, museum visits, and conventional library research to create their own Web-based exhibitions. They selected images related to a theme of their choice and wrote the texts that introduced the exhibit and accompanied each image. The special challenge of the course was to enable students to bring what they had learned in the classroom to a wider audience, to "transform students into teachers," as one student put it.

I should point out that I had never previously taught a course on African art; nor did I have any training in this field, although I had put together for classroom purposes a few small exhibitions of African art in the Bayly Museum at the University of Virginia. Undertaking such an ambitious project might seem daunting, but I discovered that almost any Africanist can do this, thanks to the wealth of excellent available resources. For the past fifteen years African art scholars have produced a body of outstanding literature that is readily understandable by nonspecialists, especially the extensive and superlative set of articles in the new *Dictionary of Art* (Turner 1996). Scholarly presentations on African art are also a regular feature at the annual meetings of the African Studies Association. Moreover, there are an increasing number of African art exhibitions at major museums that enable firsthand contact with the exhibition environment, as well as a growing presence of African art on the World Wide Web.

For several years, I had acquainted myself with African art studies by including some slide images taken from books on African art in my lectures on African religions. My exhibitions at the Bayly Museum utilized objects from the museum's small collection and required more specialized study. Having learned a great deal about African art in the process, I wondered how I might bring the same educational process into the classroom. Creating an exhibition of African art involves detailed library research, the writing of short and informative label texts, and the combining of objects creatively around a general cultural theme. Such an exercise enables students to deal with African art objects firsthand and to apply what they learn about African religions and cultures in a practical fashion. It also enables them to wrestle with the important issue of "representing" African cultures in a Western technological medium. And they do not just discuss the issues of representation; they are directly involved. Wellesley College has already had some success with an art history class whose students created an exhibition of African art in the Jewett Museum. Unfortunately, at the University of Virginia the distance between the museum and its cramped storage facility made such a project unfeasible.

Why not, then, try to use imaging technology instead? Making a virtue of necessity, this would enable each student to be his or her own curator and allow access to a large and superlative collection of "objects" to study and exhibit. Although the students would not be producing exhibitions in an actual museum environment, the scholarly tasks of producing an electronic exhibition are nearly the same with the added advantage of learning computer-imaging skills. Aiming the projects beyond the classroom at a general audience would require students to think self-consciously about the scholarly goals of their work. The whole process would raise the level of student participation in the scholarship of the subject far beyond the usual methods of course examinations and term papers written only for the instructor.

In spring 1996, twenty-one students and I set out to see how this course idea would work. At this point I possessed only basic word-processing and email skills; as it turned out, so did the students. Weekly training sessions in HTML, image processing, and Web page construction in a computer lab were therefore essential. During the semester prior to offering the course, I acquired basic computer and HTML skills but needed reinforcement during the semester in the computer classroom with the students.

My participation in these labs as a learner alongside the students helped build student confidence in tackling the sometimes challenging technological features of the course. I was also able to appreciate the difficulties students encountered in learning these procedures, which helped me to advise the computer instructor on his teaching methods and the sequence of skills to be taught. We soon learned that students need written step-by-step instructions for reference after they leave the computer training session. Executing the computer procedures correctly once or twice in the classroom does not mean students have learned enough to repeat the techniques several days later. Written instructions were attached to the course home page after each computer session. Student participation has been facilitated by today's online Web editing software programs, which are simplifying basic HTML procedures and making them more manageable.

One of the best ways students can learn about another culture is by studying the images produced by the artists of that culture. In portraying the world through images, artists express a great deal about themselves and the societies in which they live. Images give students direct visual contact with the societies to be studied. With something visually "concrete" before them, students respond immediately and are able to reflect on cultural differences and similarities.

For these reasons, it is difficult to overestimate the educational power of the study of images, especially in the contemporary image-rich world. When linked to standard print publications, such as African art exhibition catalogs and current scholarly discussion about the representation of Africa in the Western museum environment, the classroom study of African art becomes a fascinating and illuminating subject for teachers and students alike.

Nevertheless, because of the long-standing prejudice against images in academia, except in departments of art history, the case must be made for the educational value of images in the humanities. Barbara Stafford's recent book *Good Looking: Essays on the Virtue of Images* (1996: 4) does so in the strongest terms. She argues that "imaging, ranging from high art to popular illusions, remains the richest, most fascinating modality for configuring and conveying ideas." She challenges the supposed primacy of language and the printed word, arguing that the study of images reveals not only the surfaces of things but also the reflexivity of cultures as they represent and portray themselves normatively. For example, in Mende society masquerades, Sowei masks exemplify the moral and aesthetic norms of female beauty. Images thus invite serious, often critical, thought, not just emotional responses, and thus can lead us to a deeper understanding of the society that made them. Stafford (1996: 3) calls on "established and aspiring imagists across disciplinary boundaries to confront the fundamental task of remaking the image of images." She argues that in noticing differences between cultures through a perusal of their images, we also begin to notice certain likenesses and to make deeper connections, thus transforming our understanding and sometimes ourselves in the process. Through studying images of "others," Stafford (1996: 203) suggests, we begin to "fit our local perspectives into a bigger picture of humanity."

With Stafford's views in mind, I focused the course around a number of preliminary questions, guided by the scholars' articles in Appendix A. How much can an African art object tell us about the society from which it comes? How have museum exhibitions and African art scholars tried to use images to understand cultural otherness? How have museum exhibitions of African art changed and developed over the years? What stereotypes should be avoided? How can visitors to museums, real or virtual, make connections with the objects in the exhibit?

For the first few weeks, each class began with a brief student presentation of two objects from the two textbook museum catalogs. This exercise gave students some practice at presenting African art to their peers, which helped to facilitate discussion and reflection on the strengths and weaknesses of the catalogs' format, style, and label content. Students brought the catalogs to class and had them open on their desks. They were each able to speak to specific issues, guided by other students' presentations. Informed by scholarly essays on the history of African art studies and on museum representations of African culture, the student critiques became more sophisticated as the students became more adept at sorting out effective label texts. Gradually, the class and I were able to develop a consensus about the most useful components of a written label. This process led to the following guidelines:

- Since objects of traditional African art are generally made for use in specific contexts that are often ceremonial and religious, the museum label should describe certain prominent features of the object, such as shape and artistic detail relative to contextual social, moral, and religious ideas and actions. This description helps the viewer to "see" the object within its own cultural setting and to reflect on connections among different cultures.
- If possible, the label should quote a relevant statement (proverb, poetic verse, myth text) taken from the society itself or an informant's words concerning the object or context. This statement must be concise and address an audience that possesses little or no knowledge of African art.
- The label, of course, represents the exhibit curator's own knowledge and is necessarily interpretive.

After some practice in evaluating catalog labels, the students became adept at applying these principles to their own work. The following example is taken from the exhibition *The Many Faces of Africa* by Atalaya Jones:

> The Nuna people carve wooden masks to represent protective spirits that take animal form. The wing-shaped Hawk mask portrays one of these spirits. The mask is danced to gain the protection of the spirit for the clan, family, or community. The spirit provides for the fertility, health, and prosperity of its owners and the continuity of life. This mask is danced by men and performed at boys' initiation ceremonies, the funerals of elders, and market day entertainment.
>
> Although the typical Hawk mask is carved with a curved hawk beak, this one has an animal snout. The black and white geometric patterns on the wings of the Hawk are signs that represent a proverb. The zig zag lines on the face of the Hawk signify the "path of ancestors," a moral path that is very difficult but one every Nuna must follow to succeed in life.

Limiting the initial student presentations to about ten minutes of the class period allowed time to begin a survey of African art objects via conventional slide-projected images and lecture format. I was both guided by and limited to the digitized image collections for which the University of Virginia has copyright access. At present, the fair-use clause of the copyright law is interpreted in such a way that a limited number of digitized images may be taken from a published source for instructional use if access is restricted by a password valid only for the students in the course. (As the fair-use guidelines are in the process of change, teachers should check their institution's policy on this matter.)

Since the images to which I had access were those the students would use in their exhibits, my first task was to teach them as much as possible about the main features of the objects and their contexts of use. The Fowler Museum's collection is especially strong in the areas of Yoruba and Asante cultures; the Hampton University Museum and Bayly Museum collections focus mainly on the Kuba and include typical objects from a variety of West African societies. Fortunately, the Yoruba, Asante, and Kuba cultures are also among the best represented in scholarly research, so the students could become engaged in the scholarship on these objects in significant detail using conventional library resources.

I began by presenting a general overview of the various types of African art (masks, headdresses, figure sculptures, ancestor figures, royal emblems, animal figures, textiles, metalwork, clay sculpture, pottery) and ceremonial contexts (initiation, seasonal ceremonies, funerals, public festivals, altars, and shrines), using images from a wide range of western and central African societies. Then we turned to some of the readings on exhibiting African art in order to introduce that topic. For the next four weeks, we concentrated on the art of Asante, Yoruba, and Kuba. Three lectures on masks and two on images of ancestors followed, interspersed with student critiques of catalog presentations of these subjects. These activities provided sufficient background knowledge for the visits and talks with curators at the National Museum of African Art, the Virginia Museum of Fine Arts, and the Bayly Museum a week before midsemester exhibitions were due. Afterward, we delved deeper into questions of exhibiting and describing African art, as well as into certain cultural institutions such as the ritual and symbolism of kingship and the use of art objects in divination and healing rituals. Occasionally, we spent a whole class on a single object to see how far the current scholarship and our own thinking could take us toward understanding the object and its context. Finally, we took a brief look at the work of two well-known Yoruba artists, Olowe of Ise, who died in 1938, and contemporary carver Lamidi Fakaye of Ibadan and Ile-Ife.

The focusing framework in the lectures and student presentations was twofold: (1) the aesthetic and symbolic characteristics of the object and (2) its social and ritual context. Here is how one student described this dual focus in her exhibition statement on *Art of Crisis: An Exploration of African Art,* by Gina Ranieri Wells:

> My aim is to synthesize formal artistic concerns with an understanding of the utility of the sculpture. Most African art serves a utilitarian purpose, and an examination of that purpose in conjunction with its form, attention to detail, and overall vitality, is essential to understanding the art of Africa. The object's intended use contributes to its distinctive shape. It is important to consider many issues when viewing the exhibition: who made the object (or commissioned it to be made), why was it made, and how, when and where it is used. Answers to these questions are an integral part of understanding this exhibition.

Art of Crisis displays twelve works representing societies of the Yoruba, the Asante, the Baule, and the Mijikenda peoples. Each of these societies places a special significance on art in the culture; the works represent some attempt to resolve a particular conflict that arises in the everyday life of a community.

Because the students had to present a small electronic exhibition by midsemester, they were encouraged to begin thinking about the choice of exhibition theme soon after the semester started. The two textbooks for the course, Sieber and Walker's (1987) *African Art in the Cycle of Life* and Woodward's (1994) *African Art: The Virginia Museum of Fine Arts,* are broad in scope and served as excellent introductions to a range of thematic subjects and to contrasting presentation styles. The students chose their exhibition themes on the basis of their own interests and on what seemed to them to be visually interesting and culturally important. Consultations with me helped clarify their ideas and identify the relevant source material.

The process of choosing an exhibition theme, defining its general nature and scope, and selecting the objects to portray led to the recognition that every exhibition of African art is a curator's "choice"; hence every exhibition displays the curator's own perceptions and priorities in understanding African cultures. Students created written explanations of their themes to introduce the exhibits. They also attached their names to their exhibits, as some museum curators are beginning to do.

Here is an example from an exhibition titled *Keeping the Dead Alive: Ancestor Images in Sub-Saharan African Art,* by Opeyemi Adamolekun:

> In contrast to Western perspectives, in most African societies one's lifetime is not linear but a cycle that has no beginning and no end. A person's death is related to another's birth. Examples abound of the different myths and customs that characterize how various African societies view the dead and death. One thing that is common is that the dead are still very much a part of the lives of the living. Thus, depending on the customs, we see different attempts to keep the dead as a part of the land of the living. Ancestors are represented in different forms and for different reasons in various African societies. Some images are to appease the ancestors as the Commemorative Post of the Mijikenda; others are masks such as the Egungun Mask of the Yoruba which are danced to resurrect the spirit of that particular ancestor while others, such as Reliquary Figures, serve as a storage vault of the ancestor's remains. Using ancestor images from the different sub-regions of Sub-Saharan Africa, this exhibit attempts to show how the dead are kept alive and the various rituals and customs that surround the preservation of the spirit of the dead.

One of the more difficult tasks was for students to include their own perceptions in the exhibit and thus to connect with the objects and the viewer. One of the reasons for adopting the impersonal voice of the museum curator was the value they placed on interesting and reliable scholarship. They felt a professional sense of responsibility for their exhibits, realizing that other students around the university (and potentially around the world) could access their work. Given their contact with museum curators and engagement with the most recent published research, they came to see themselves as active participants in the world of African art scholarship and curatorship. The Web had "transformed them into teachers." To me, this was one of the unexpected and stunning results of student academic involvement with the educational features of the Web.

Having engaged in a scholarly research project and created their own materials for the Web, students were fully aware of the difference between this activity and simply downloading information from it. Indeed, they were now more able to evaluate other materials on African art on the Internet, as they had done with the scholarly museum catalogs in class. They were asked to critique anonymously each other's midterm exhibitions for design, organization, and content, as well as other exhibitions on the Web. The students proved remarkably successful in doing this and provided helpful criticisms and suggestions for improvement. They also learned firsthand that the information on the Web is only as good as its sources no matter how fancy the Web pages appear on the screen.

Although the students recognized that their scholarly product was a virtual one, they were prepared to have it evaluated by other faculty members. Such evaluations are easy to do online and are a simple device for engendering faculty collegiality and interdisciplinary teaching.

The course was fundamentally project-oriented, and most teaching was related to particular tasks. Whether it was a specific computer skill, a guide for writing object labels, or the best scholarly studies, everything in the course served as a resource for the final project. I found this a refreshing and effective mode of teaching. I was no longer teaching for the sake of testing or paper writing but for the sake of project effectiveness and collaborative learning. Students themselves brought resources to the class, observations about interesting museum exhibitions they had seen, and Africa-related Web sites they had discovered.

In addition to published material and my lectures, the resources for the course included the student exhibitions themselves. I deliberately set up the course with a roster listing each student's project on the course home page so that students would have the opportunity to consult each other's work. I, too, frequently monitored their projects, giving suggestions that all could read and respond to via the class email account. The class addressed the issue of plagiarism at the outset. Students liked the possibility of accessing each other's work and decided that borrowing each other's Web design techniques was both permissible and helpful. They drew the line at borrowing each other's exhibition themes and label content. During the lab sessions, students frequently assisted each other in image processing and Web construction techniques. In this way, the least experienced students caught up and gained confidence with the computer. Looking at each other's work also stimulated their efforts and raised the level of their academic expectations.

Students also sought to improve the look of the objects on the Web page. Some students removed background material from around the objects in the photographs, making the images into what are called transparencies, and placing them against Web-page backgrounds of various colors and patterns so that the objects appeared to float in space, almost three dimensionally. Students found this effect artistically attractive but worried about the distortion involved. Consequently, they chose to include interpretive field photographs of objects in their contexts of use, such as masks shown being worn by dancers. Using these images via links within the object labels allowed the students to acquaint the viewer with images of an object's actual life setting. This technique also gave students the opportunity to write additional material about cultural context.

One student addressed these issues specifically in "A Note from the Curator" in the exhibit *Crossing Over: Masks and Initiation Rites and Secret Societies,* by Daniel Haithcock:

This Web project has been designed with the goal of educating visitors about the cultures and ideals involved in African art. . . . In order to appreciate African art fully, one must discover the original purpose of the object and explore the culture that created it. Although the total experience of an object can never be replicated once it has been removed from its original context, supplementary information is crucial for its appreciation. To this end, several additions have been made to the traditional museum approach to exhibiting African art. I have attempted to use longer, more educational labels that describe more about the cultural context of the object and less about the aesthetic qualities. When available, I have included photographs showing how the masks were meant to be displayed by their creators. My desire is that as you view the beautiful masks exhibited here, you will also acquire a greater appreciation of the culture that created the masks and the manner in which they are used. I realize that by changing background colors and through my treatment of the images, I have also added yet another foreign context to an object already robbed of its true existence. My only hope is that the context I create enhances your desire to learn more about the mask and the culture that created it.

It is necessary, of course, to ask how well this class in African art "taught" about Africa. Since approximately one-third of the students' time was taken up with learning and applying the technology of image processing and Web-page construction, a certain amount of course content had to be compromised. Extensive reading in African religions and culture was sacrificed, as was a broader range of art objects, for the sake of completing the exhibitions on time. Students also became acquainted with the odd fact that some of the most popular art objects in Western collections, such as the Okuyi mask of the Puni, have received little attention in the literature; others, such as the Sowei mask of the Mende, mentioned at the beginning of the chapter, have received volumes. Consultation with the instructor helped avoid the use of too many of the less well researched objects. Given the project-driven character of the course, students also tended to restrict their attention to what they needed to know about the twelve objects in their exhibits, neglecting a deeper and more comprehensive understanding of African art and culture.

Nevertheless, the exhibits achieved considerable depth and focus. The insertion of links within the object labels gave students the opportunity to add additional pages, without infringing on the exhibition format, in order to include the results of more extensive research as the semester progressed. This technique greatly enriched the exhibits and enabled the better students to write short essays on each of their twelve objects. Fortunately, most students reached the peak of the computer learning curve by midsemester, so they could devote more time to the selection of objects and their library research. Some felt distracted by trying to do library research and learn computer skills at the same time. This problem will be addressed in future courses—perhaps by concentrating first on research and later on computer skills.

To conclude, I believe that technology is best used in the classroom in as interactive, creative, and collaborative a way as possible. On this pedagogical potential, I can quote with approval a statement by Terry Crane (in Oppenheimer 1997: 47), an Apple vice president: "Instead of isolating students, technology actually encouraged them to collaborate more than in traditional classrooms. Students also learned to explore and represent information dynamically and creatively, communicate effectively about complex processes and become more socially confident." Classroom use of the Internet as an information resource is becoming increasingly valuable; even more valuable is the opportunity for students to become active participants in the Internet's resources by designing and creating original educational material, whether for local use within the classroom or the school as a whole or for the Web-viewing public around the world. Despite the considerable amount of preparation involved, especially at the university level, making use of this technology offers teachers of African studies significant educational results both in the classroom and beyond.

NOTES

1. The Museum Educational Site Licensing Project is a national demonstration project sponsored by the Getty Information Initiative to address key issues in the

educational use of museum images and related information delivered over computer networks. The Museum Educational Site Licensing Project will define the terms and conditions under which digitized museum images and information can be distributed over campus networks for educational use. The pilot project will test the distribution of art images and information from seven museums to seven universities, including American University, Columbia University, Cornell University, University of Illinois at Champaign-Urbana, University of Maryland at College Part, University of Michigan, and University of Virginia. The seven participating museums are the National Museum of American Art, National Gallery of Art, Library of Congress, Museum of Fine Arts Houston, Fowler Museum of Cultural History, George Eastman House, and Harvard University Art Museums.

APPENDIX A: EXHIBITION GUIDELINES

MIDTERM EXHIBITS

Midterm exhibits should consist of six images with descriptive labels. The images may be left-justified or placed in any position on the Web page in relation to the label. The images should be imported in both small gif form and the larger jpeg format so that the viewer can study the object in greater detail. The exhibit should open with a title, followed by an opening statement, two or three paragraphs in length, that explains the exhibit's theme. A key image might follow immediately below the exhibition title (or stand next to it) as a way of visually conveying the theme of the exhibition. The six images should be taken from at least four different societies. A map locating the societies represented in the exhibit is not necessary for the midterm.

FINAL EXHIBITS

The final exhibitions should be expanded and revised versions of the midterm exhibitions, made slightly more complex with more descriptive information and about double in size, or approximately twelve images.

First, consider whether your exhibition theme should be slightly revised to include the six additional objects. You may also choose to reduce (or expand) the number of societies represented in your exhibit (the final exhibition should present images from at least two different societies). Your final exhibit should relate the objects to their social, moral, and religious contexts, as well as to pertinent aspects of Western culture and human life in general. Here your exhibit can express a distinctive point of view in addition to conveying artistic and cultural information. Reread Warren H. Robbins's article "Making the Galleries Sing: Displaying African Art" and the articles by Susan Vogel and Ivan Karp.

Second, review the design, structure, and organization. Make a separate title page, presenting the title (with perhaps a subtitle), your name, and an image that conveys the general theme of the exhibit. If there is enough space, write a statement—short enough so that it appears on the title page, without the need to scroll too much down the page—to introduce the theme. At the bottom of the title page, include three or four links to the various parts (pages) of your exhibition, each part having its own title. These same links should appear at the end of each section of the exhibit so that the viewer can navigate from one section to another and return to the title page. As a general rule you should place your labels next to the images so that the viewer can view the image and the label together. Each thumbnail image (gif) should be linked to a larger, more detailed version of the image (jpeg). Linking can be done by "wrapping" the jpeg image anchor around the gif or by "mapping" the gif image so that it links to the jpeg. If you like, make your images into transparencies and place them against a particular background, for example, an African fabric, to enhance the aesthetics of your exhibit. This task is time consuming, however, and should not be undertaken at the expense of the research and writing components. Your exhibit should contain a map of Africa locating the societies whose objects are represented. The best method is to use the scanned maps provided in your image collections and type the names of the societies in the appropriate locations.

Third, address the textual content by making the labels more complex. Each label should begin with the name of the object, the society or culture from which it comes, and the nation-state to which it belongs. Include a brief statement to explain how the image fits into the overall theme. Also include an image source or museum credit line, for example, "Hampton University Museum." The labels should contain links to bibliographical references, either at the end of the label or within the body of the text. There should also be links to "further information" concerning some major point (or points) that appear in the label. Be sure to include a link at the end of this page that returns the reader to the label. You might find it useful in some cases to crop the jpeg image and enlarge one or more parts of it so that the viewer can focus on a specific feature or features. You should put a link with the text label to this part of the image and add a few more lines of text describing this feature, then create a link that returns to the original label.

Fourth, since there are very few contextual photos in the Fowler Museum images, you will need to scan them from published sources. I have already provided some in your digitized image collection. One of the most extensive sources is Michael Huet, *The Dance, Art, and Ritual of Africa* (1978). Most of the recent books on African art also contain excellent photos showing the objects in context. The journal *African Arts* is full of field photographs; consult the complete index to *African Arts* in your course packet. Providing many context photos is time consuming and should be low on your list of priorities.

APPENDIX B: ITEMS IN
ASSIGNED-READINGS PHOTOCOPIED PACKET

Brenson, Michael. 1990. "Art View: Appraising African Art Through Western Eyes." *New York Times* (Sunday, October 7): 38–40.

Drewal, Henry, John Pemberton III, and Rowland Abiodun. 1989. "Yoruba: Nine Centuries of African Art and Thought." *African Arts* 23, 1: 68–77.

Karp, Ivan. 1989a. "Culture and Representation." In *Exhibiting Cultures: The Poetics and Politics of Museum Display*, ed. Ivan Karp and Stephen D. Lavine. Washington, D.C.: Smithsonian Institution Press.

———. 1989b. "Other Cultures in Museum Perspective." In *Exhibiting Cultures*, ed. Ivan Karp and Stephen D. Lavine. Washington, D.C.: Smithsonian Institution Press.

Pemberton, John, III. 1989. "Art and Rituals for Yoruba Sacred Kings." *Art Institute of Chicago Journal:* 97–111.

Robbins, Warren M. 1991. "Making the Galleries Sing: Displaying African Art." *Museum News* 73, 5 (September–October): 36–41.

Sieber, Roy, and Roslyn A. Walker. 1987. *African Art in the Cycle of Life.* Washington, D.C.: Smithsonian Institution Press.

Thompson, Robert Farris. 1973. "Yoruba Art Criticism." In *The Traditional Artist in African Societies,* ed. L. d'Azevedo. Bloomington: Indiana University Press.

Vogel, Susan. 1987. "Introduction." In *Perspectives: Angles on African Art.* New York: Center for African Art.

———. 1988. "Introduction." In *Art/Artifact: African Art in Anthropology Collections.* New York: Prestel Verlag and Center for African Art.

———. 1989. "Always True to the Object, in Our Fashion." In *Exhibiting Cultures,* ed. Ivan Karp and Stephen D. Lavine. Washington, D.C.: Smithsonian Institution Press.

———. 1990. "African Sculpture: A Primer." In *Closeup: Lessons in the Art of Seeing African Sculpture,* ed. Jerry L. Thompson and Susan Vogel. New York: International Museum of African Art.

SUGGESTIONS FOR FURTHER READING AND RESOURCES

GENERAL

Barbier, Jean Paul. 1993. *Art of Côte d'Ivoire.* Geneva: Barbier-Mueller Museum.

Bay, Edna G. 1985. *Asen: Iron Altars of the Fon People of Benin.* Atlanta: Emory University Museum of Art and Archaeology.

Boone, Sylvia. 1986. *Radiance from the Waters: Ideals of Feminine Beauty in Mende Art.* New Haven: Yale University Press.

Cole, Herbert M. 1985. *I Am Not Myself: The Art of African Masquerade.* Los Angeles: Museum of Cultural History, University of California.

———. 1989. *Icons: Ideals and Power in the Art of Africa.* Washington, D.C.: Smithsonian Institution Press.

Herreman, Frank, and Constantyn Petridis. 1993. *Face of the Spirits: Masks from the Zaire Basin.* Gent: Snoeck-Ducaju.

Huet, Michael. 1978. *The Dance, Art, and Ritual of Africa.* New York: Pantheon.

Karp, Ivan, and Stephen D. Lavine, eds. 1991. *Exhibiting Cultures: The Poetics and Politics of Museum Display.* Washington, D.C.: Smithsonian Institution Press.

McGaffey, Wyatt, and Michael D. Harris. 1993. *Astonishment and Power: Kongo Minkisi—The Art of Renee Stout.* Washington, D.C.: Smithsonian Institution Press.

Nooter, Mary H. 1993. *Secrecy: African Art That Conceals and Reveals.* New York: Museum for African Art.

Northern, Tamera. 1984. *Art of the Cameroon.* Washington, D.C.: Smithsonian Institution.

Oppenheimer, Todd. 1997. "The Computer Delusion." *Atlantic Monthly* (July): 47.

Perrois, Louis. 1986. *Ancestral Art of Gabon.* Geneva: Barbier Mueller.

Philips, Ruth B. 1995. *Representing Women: Sande Masquerades of the Mende of Sierra Leone.* Los Angeles: UCLA Fowler Museum of Cultural History.

Price, Sally. 1989. *Primitive Art in Civilized Places.* Chicago: University of Chicago Press.

Roy, Christopher. 1987. *Art of the Upper Volta Rivers*. Iowa City: University of Iowa Press.

———. 1992. *Art and Life in Africa*. Iowa City: University of Iowa Press.

Sieber, Roy, and Roslyn Adele Walker, eds. 1987. *African Art in the Cycle of Life*. Washington, D.C.: Smithsonian Institution Press.

Stafford, Barbara. 1996. *Good Looking: Essays on the Virtue of Images*. Cambridge: MIT Press.

Thompson, Jerry, and Susan Vogel, eds. 1990. *Closeup: Lessons in the Art of Seeing African Art*. New York: International Museum of African Art.

Thompson, Robert. 1974. *African Art in Motion*. Los Angeles: University of California Press.

Turner, Jane, ed. 1996. *Dictionary of Art*. New York: Macmillan.

Vogel, Susan. 1981. *For Spirits and Kings*. New York: Metropolitan Museum of Art.

———. 1986. *African Aesthetics*. New York: Center for African Art.

———. 1987. *Perspectives: Angles on African Art*. New York: Center for African Art.

———. 1988. *Art/Artifact: African Art in Anthropology Collections*. New York: Prestel Verlag and the Center for African Art.

Woodward, Richard B. 1994. *African Art: Virginia Museum of Fine Arts*. Richmond: Virginia Museum of Fine Arts.

ASANTE

Appiah, P. 1979. "Akan Symbolism." *African Arts* 13, 1: 164–167.

Cole, Herbert M., and Doran H. Ross. 1977. *The Arts of Ghana*. Los Angeles: Museum of Cultural History, University of California.

Garrard, Timothy F. 1979. "Akan Metal Arts." *African Arts* 13, 1: 35–43.

Kyerematen, A.A.Y. 1964. *Panoply of Ghana*. London: Longman.

McLeod, M. D. 1981. *The Asante*. London: British Museum.

Rattray, Robert S. 1923. *Ashanti*. Oxford: Clarendon Press.

———. 1927. *Religion and Art in Ashanti*. London: Oxford University Press.

Ross, D. 1977–1978. "The Iconography of Asante Sword Ornaments." *African Arts* 11, 1: 16–25.

———. 1982. "The Verbal Art of Akan Linguist Staffs." *African Arts* 16, 1: 56–65.

Sarpong, Peter. 1971. *The Stools of the Akan*. Accra-Tema: Ghana Publishing.

YORUBA

Abiodun, Rowland. 1989. "Woman in Yoruba Religious Images." *African Languages and Cultures* 2, 1: 1–18.

Abiodun, Rowland, Henry Drewal, and John Pemberton III. 1991. *Yoruba Art and Aesthetics*. Zurich: Reitberg Museum.

———. 1994. *The Yoruba Artist*. Washington, D.C.: Smithsonian Institution Press.

Drewal, Henry, and John Pemberton III, with Rowland Abiodun. 1989. *Yoruba: Nine Centuries of African Art and Thought*. New York: Center for African Art.

Drewal, Henry, and Margaret Thompson Drewal. 1983. *Gelede: Art and Female Power*. Bloomington: Indiana University Press.

Fagg, William, and John Pemberton III. 1982. *Yoruba: Sculpture of West Africa*. New York: Knopf.

Lawal, Babatunde. 1996. *The Gelede Spectacle*. Seattle: University of Washington Press.

Thompson, Robert F. 1971. *Black Gods and Kings*. Los Angeles: University of California Press.

14

USING H-AFRICA
IN A VIRTUAL COURSE

ROBERT G. WHITE

Rapid developments in the use of electronic technology in the classroom at the end of the twentieth century herald a fundamental shift in our approach to teaching about Africa in the twenty-first century. The California State University system, like many others in North America, is focusing both money and attention on the use of electronic technology in the classroom. A major motivation is the impending tidal wave of new students demanding access to higher education in the early part of the twenty-first century. Intrigued by the rhetoric, and in need of both money and attention, I decided to see if I could catch this wave for my own course on Africa. So with much enthusiasm but little knowledge of computers or the Internet, I set out to design a "virtual" course on Africa, one that would meet only in cyberspace. It would thus be available to anyone, any time, any place. How was it constructed? What was it like? Was it worth doing?

The central feature of the course was a virtual office, or home page, for the course. I spent a lot of time on this, and in retrospect, I am not sure if it was worth it. I wanted a picture of a real office with a map of Africa on the wall, some African artwork, a computer, newspapers, and so on. The computer screen, if you click on it, is a link to the H-Africa home page. The newspaper on the desk is a link to Africa Online. The map on the wall is a link to the University of Pennsylvania's country-specific sites. I asked students to read and follow the news from Africa on a regular basis, and many of them did. I also occasionally forwarded to them articles that were especially pertinent from listservs to which I subscribed.

Since I wanted to incorporate H-Africa—a subscription-based, mediated list on the Internet that offers academic information and discourse on various Africanist topics—as a central feature of the course, all students were required to subscribe to it. I regarded this list as essential because it could introduce students to the ongoing dialogue about Africa among Africanists from many disciplines around the world. It also provided direct access to the many links on the H-Africa home page. One of the early assignments, after students sent me an email and subscribed to H-Africa, was to access the H-Africa home page and print "A Brief Citation Guide for Internet Sources in History and the Humanities" (Version 2.1) by Mel Page. This excellent and useful article provided the students and myself an entry point into Internet sources, as we were all encountering this new medium at about the same time.

The ongoing discussions on the list about a particular topic (threads, as they are called) were incorporated into the course where appropriate, although not as fully or as effectively as I had planned, for reasons I will discuss further on. One particularly interesting thread was a dialogue about European and North American images of Africa as revealed in fiction and film. This fit with the way I usually start my Africa survey course, that is, with a discussion of the images of Africa we carry around in our heads, images that serve as filters for information we receive about the continent. Beginning with the stereotypes enables the class to bring prejudices out in the open early in the course and allows me to introduce the notion of Euro- and Afrocentric approaches in the study of Africa.

In using these threads from the Internet, the instructor must maintain some flexibility. Threads appear more or less spontaneously, and not all of them fit easily into the course outline. Moreover, some of these discussions are fairly esoteric and likely to be of interest mainly to scholars in the field, and often only to some of them. Nevertheless, some discussions might intrigue a couple of students, so enough flexibility should be permitted to allow those whose interest is piqued to pursue a particular thread as part of their coursework. Providing such choices gives the course a student-centered orientation, empowering members of the class to use the Internet to shape the course beyond the basic information that the instructor wishes them to learn.

As an aside, let me relate an interesting experience from the first time I incorporated any electronic technology—except for slides and video—in my course. I had all the students open their email accounts, and I put them on a class email list. I then forwarded all kinds of information from the various lists to which I subscribe. There were two reactions, both quite interesting. First, midway through the course I faced a rebellion; the students were mad, and they were mad at me! It seemed that I was clogging their mailboxes with far more information than they could possibly digest or even read, sometimes even exceeding their disk quotas so that they could not receive mail from any source. They had been chained to the computer by my well-meaning desire to give them as much information as possible. I learned an important lesson from this: Students are not as keenly interested in the topic as their instructor, and the ease with which email can be for-warded leads to too many "electronic" handouts. As one student pointed out to me, if I had had to photocopy every article I sent them, they would have had only one or two instead of twenty per week.

Second, although not by design, I left the students on the email list after the course ended. Since they were still there, and it was so easy, I con-tinued to send them articles, at a greatly reduced rate, carefully selected for their relevance to topics we had discussed in class. For several weeks into the new semester, I continued to have email conversations with many of the students from the class. Some time toward the end of the next semester, I ended the list, although I continue to receive email from several of the stu-dents. Of the sixteen students in the class, two joined the Peace Corps with Africa assignments, two went to Africa last summer with Operation Crossroads Africa, and two more will shortly be going to Africa with the Peace Corps. Was the introduction of electronic technology partially responsible for this? In twenty-five years of teaching, I have never had that many students go to live and work in Africa so soon after finishing my course. My hunch is that the introduction of electronic technology via email had something to do with what occurred. Perhaps the introduction of electronic technology and the immediacy of information that it seems to provide stimulated a greater degree of interest than my well-worn lectures of the past.

Returning, however, to the content of the virtual course: The first assignment was for students to send me an email message introducing themselves and saying something about their interest in Africa. I then for-warded these introductions to everyone in the class, a very easy task because of the email list. After this, most of the assignments took the form of Web quests. A good source for information on Web quests is *The Web Quest Page* by Bernie Dodge (see bibliography). The introductory Web quests were designed to familiarize students with a few of the best and most easily accessible Web sites on Africa. Some of these are linked to the H-Africa home page, so students did not have to search far afield for them. These sites, and there are many of them, contain vast amounts of informa-tion, including links to other sites. In the first Web quest students were required to spend an hour or so at each of two or three sites, browsing to see what data were available and comparing the sites. They were asked to make this comparison in terms of the kind, quality, and quantity of infor-mation to be found. Did they have searchable databases? What links did they have to other sources? Which one did they like best? Why? To orga-nize this assignment, I asked the students to use a separate sheet of paper for each site. At the top of the paper, they were to put the Internet address (URL) and the name of the site. On the rest of the page they recorded their notes about what the site contained as well as their ultimate evaluation of it.

The purpose of this exercise was to provide students with a critical attitude and the skills to evaluate any Web site, both of which they would increasingly need for the course and for future work on the Internet.

A second introductory Web quest involved becoming familiar with African map resources. Over the years, I have found that students come to their first class on Africa with an appalling ignorance of African geography. Frequent references to the large map in the lecture hall during lectures and discussions, coupled with frequent map quizzes, helps to fill this gap in their knowledge. I sent them to the University of Pennsylvania site, to the country-specific links, and asked them to print a map of a particular country and a general map of Africa. Each student was assigned a different country to "explore." They were then asked to note a number of geographical features (rivers, mountains, deserts, etc.) for their assigned country, what other countries bordered it, and so on. They were asked to post these maps where they would see them every day—above their desks, on the refrigerator door, by the bathroom mirror. I hoped that these maps would take the place of the map in the lecture room (which I often forget to turn over when I give a map quiz).

In the final analysis, I do not think this Web quest assignment fully, or perhaps even adequately, replaced the traditional approach, and I am still unsure how I will take care of this problem when I teach the course again. A colleague recently suggested to me that it should be possible, and not too difficult, to construct an online map quiz, since all the questions have yes or no answers. Students could take this quiz when they wanted, but at least every week. Although this approach has its merits, I wonder how I can monitor whether they are taking the quiz with a map in front of them. After all, they will not be in the lecture hall but in the computer lab or at home. With this in mind, I have decided to experiment with open-book quizzes, since the point, after all, is to require the students to study and become familiar with the map, not to memorize it.

After these introductory assignments, which took longer than I anticipated in the first iteration of the course, the students moved to more advanced Web quests. One of these was about the crisis in the Great Lakes region. Using links from the H-Africa home page and postings to the H-Africa list from various scholars and journalists, students received current news and background information on the events in Rwanda/Burundi. They compared news from different sources, including the UN Relief Web and major nongovernmental organizations (NGOs) like Interaction. They also found important background information from the African Policy Information Center and the Association of Concerned African Scholars home pages. Students were asked a number of questions, such as, What is the historical background of this region? Who were the colonial powers, and what was the nature of their rule? What was the independence struggle like here? What postindependence developments have a bearing on the current crisis? What is and has been the role of outside powers?

An interesting extension of this assignment, which did not occur to me until later, would have been to ask the students to propose ways to solve the crisis. They could have worked collaboratively, communicating through email. For this extended assignment, they might have been asked questions such as, What would be the key elements in such a proposed solution? Who would be likely to support or oppose it? Why? I mention this because the technique of posing problems for students to solve has often proved an effective way to involve them as active learners, especially if the problem is real rather than hypothetical. Working collaboratively stimulates motivation, teaches students to cooperate in intellectual endeavors, and helps establish personal relationships based on their study of Africa. (In a virtual course, this kind of class unity is difficult at best to muster, so it certainly should be encouraged.) Other Web quest assignments that might foster group work could include the discussion of political economy issues relating to Nigeria, South Africa, Sudan, Western Sahara, and so forth.

The final assignment was to construct a home page focusing on their special interest in Africa. I was quite surprised by the high quality and broad variety of topics covered by the students. One focused on Africa and the Diaspora. Another, by a soil science major, focused on the soils of Africa; another on Hillary and Chelsea Clinton's trip to Africa. All of them contained graphics, text, and links I had never seen before.

I have a few recommendations for future versions of this course. The most important would be tighter organization and more explicit instructions for the students. The beginning point should be how to open a student email account. Other elementary matters would include an introduction to the Internet and how to use Netscape (or whatever Web browser is being used in the institutional setting). This introduction would enable the instructor to quickly identify those students who have some knowledge of computers and the Internet and make them resources for the neophytes. The instructor should also tell students how to print out important reference information such as the citation guide and Netscape's "how-to-use" file. They should certainly also familiarize themselves with the lab computers they will be using. These computers are frequently configured differently and are not necessarily as good as the equipment on a university professor's desk. The instructor of a virtual course should reply quickly and positively when students send him or her email and acknowledge that assignments have been received. For easy access, important sites need to be directly linked to the instructor's home page so that students do not have to copy long Web addresses and the instructor does not have to write them out. Finally, the virtual Africa course instructor needs to keep a file drawer full of patience, expect plenty of frustrations, and advise students to do the same.

There were three tasks I did not assign but would like to develop for another time. They have special appeal for students on my North American campus and fit the department's emphasis on social responsibility, political advocacy, and a sustainable society. One assignment would be to examine environmental problems in Africa, including issues such as oil production, environmental degradation, and human rights in Nigeria and perhaps the continental ban on the sale of ivory, where interesting contrasts can be drawn among countries such as Botswana, Zimbabwe, and South Africa, on the one hand, and Kenya, Tanzania, and others, on the other hand. I also want to explore with students how to lobby or advocate for African issues at the national level. Here students would research an issue and write to appropriate members of the U.S. Congress, their own representatives, or members of the subcommittees on Africa. Finally, judging from student interest, I think an assignment could be fruitfully constructed around the topic of women in Africa.

Given the substantial amount of work involved in preparing and teaching the course, it is appropriate to ask if it was worth doing. I did not have a formal evaluation, pre- and posttest, to determine how much students learned about Africa in this course compared to the traditional lecture and discussion course, but I can make some observations based on conversations with students and my nearly three decades of teaching experience. The answer, I think, is that it was definitely worth doing, but not for the same reasons that so many high-level university administrators in the California State University system and elsewhere in North America think, a point I will return to in a moment. It is clear that many students are quite keen on using electronic technology, and a number of them have increasingly sophisticated computer skills. Some students had little or no knowledge of email or the Internet, but several knew much more than I did. In fact, I often turned to them for help myself, and they frequently helped other students in the class. I believe it behooves us to incorporate more of this technology into our courses, not only to increase student capacity but to make better use of these resources ourselves.

That it is a striking advantage for us as teachers to have almost instant access to the vast and growing amount of information on the Web cannot be denied. So, yes, developing virtual courses or simply using the Web more frequently in our more conventional courses is definitely worth doing. If it is true, and I think it is, that we are just beginning to see the global significance of the Internet for the academic enterprise, then Africanists must take the lead in applying it to our teaching about Africa. If we do not, the marginalization of Africa that we see in the national and international arenas, and in the media, will continue and Africa will end up being marginalized again, this time in the virtual but nonetheless powerful realms of cyberspace.

Another reason for adopting such an approach is that although I do not think students learned as much content about Africa as in a traditional lecture course, they learned other skills, such as how to send email, how to do research on the Internet, how to build a home page—skills that they considered extremely important for their own purposes. I was amazed by how much students appreciated the technology component of the course. It does, however, trouble me that so much time was spent on technology skills at the expense of course content. I expect the balance will shift back toward content in the future for two reasons. First, students are in a period of transition, as we are, and will be coming to classes in the future with more skills in electronic technology, and we will spend far less time with them on that topic. Indeed, if the behavior of my seven-year-old daughter and her friends is any indicator of the future, we are going to have to run very fast to keep up. Second, I can already see how tighter organization, clearer assignments, and more explicit directions can minimize the time spent on technology skills. As the course is better developed, the technical skills will be more naturally developed through the assignments themselves.

Finally, and this is an advantage of great interest to university administrators, a completely Web-based course can be available to distance-learning students if they have access to the Internet. These students' work schedules or family responsibilities may conflict with the fixed time traditional classes are offered, or they may be students who cannot get to the physical campus because of weather, distance, or disability. The issue of distance learning probably deserves further discussion. It is particularly important for a rural campus like Humboldt State University, isolated as it is on the foggy, rainy, and windswept north coast of California, with a huge geographical service area. I think such courses may, in the future, be an important educational asset for many parts of North America and, indeed, for Africa itself. Moreover, if we move from the introductory-level course to more advanced and specialized courses, the pool of interested and prepared students may be too broadly distributed geographically for the courses to be offered in the traditional manner. Further information on the potential of distance education can be found on James J. O'Donnell's home page at the University of Pennsylvania.

One problem of such virtual courses needs to be carefully considered. There is a limit to how many students a professor can have in an online course, and that limit, I now strongly believe, is lower than for a traditional lecture course. One colleague puts the limit at forty students, saying that even with a student assistant and computer-graded examinations, he nearly killed himself with this number in an accounting course. He is not sure he would do such a course again because it was so much more work than his traditional lecture course. He did not take into account the additional preparation time required for course development. Perhaps these are the comments of any instructor operating in a new medium. After a few semesters, perhaps they will disappear, but I do not think so. The main point here is that although online classes may be richer and more interesting for some students and professors, and certainly more accessible for some students, they are not likely to produce the kind of large-scale productivity gains that many in higher education administration seem to expect. I think some of these administrators have been nipping from a bottle of "Silicon snake oil" (Stoll 1995) when they should have been considering Clifford Stoll's second thoughts on the advantages of the information highway.

SUGGESTIONS FOR FURTHER READING AND RESOURCES

African National Congress Home Page. http://www.anc.org.za.

African Policy Information Center. http://www.igc./apic/index.html.

African Virtual University. http://www.worldbank.org/html/emc/documents/afvirtual.html#TOC.

Africa Online. http://www.africanews.org/.

Association of Concerned African Scholars. http://www.prairenet.org/acas/.

Dodge, Bernie. *The WebQuest Page.* http://edweb.sdsu.edu/webquest/webquest.

H-Africa. http://www.h-net.msu.edu/~africa/.

Interaction. http://www.interaction.org.

O'Donnell, James J. "New Tools for Teaching." http://ccat.sas.upenn.edu/~jod/teachdemo/teachdemo.html.

Pfister, Roger. 1996. *Internet for Africanists and Others Interested in Africa.* Basel: Basler Afrika Bibliographien.

Political Resources on the Net. http://www.agora.stm.it/politic/zaire.htm.

Stoll, Clifford. 1995. *Silicon Snake Oil: Second Thoughts on the Information Highway.* New York: Doubleday.

United Nations Relief Web. http://www.reliefweb.int/emergenc/greatlak/latest.html.

University of Pennsylvania. http://www.sas.upenn.edu/African_Studies.

USAfrica. http://www.usafricaonline.com/.

15

NEW TECHNOLOGIES (AND PRETTY PICTURES) FOR TEACHING AFRICAN PHYSICAL GEOGRAPHIES

GARTH MYERS, JACK LIVINGSTON, AIMEE STEWART, AND SARAH SIGNISKI

The teaching of Africa's geography is being transformed by two currents of change in the discipline. First, geography is becoming more technology rich. Second, geographers are becoming more interested in theory and philosophy. Both sets of changes affect how Africa's geography is taught at the university level. This chapter addresses the redefinition and reorientation of an undergraduate course entitled Physical Geography of Africa at the University of Kansas by Professor Garth Myers and three graduate students. Remaking this course has involved rethinking the technology and philosophy of instruction in light of the two currents of change just outlined. We want to suggest in this chapter that there are possibilities for interchange between geography's technological revolution and its theoretical turn and that classrooms provide valuable contexts for these interchanges. We begin by addressing the very basis of Myers's course as an introduction to Africa's environments. This reconceptualization led directly to changes of instructional instruments and methods. Some new methods involved incorporating uses of new technologies, our primary area of concern here. Several of our moderately high-tech student projects that take their cues from some more philosophical or theoretical research by geographers in Africa can, we believe, be replicated in other types of courses about Africa's environments.

As our title suggests, the broader purpose we have in mind in this chapter is a transformation of how we teach students about Africa's geogra-

phy from so great a distance and given the stereotypes and misunderstandings of African environments with which many students enter the classroom. For instance, in African studies geography, one rather weighty philosophical and moral issue brought on by advanced technology concerns
what might be called the right to look, since the "data capture" of satellite
imagery usually takes place without permission from those whose fields,
farms, or homes are "captured" in the process. Thanks to *National
Geographic* and the Discovery channel, most North American undergraduates come to the study of Africa's physical geography with a lot of pretty
(or not so pretty) pictures in their heads of what Africa is like. We see our
course and its projects as a means of challenging students' stereotypes
about the continent: We want them to be able to think critically about the
pretty pictures and fancy maps they see. We believe that the ideas behind
these projects are crucial to successful university (and even high school)
courses or units on the African environment.

RETHINKING GEOGRAPHY TEACHING

The course revision began with Myers's decision to place more emphasis
on African points of view and African scholarship about the physical environment. The aim in doing this is to make North American students more
graphically aware of African science scholarship by putting it in their hands
as a counterweight to misconceptions many of them have about African
agency within African development-environment issues. African geographers and earth scientists work in a context where development is necessarily always present in their writings on the physical setting (Darkoh 1986).
Their work, together with an introduction to African indigenous technical
knowledge of the environment in lectures, can provide North American
undergraduates with a more complete picture of Africa's physical-environ-
mental problems and challenges (James 1991, 1993, 1994; Samatar 1993;
Moyo 1991).

There are a number of good textbooks for African geography, but most
are not written by Africans, are really for human geography classes, or provide only a cursory chapter or two on the environment (see, for example,
Binns 1994; Stock 1995; Aryeetey-Attoh 1997). Those that do provide
more information often presuppose a greater knowledge of both Africa and
of physical geography than most North American undergraduates possess
upon walking into a course such as ours (Grove 1993). Inevitably, instructors must search for fairly nontraditional textbooks. There are several
excellent possibilities. One is William Adams's (1992) *Wasting the Rain:
Rivers, People and Planning in Africa*. Even though this book has an

explicit focus on water resources development, it effectively covers the continent's climates, soils, landforms, and vegetation in easily accessible language. Moreover, Adams engages development issues that can sustain most students' interest in Africa's physical geography. Another possible nontraditional textbook is Melissa Leach and Robin Mearns's *The Lie of the Land: Challenging Received Wisdom on the African Environment* (1996). It may be a bit challenging for some undergraduates, but it too engages development issues in an accessible manner. Recent books produced by Valentine Udoh James (such as his 1993 book, *Africa's Ecology*) might serve as substitutes for either the Adams book or the Leach and Mearns volume.

In our class, the eventual choice for a textbook was *State of the Environment in Southern Africa,* a collective product of the Southern African Research and Documentation Center (SARDC) published in Harare, Zimbabwe, and distributed through the African Book Collective (SARDC 1994). The book's authors and collaborators are overwhelmingly citizens of the Southern African Development Community (SADC) member countries and scientists based in universities or government units in southern Africa. The book is well written, readily grasped by students, and favorably regarded by them; furthermore, it makes direct connections between basic physical-geographic concepts and environmental problems associated with the human impact on physical processes. The book is focused on only one region of the continent and may skew students' appreciation of the continent as a whole somewhat. However, this regional focus, when combined with continent-wide lectures and other readings (or perhaps one of the more continent-wide texts previously mentioned), actually enables more than the overly generalized inventory of Africa's resources often found in many introductory classes. Southern Africa is relatively well represented in terms of electronic data and other online resources; therefore, the SARDC book's other advantage is that its approachability makes it useful for students' projects that use these electronic data.

The project components of the reconfigured course have their basis in the belief that the learning process is advanced most effectively in small-group work that gives students more of a hands-on feel for African environments. Group work can also serve to demystify the professor's expertise and restructure the power dynamics of the classroom in students' favor. The eleven projects in our class are designed for students to build from strength to strength, gaining confidence in their knowledge base as one set of information is layered on another. The first six projects function as one unit and the next four as another unit; the eleventh and final project is a research paper based on the experiences with the ten small projects, the textbook, and an extensive collection of recommended and reserved readings.

The first unit of projects involves several steps:

1. Analysis and creation of diagrams that describe various climates in Africa.
2. Assessment of how vegetation changes with the seasons in those climate settings, using satellite imagery.
3. Use of topographic maps from the continent to assess the interrelationships between the climate and vegetation patterns seen in projects 1 and 2 and the landforms or topography in those or similar settings.
4. Analysis of stream and drainage patterns using computer-based map software.
5. Classification and evaluation of soil properties using a selection of handouts on soils together with Internet maps showing the intensity of cropland utilization.
6. Assessment of the geography of protected forests and other protected lands, using both Internet databases and computer-based maps.

One-third of both midterm exams consists of take-home essays and problems asking students to pull together their projects and apply what they have learned. The second unit of projects includes an exploration of methods for doing library research on Africa and finding and using African news sources for environmental research as well as semistructured debates on the topics of wildlife conservation and water resource development. This second unit's main objective is to point students toward their final project, the integrative term paper.

TECHNOLOGY PROJECTS

Since the most challenging and innovative projects are those that attempt to integrate new geographic technology with more philosophical lecture and project content, we now turn to the positive and negative experiences we have had with these attempts. Each project lays the groundwork for the next. In their first project, students collaborate to devise climatic diagrams for four locations in Africa. These locations are chosen to represent rain forest, savanna, semidesert (steppe), and so-called Mediterranean environments—in this case, South Africa's Cape scrublands. (One might add a desert case, as well, so that Africa's main environment types are all represented.) These climatic diagrams (or climagraphs) chart the annual temperature and precipitation regimes at the four sites based on a climate data set available in an old edition of *Africa: Oxford Regional Economic Atlas* (Ady 1970). The rainfall and temperature statistics in the atlas are for 1940–1965, making them useful for comparative purposes with more recent climate data. Almost any good world atlas or introductory physical geography textbook presents and discusses climate diagrams, and instructors can easily adapt data from the African examples in those texts to enable students to make their own climagraphs.

Working in the same small groups for project 2, students then take their climagraphs into the department's Geographic Information Systems and Image Processing Laboratory to work with some vegetation maps for those locations. This second project has been highly successful, so we discuss it in a little more detail. It utilizes maps available on the Internet site of the African Data Dissemination Service (http://edcintl.cr.usgs.gov/adds/adds.html). This Internet site is full of useful maps and information for introductory courses on Africa, and it can also be valuable for more complex projects like our project 2. The site now has available monthly maps of vegetation greenness data going back to 1981 for nearly every African country, even island states such as Comoros or Seychelles. These maps are based on data from the Advanced Very High Resolution Radiometer (AVHRR), a satellite-borne instrument used to measure reflectance in different bands of the electromagnetic spectrum. Indices developed mathematically from AVHRR data are sensitive indicators of the presence and condition of both crops and natural vegetation on the landscape. One popular index based on a comparison of how different things on the ground reflect light is called the Normalized Difference Vegetation Index (NDVI). We do not require students to learn the mathematics behind NDVI, but we do use the Web site's NDVI maps, color coded to show NDVI values. Basically, what students can gather is this: The greener the map, the greener the vegetation in that part of Africa in any month of a particular year; alternatively, the browner the map, the less vegetation or greenness in that part of Africa in the same period.

Images of NDVI values like those at this Web site are helpful in assessing such concerns as the impact of climate on vegetation, the extreme seasonal differences in vegetation greenness, and the extreme year-to-year variability of vegetation greenness across much of Africa. Learning to analyze the NDVI values can help students develop a more critical analysis of environmental issues such as drought, desertification, or deforestation. In project 2, students examine monthly vegetative cover changes over the four locations from their climate diagrams. By examining patterns of crop and other vegetation change, students are able to compare the climates of the different locations. They also explore differences between their climagraphs (1940–1965 data) and the climate pattern suggested by the NDVI maps (1981–1995 data). They then compare their climate diagrams and the NDVI maps with the SARDC textbook's classification of ecozones (different types of environments) in southern Africa to assess relationships between the book's ideal-type vegetation classification and the green (or not-so-green) contemporary reality.

The Internet site used for this exercise provides other user-friendly access to information about African countries; students can gather information on this site that would otherwise be extremely expensive to obtain. Instructors might also use many other country-specific or regional data from the site. Data sets are updated continually, and the site improves with time; so it will continue to be a useful tool in the foreseeable future. The Web site is accessible from any machine that has an Internet hookup and Web browser software such as Netscape or Internet Explorer. It is highly recommended that instructors examine the possibilities for utilizing it in their classes.

Difficulties, of course, can arise from using an independent online information service. In fall 1996, although the data were readily available prior to the assignment of project 2, problems at the Web site itself prevented access over a four-day period, forcing modification of the course schedule. Once the site became available again, students were able to take full advantage of the technology, but the experience provides an immediate caution to those who want to jump on the technology-in-the-classroom bandwagon: Technology does not always work right, and even when it does, it can do so painfully slowly, wasting valuable class time. The instructor should be prepared to use any downtime wisely, preparing the class for data use or even looking ahead to the next part of the assignment if the Web—or his or her equipment—should disappoint.

The exercise also works from the assumption that beginning students of Africa's geography, once they have struggled to take in the technological and scientific information of the NDVI maps, barely have time to think critically about the political-economic context of the data and its collection. We thus hold off on asking for that level of critical analysis at the beginning of the course, something we believe is essential for the course's ultimate success.

In their third group project, students work in teams to analyze rivers and drainage on topographic maps for southern Africa. Almost any topographic maps from the region will do the job. Students develop basic physical geography skills in classifying drainage basins, stream orders, drainage density, and relief ratio in order to evaluate the potential for flooding and erosion, all the while keeping their climate and vegetation data sets in mind. This is a very conventional physical geography exercise without the new technology, and students occasionally find it tedious. Yet this project is one with a steady learning curve that endures and is critical for the very next project of the term.

Project 4 is another very successful technological project. It uses the technology of Geographic Information Systems (GIS) to bring together various types of data about the physical geography of Botswana, allowing the students to evaluate the nation's hydrology in detail based on their work with the topographic maps in project 3. GIS is a collection of hardware, software, and data that are combined for the purposes of map display and analysis. A full GIS allows for mathematical analysis of many elements of a region, but we do not expect any particular mathematical sophistication from students, preferring instead a more user-friendly GIS software system for this level of instruction. ArcView software (developed by the Environmental Systems Research Institute in Redlands, California, and sold all over North America in software stores) enables the display and visual analysis of data from the Africa Data Sampler CD-ROM. The Africa Data Sampler, available via catalog or directly from its producer, the World Resources Institute, is self-described as a "Geo-Referenced Data Base for All African Countries" (World Resources Institute 1995). This CD-ROM provides country-based data for population, conservation, land use, land cover (forests), and other aspects of physical geography.

As with other GIS data, the CD-ROM's data are organized into what are called themes and coverages. A theme is the category of information in the data set, for example, population density. The visual displays of theme data are called coverages because a basic idea of GIS is that computer technology allows us to lay one theme on top of another (i.e., *cover* it), then peel it off at the click of a mouse. For instance, with the CD-ROM map data for Botswana, students can click on an ArcView icon to lay down a coverage of protected areas and national parks of Botswana on top of its stream network, or vice versa; alternatively, students can make some clicks and thereby see one theme without the other. ArcView also allows students to zoom down in one area of Botswana—in our project, it is the Okavango Delta—to an incredible level of detail, enabling them to understand both the big picture of hydrology in Botswana and the fine braiding of stream channels as the Okavango River opens into its inland delta. These types of visual manipulation of scale and coverage are impossible with conventional maps.

In our exercise, students begin with detailed instructions on starting the software and opening the project. We provide a list of general hints for operating the software, such as displaying different types of data (or "themes"), zooming in or out of a particular area, and selecting a feature, then displaying its attributes. The students compare regions, attempt to explain the relationship among different features (streams, wetlands, elevation, and population) in key areas, and speculate on why different data sources classify some wetlands differently. Although previous lectures, projects, and handouts introduce some basic concepts about hydrology, we operate on the assumption that students know nothing about the technology (ArcView, Windows, or even turning on the computer). This seems to contribute to the project's success, since students are not intimidated from the beginning by the project's tools. Students are able to work through the questions with few technological problems; in our experience, instructional assistance has been limited to elaborating on questions or principles of physical geography. The project is short enough to be completed during class time (eighty minutes), so unforeseen problems with the computers or software can be addressed immediately. The SARDC textbook also provides a valuable backdrop for questions about water resources development and water demand in Botswana.

The Africa Data Sampler also allows for more sophisticated integration of its data sets with other GIS software packages. Some of the graduate students who sat in on this undergraduate course in fall 1996 used the CD-ROM data in this manner. Otherwise, we leave this complex use of computer science to higher-level courses than this one. The CD is currently used by the World Health Organization (WHO), the World Bank, and the Food and Agriculture Organization (FAO) for various development applications, so using it as a teaching tool fits in with pragmatic concerns of our students about their future employability. It is fairly inexpensive (about US$150 at the instructor price), especially considering what it can provide for the classroom.

The hardware and software requirements for this CD-ROM are fairly extensive, however. Instructors must investigate the capabilities of the computers in their institutions before diving into this purchase. Users need to have a CD-ROM drive linked to an IBM-compatible PC with a minimum of eight megabytes of RAM. Software must include MS-DOS version 5.0 or later, Microsoft Windows version 3.1 or later, and some version of ArcView software. The CD was produced for use in ArcView version 1, but we have used it without any difficulties in both ArcView version 2.1 and the newer ArcView version 3.0 software. In addition, the World Resources Institute recommends that the computer's processor be an 80486 or higher IBM-compatible version, and that the color monitor possess 256-color graphics and 640 x 480 resolution. Display will be much more limited on a 16-color monitor. Most university computer laboratories will have machines that meet these requirements, and most geography departments (as well as environmental studies or other geosciences programs) should have these software packages.

We have imported data from the CD-ROM located on our department's file server onto all of the department computer laboratory machines so that many students can work at one time on their projects. The process of importing data or downloading it is not as simple as the CD-ROM's user guide might lead one to believe, so users ought to be forewarned of the time commitment involved in such an undertaking. Alternatively, we have found that use of the CD-ROM is faster and more effective on just one machine with its own CD drive. This approach can be helpful to professors in making class presentations, or this approach can be taken when it is possible for students to be assigned individual projects to be done on their own time in a lab setting.

Exercise 5 concerns soils. The aim is to introduce students to the complexities of soil classification (especially the problem of scale in analysis of soil types) and to begin to develop their appreciation for the intersection of soil types with land cover, vegetation, and agriculture with a focus this time on Malawi. Malawi has a diversity of soils that makes it fairly representative of the continent; it also presents African soil degradation issues in (literally) stark relief. Electronic data available for Malawi through the Africa Data Sampler CD-ROM and on the Africa Data Dissemination Service Internet site are relatively comprehensive in comparison to what we find for most African states. However, one key shortcoming of the project is that soil map data are as yet unavailable electronically for any African country as far as we know. Another key shortcoming stems from the fact that a myriad of overlapping and conflicting soil classification systems have been applied to Africa, making this a subject that is difficult to simplify if one wants to prepare students to be analytical.

As a result, students are at present forced to flip through a series of handouts on Malawi's soils and on soil characteristics generally, all the while comparing these with the Internet and CD-ROM data on land cover, greenness, and the intensity of cropland use. The purpose is to get students to think critically about the often contradictory relationships between soil quality and the intensity of land use. When this information is paired with political-economic analysis via readings and lectures, it is difficult to miss how interrelated Malawi's human-political geography is with its degradation problems. (Similar lessons could be drawn, and computerized, for other southern African countries, such as Zimbabwe and South Africa. See Moyo 1991; and Harris, Warner, Weiner, and Levin 1995.)

In fall 1996, frustration with all the handout-flipping, when combined with the intricacies of soil classification in which students became enmeshed, meant that some students lost sight of some of the deeper connections we wanted the class to make. In the future, we are planning to develop an electronic version of a soil map of Malawi, to be worked into GIS software in combination with the other spatial data in the exercise. More explicit pairing of the soil assignment with readings in the Leach and Mearns textbook that discuss how soil erosion has been conceptualized in southern Africa over time also provides an opportunity for deeper critical thinking about the pretty pictures available for student perusal. For instance, the language used in British colonial studies of soil classification or erosion make for a lively comparison with the categories used on today's high-tech maps.

Students then expand their appreciation of this subject in the more user-friendly exercise 6. In this exercise, students use the Africa Data

Sampler CD-ROM, Food and Agriculture Organization soil maps, and modified, downloaded files from the Africa Data Dissemination Service Web pages to examine aspects of land use and conservation in Malawi. Unlike the CD's complicated downloading process, the Web site's ArcView data file requires only minimal manipulation when downloaded, and the instructions given on screen are fairly easy to follow. The receiving machine, of course, must have ArcView software and adequate memory (the necessary size varies by country for these files). Cropland use-intensity maps (which classify land by what percentage is being used for crops) are not available online for very many of the countries listed on the Africa Data Dissemination Service site, Malawi being a current, notable exception. The CD's themes and the Web site's cropland use-intensity theme are viewed and manipulated in ArcView. In the SARDC textbook, the students are provided with descriptions of the International Union for the Conservation of Nature (IUCN) protected-land categories for all such locations in Malawi. IUCN classifications, together with the textbook's analysis, give the students the means to evaluate the quality of protected lands in terms of national conservation goals and international conservation criteria.

The students first examine the relationships between regional population densities, soil quality, and cropland use intensity. Students use knowledge gained in exercise 5 to evaluate which regions of the country possess the highest-quality soils. They then consider how soil quality relates to population. (In the case of Malawi, relatively high population densities are present on lower-quality lands.) Finally, the students examine the cropland use-intensity data from the Web site. The combination of data sets can begin to suggest areas of potential land use conflict and population pressure in the country, to be seen in the light of readings and lectures on political approaches to environmental geography (for example, Blaikie 1995; Carney and Watts 1990; and Moore 1993).

In the second part of the exercise, the students examine the extent of protected lands in Malawi using both national and international classification schemes. The students first assess the extent of national parks, forests, and wildlife refuges as classified by the government of Malawi. They then analyze how the national classification compares to IUCN classification and consider the environmental, economic, and political implications of each class. The Data Sampler CD also indicates additional lands in proposed status and the classifications for these proposed lands. The students evaluate how the addition of the proposed areas would change the landscape of conservation in the country. Finally, the students must speculate on the future course of conservation in Malawi and how population pressures and political economy might effect this course.

Students tie all of the technology-related projects together in a take-home essay as one-third of their second midterm. The essay addresses "how to do a GIS in your head" and how to relate the overlaid coverages of information they have gained to the practice of environmental management. For their essay in fall 1996, students were asked to create a budget for environmental management in Malawi, making cases for both regional (northern, central, and southern provinces) and systematic (soil conservation, water resources, forest protection, and ecotourism) priorities. Last, they were asked what "coverages" were missing from their "GIS in the head" about Malawi, based on their reading of pages 21–64 in the SARDC textbook. These are the chapters called "Learning from History" and "The Evolution of Policy," which taken together lay out the political history of environmental management in southern Africa and make a case for indigenous technical knowledge while setting up current environment-development dilemmas for the students.

The purpose of the essay is to juxtapose the "remotely sensed" environmental knowledge students obtain in the technology projects with critical thinking about indigenous technical knowledge or social history from textbook and lecture materials. In fall 1996, although most students' essays accurately analyzed the technical parameters of Malawi's physical geography, none considered the ethics of technology use, and only a small minority of students took the essay to the higher level of a political analysis of the ecology. Two of these students had previously taken a course called Human Geography of Africa offered by Myers and are dedicated geography majors with an interest in Africa. We are not going to stop trying to lay the groundwork for critical, integrative thinking because of this gap but conclude that we are often more ambitious and enthusiastic for our students in this area than their commitment to or command of the subject warrants.

CONCLUSION

The discipline of geography is exploding with ideas that seem to go in two different directions at once. One direction leads toward increasing technological sophistication. Another leads toward increasing connections with philosophy and other theoretical disciplines. In the teaching of Africa's environmental geography, the dizzying pace of these changes makes classroom application of either direction, let alone both at the same time, a daunting endeavor. In practice, attempts within our class's small-group projects to integrate a more sophisticated technological and scientific approach with critical thinking about complex social-theoretical issues have had uneven results, but this unevenness can itself be considered instructive. Most students greatly enjoy working with GIS packages or examining remotely sensed data, but they are less willing to engage with how political and historical questions interrelate with the pretty pictures on their computer screens, let alone to engage the even larger questions of the sources or purposes of their electronic data or indeed the imperialist nature of a technologically based geography. After all, as most teachers know but our students rarely realize, very few African classrooms could even consider using these technological projects in their programs of geographical instruction. This problem is suggestive of a larger point that appears to set geography's two new directions at odds. Claims for GIS and associated technologies as conducive to more democratic learning, rational decision-making, and the creation of critically engaged students are, if not wholly unsustainable, frequently overstated (Pickles 1995). Students are prone to take what the technology offers as "objective" facts rather than value-laden representations.

Resistance to breaking open those representations and examining them in the classroom may be higher in the marketability-driven age of education that North American institutions have entered. Nevertheless, we continue to believe that our class (and other similar African studies classes) offer opportunities to challenge students to link technological with theoretical sophistication. When even one student argues in an essay (as one did in fall 1996) for juxtaposing a "coverage based on indigenous technical knowledge" with one based on Western science in their GIS, we feel that the course's content and implied critical emphasis have contributed to a disruption of the apparent inertia of many 1990s university students. The course reorientation is an ongoing process but one we are convinced is both necessary and valuable. We encourage instructors to experiment with the suggestions borne of our experiences.

SUGGESTIONS FOR FURTHER READING AND RESOURCES

Adams, William. 1992. *Wasting the Rain: Rivers, People, and Planning in Africa.* Minneapolis: University of Minnesota Press.

Ady, P. 1970. *Africa: Oxford Regional Economic Atlas.* New York: Oxford University Press.

Aryeetey-Attoh, Sam. 1997. *Geography of Sub-Saharan Africa.* Upper Saddle River, N.J.: Prentice-Hall.

Binns, Tony. 1994. *Tropical Africa.* New York: Routledge.

Blaikie, Piers. 1995. "Changing Environments or Changing Views? A Political Ecology for Developing Countries." *Geography* 80, 3: 203–214.

Carney, Judith, and Michael Watts. 1990. "Manufacturing Dissent: Work, Gender, and the Politics of Meaning in a Peasant Society." *Africa* 60, 2: 207–241.

Darkoh, M. 1986. "Geographic Research and National Development in Developing Countries: The Case of Tanzania." *Journal of Eastern African Research and Development* 15, 1: 20–34.

Grove, A. 1993. *The Changing Geography of Africa.* New York: Oxford University Press.

Harris, T. D.Weiner, T. Warner, and R. Levin. 1995. "Pursuing Social Goals Through Participatory Geographic Information Systems: Redressing South Africa's Historical Political Ecology." In *Ground Truth: The Social Implications of Geographic Information Systems,* ed. John Pickles. New York: Guilford Press.

James, Valentine Udoh. 1991. *Resource Management in Developing Countries: Africa's Ecological and Economic Problems.* New York: Bergin and Garvey.

———. 1993. *Africa's Ecology.* Jefferson, N.C.: McFarland.

———. 1994. *Environmental and Economic Dilemmas of Developing Countries: Africa in the 21st Century.* Westport, Conn.: Praeger.

Leach, Melissa, and Robin Mearns, eds. 1996. *The Lie of the Land: Challenging Received Wisdom on the African Environment.* Portsmouth, N.H.: Heinemann.

Moore, Donald. 1993. "Contesting Terrain in Zimbabwe's Eastern Highlands: Political Ecology, Ethnography, and Peasant Resource Struggles." *Economic Geography* 69, 4: 380–401.

Moyo, Sam. 1991. *Zimbabwe's Environmental Dilemma.* Harare: SAPES Books.

Pickles, John, ed. 1995. *Ground Truth: The Social Implications of Geographic Information Systems.* New York: Guilford Press.

Samatar, A. 1993. "Structural Adjustment as Development Strategy? Bananas, Boom, and Poverty in Somalia." *Economic Geography* 69, 1: 25–43.

Southern African Research and Documentation Center (SARDC). 1994. *State of the Environment in Southern Africa.* Harare: SARDC.

Stock, Robert. 1995. *Africa South of the Sahara: A Geographical Interpretation.* New York: Guilford Press.

World Resources Institute. 1995. *Africa Data Sampler: A Geo-Referenced Database for All African Countries* (CD-ROM). Baltimore: WRI.

PART FOUR

BROADER APPROACHES TO TEACHING ABOUT AFRICA

16

TEACHING AFRICA THROUGH CULTURE AREAS AND LITERARY TEXTS

RALPH A. AUSTEN

When I was a grammar school student shortly after World War II, Africa appeared on our curriculum only under the rubric of geography; it was an interesting space on the map but not the site of any autonomous history or culture that we needed to learn about. Since that time the more active entry of Africa, Africans, and African Americans into world and national affairs does not allow us to give the continent such limited attention. Furthermore, teachers at all levels of education now have access to a plenitude of materials on African history and culture. Yet it is not clear that we have come to any understanding of how to organize and focus teaching of Africa that clearly transcends geography.

The first portion of this chapter discusses some of the philosophical issues involved in defining the approach of a university course on Africa. The second section describes my own—far from perfect—response to these issues in the form of a course organized around specific culture areas that attempts to integrate historical and anthropological accounts with indigenous literary texts.

THE DILEMMA: INVENTING, PROCLAIMING, AND DECONSTRUCTING AFRICA

The subtitle of this section indicates some of the dominant approaches to Africa in current scholarship and teaching. Stated simply, "invention" refers to the images imposed on Africa by Europeans and European Americans, "proclaiming" refers to the counterdefinitions offered by

African and African American cultural nationalists, and "deconstructing" in this context (as opposed to formal literary theory) refers to critical analysis of the basis on which both preceding sets of definitions have been developed. Most contemporary Africanist scholars identify instinctively (but not explicitly) with the last position. However, as teachers of African studies courses, this stance presents us with the dilemma of maintaining some sense that there is a real subject out there without backing into the firing range of our own critical weapons. To put it another way, we are in danger of falling into a nihilist trap where all we seem to be teaching our students is suspicion of everything they read or even spontaneously say about Africa.

One reason we risk such danger is that the suspicions are generally well grounded. In most European and European American social theory, Africa does remain the quintessential "other," the realm that has to become "civilized" and "developed" rather than possessing any positive dynamic qualities of its own. It is also true that most students, even at the University of Chicago, have never even heard of these theories and are thus somewhat put off by our efforts to "deconstruct" them. Nonetheless, when these same students begin to write papers they instinctively label all African communities as "tribes," all languages as "dialects," all cultural practices as "custom," and everything that preceded contact with the centers of European or Islamic civilization as "tradition," by which they mean something that is usually "primitive" and always ahistorical.

We have even become very "reflexive" in teaching what used to be considered the basis of culturally relativist African studies, that is, anthropological theory. Anthropology, above all other disciplines, is regularly indicted "for its complicity in colonialism, for its alleged part in the creation and domination of the 'other.'" Even when, as in the preceding quote (from John and Jean Comaroff, with whom I regularly teach African civilization), we feel that these charges are exaggerated; it remains part of our pedagogical obligation to explain their basis to students.

The irony of such a critical effort is that it can be applied with almost no adjustment to the black "proclaimers" of Africa on either side of the Atlantic. Their most famous theory, and one that still exercises fascination despite decades of denunciation from all quarters, is Negritude. Negritude emerged from the very exciting cultural encounters in the Paris of the 1930s and 1940s among Africans, black West Indians, and the Harlem Renaissance-in-exile. It produced poetry of lasting value and constituted a critical moment in the process of defining African identity. However, the immediate identity patented under this label simply embraces the negative European stereotypes of Africans as sensual, nonrational beings and romanticizes them into positive virtues.

Far less appealing, from my point of view, is the current "Afrocentric" doctrine, which identifies Africa with ancient Egypt and attributes to this commanding center not only the entire culture of the sub-Saharan portions of the continent (which thus become devalued) but also the leading role in the grand narrative of world civilization. This idea represents little more than an appropriation of the discourse of Western racism by its victims. The purpose of an African studies course should be the subversion of this discourse rather than the reversal of its directional arrows. Like Negritude (with which it was historically linked in the person of the Senegalese writer Cheikh Anta Diop), Afrocentrism has an important place in the intellectual history of modern Africa; but I cannot, in good conscience, adopt it as the basis for teaching that history.

One way out of this dilemma might be to use contemporary African culture theorists who speak to questions of identity from a position based on both external critique and internal experience. V. Y. Mudimbé's (1988) *The Invention of Africa* is generally considered the canonical text for this approach. With all due respect to Professor Mudimbé's impressive learning and intelligence, I think that this book is consumed by the very problems it sets out to attack. The work contains some useful tools for deconstructing what Mudimbé (borrowing from Said) calls "the colonial library" of Africanist concepts. But Mudimbé is far from the clearest guide to this library; nor does he ever work out his own ambivalent stance toward various forms of Negritude. With Mudimbé we are thus caught in a dilemma of simultaneously proclaiming and deconstructing Africa, a situation that is extremely instructive for anyone who wishes to explore some of the most sophisticated contemporary African and African American thought but that provides little positive direction for organizing our own teaching of the African heritage.

In the end, therefore, each of us can come up with only partial solutions to the definition and organization of what we teach in the hope that students can somehow achieve a simultaneous intimacy with African culture and critical distance from any overly systematic constructions of this culture. My own approach to the teaching of Africa over the past thirty-plus years has more often exemplified or added to the dilemmas just discussed than offered any solution to them. In the 1960s I based my courses on a narrative survey of the entire continent (including Egypt). Later I shifted to a more analytic emphasis on political economy. The first approach was abandoned because it seemed to drown students (even those I taught at African universities) in a sea of geographic, political, and ethnic units. The economic approach suffered from the depressing nature of much of the subject matter, a growing lack of confidence in the theoretical tools used to explain this situation, and finally (perhaps as a result of the two previous conditions) a growing disinterest in these approaches among students who enrolled in courses on Africa.

My preferred approach over the past decade or so has thus shifted to culture with an emphasis on literary texts and a relegation of both history and anthropology to the role of background for understanding such texts. I make no claims for this approach other than that it works relatively well for me. Moreover, it raises its own dilemmas about the "invented" category of "African great books' as well as the capacity of specific written documents either to contain the most critical elements of African culture or to convey whatever they contain to North American students. However, rather than treating such further problems in the abstract, I will touch on them in describing what I actually do in my teaching.

A SOLUTION: CULTURE AREAS AND LITERARY TEXTS

The two areas through which I have exercised my approach are the Mande region of West Africa (centered on present-day southern Mali and northern Guinea) and the present-day Republic of South Africa. My first choice grew directly out of experience in teaching (only subsequently did I begin doing research there). South Africa is something of an obligatory subspecialty for anyone studying the continent. The approach could obviously work in many other areas or configurations of Africa as long as a reasonably appealing set of literary texts is available and they can be used to deal with issues that represent a fairly wide range of African historical and cultural experience. Among the two options that I have used, the Mande region provides a better integrated teaching unit, and I will give it somewhat greater attention. However, this choice probably reflects more my own efforts and proclivities than the intrinsic character of the two regions.

Another key to my choices is the undergraduate education system at the University of Chicago. Africa is taught here as one option in a college-wide "non-Western civilization" requirement. Thus the students do not concentrate in any particular discipline or area studies program, and the courses are expected to combine a variety of social science humanities approaches. The university also operates on a quarter system, so a year-long civilization sequence can easily be divided by subregions and disciplines (the African Civilization course tends to follow both subregional and disciplinary divisions).

The format of the course, as I teach it, consists of two lectures and one discussion session per week. The lectures mainly deal with historical and anthropological issues but always conclude with an introduction to the text, which is the subject of that week's discussion session. Students are normally expected to write two short papers per quarter dealing with the discussion texts (they are given suggested questions to address). They are to be completed before the discussion. These papers are difficult (although the better students do develop a comparative basis for writing them as the quarter progresses), but they do ensure substantive student input to the discussions. Students can meet all course requirements by writing four such papers but are encouraged to take an in-class final, in which they deal synthetically with material that has already been discussed. Although many students are convinced that even this number of papers is preferable to the trauma of exams, the grades on the final are generally better than those on the papers.

Whichever region of Africa I choose, I attempt to follow both a historical sequence and to cover a related range of social-cultural settings. I begin by discussing village society and the earliest known forms of local social structures, then move on to the formation of indigenous states, African confrontations with world religions and literacy, experiences with (and struggles against) colonialism, and problems of postcolonial development. There is an obvious danger that such an ordering may play into a Eurocentric view of inevitable progress from "tradition" to "modernity." However, my experience is that students become highly sensitized to the persistence and dynamic nature of the "traditional" while all too readily (given the substantive dilemmas of contemporary Africa) appreciating the limitations of "modernization."

There is no space here to go into detailed analysis of all the literary texts I use (see bibliography at the end), so I will limit myself to discussing the genres represented by these readings and the work they are supposed to do in the course. In general they parallel the substantive sequence of the course, beginning with various genres of oral literature; moving on to early, world religion–inspired writing; and concluding with modern autobiographies and novels. However, in the Mande case I begin with a late-colonial autobiography/coming-of-age novel (Camara Laye [1987], *The Dark Child*) because it is an easy introduction to many of the issues of the course and can be revisited in more critical (but still appreciative) terms as the quarter progresses.

One area of frustration in both versions of this course is finding literary texts to represent village agricultural life, the most common setting of African societies. It may well be that literature generally focuses on the dramatic and disruptive rather than the everyday (thus the best African depiction of rural existence may be Chinua Achebe's [1959] *Things Fall Apart,* with which one might begin a sequence based on Nigeria or Igboland). In the Mande region we do have versions of a creation myth that present the cycles of agricultural and sexual reproduction in complex and even dramatic terms—Griaule (1965), *Conversations with Ogotemmeli,* and Dieterlen (1957), "The Mande Creation Myth." But the genesis of both these texts is highly problematic, and they raise as many questions about

European "inventing" of Africa as they reveal about local beliefs. I thus prefer to discuss these texts in lecture rather than expect students to analyze them independently.

Short oral narratives ("folktales") make for quite engaging reading, but in order to be of use in a course like this, they need to deal with more complex social issues than is often the case with "animal stories" or moralizing narratives aimed at children. Among the Mande, however, there are many such tales that deal with hunting (e.g., "Mande Fabori and the Animals" [Jackson 1982]) and that thus raise very complex issues about critical relationships throughout the culture: between humans and the uncultivated wild; among gender power, parental bonds, and sexuality; and between occult knowledge and social roles. In the South African course I begin the quarter with a brief but somewhat difficult Bushman/San tale ("Mantis Steals Ticks' Sheep" [Bleek 1924]) that provides some sense of the values of the aboriginal hunter-gatherer peoples of the region as well as their views on both creation and their often violent confrontations with other peoples (both African and European) within the region.

The richest genres of African oral literature are its poetry and epics. The poetry is almost impossible to present for student analysis, but in both the Mande and South Africa cases I provide examples and discuss it in lectures. Both regions have developed major indigenous states whose rulers are commemorated in complex and highly allusive praise poetry (Cope [1968], *Izibongo*) that students cannot be expected to read in any independent manner. In the Mande case, however, this poetry and the tale tradition have been combined into a powerful epic genre. The most famous of these heroic accounts, that of the medieval empire builder Sunjata, is accessible in a relatively contemporary version (Niane [1965], *Sundiata*) that can be used as a discussion reading and even inspires some students to take on a rendition that is much closer to the oral performance (Johnson [1992], *Son-Jara*). For South Africa, we have no such historical epics, but there is a wonderfully magical miniepic tale ("Sikhuluma" [Scheub and Zenani 1972]) that follows the steps to maturity of the heir to a generic Xhosa chieftainship. Both the "Sunjata" and "Sikhuluma" narratives also indicate how profoundly the success of their masculine heroes depends on the actions of women, so questions of gender in these societies can be foregrounded if the instructor is so inclined.

One advantage of the Mande unit is that it allows some discussion of the role of Islam in Africa. Teaching this, however, requires a one-lecture version of an entire Islamic civilization course. The Islamic texts that we read ("Jabi Ta'rikhs" [Hunter 1976a, 1976b] and "Umar Tal Biographies" [Hanson and Robinson 1991]) are much more difficult for students to deal with than transcribed oral narratives, although the effort helps them appreciate the functions and limitations of literacy as an element of "modernization." The equivalent text in my South African syllabus is Mofolo's (1981) *Chaka*, a work that is quite readable (it deals with the very dramatic life of the first Zulu king) and also raises questions about world religious influence (in this case Christianity) on very early African writers.

The colonial era in the Mande world is the subject of a marvelous, although little-known, novel (Hampaté Ba [1987], *The Fortunes of Wangrin*), a mock-epic/trickster tale about an African interpreter under French rule. For South Africa with its very large and internally divided white settler population, colonialism is a more extended and complex process. In order to get some understanding of the critical Afrikaner community, as well as issues of local slavery, I assign André Brink (1983), *An Instant in the Wind,* a modern novel dealing with the eighteenth century. For more conditions under the later apartheid regime, there are surprisingly few works of fiction available, although La Guma's (1967) novella *A Walk in the Night* is a major exception. However, there is a great choice of black and colored autobiographical works, from which I most recently chose a set of interviews with women who had moved between their rural homes and Johannesburg (Bozzoli [1991], *Women of Phokeng*) and a brief article about male sexuality in prison (Achmat 1993) to get at broader issues of both suppression and the experience of labor migration.

African imaginative literature has likewise paid relatively little attention to the anticolonial struggle. Again, however, one of the exceptions is a very compelling novel, Sembène's (1986) *God's Bits of Wood,* which deals with a 1945 railroad strike in Senegal and Mali and thus fits well into the Mande unit. For this part of the South Africa course I have used the film *Mapantsula* (Schmitz and Mogotlane 1988), which gives an excellent picture of township life and politics in the 1980s. Both these works take very optimistic views of the new national and class consciousness emerging from these historical moments, and my goal is to have students appreciate the vision of the authors while also recognizing the problems they leave unresolved or even ignore.

Such problems are very evident in the extensive and largely disillusioned postcolonial literature of tropical Africa. For the Mande world, we are fortunate to view this despair through the eyes of Ahmadou Kourouma (1981, *The Suns of Independence*). His novel beautifully plays off contemporary poverty, oppression, and corruption against the values and idiom of Mande culture, which students by this stage can recognize and interrogate for its capacity to make any sense of the new conditions it must confront. In the case of South Africa, white rule ended only in 1994. Since I last taught this version of the course one year later, I have no clear idea of what readings I would now use for the last week. However, given the continued vitality of South African universities and their connection to the Internet (particularly via discussion lists like NUAfrica and H-Africa, already mentioned in this volume), it should not be difficult to get help in locating materials.

As indicated in the discussion of South African decolonization, it is possible to use films in much the same way as written texts, for purposes of student analysis. Indeed, I am probably not unique in finding that students are often much more sensitive to the nuances of such visual presentation than they are to the language of written texts. There are many films available for South Africa—as noted, *Mapantsula* (Schmitz and Mogotlane 1988) is outstanding as a high-quality feature work made inside the country, as opposed to ethnographic, documentary films or foreign-produced features. The Mande world and its immediate surroundings (Senegal, Burkina Faso), are the major center for tropical African feature film production. Two of the films I have used in my course are *Keïta: L'Héritage du Griot* (Kouyaté 1994) and *Yeelen* (Cissé 1987). The former deals with the Sunjata epic and the bards who perform it in a modern context. The latter creates is own metahistorical epic around the occult power embodied in secret societies dominated by Mande "casted" blacksmiths. It does not fit neatly into my course organization, but I usually show it near the end of the quarter as the basis for an optional paper (even a substitute for the final exam).

In both the Mande and South African courses, I make considerable use of music tapes both as "soft" introductions to other topics and as the basis for some ethnomusicological analysis of renowned "world-beat" performers like Malian Salif Keita. This approach is promising, since many of our students do think (and even write) a good deal about popular music, but probably due to my own shortcomings in this field, I find it difficult to get good papers on the topic.[1] There is also considerable material on African (especially Mande) music now available on the World Wide Web (Kennedy Center African Odyssey can be found at http://artsedge.kennedy-center.org/odyssey.html). The Mande world and South Africa also have very rich traditions of visual art in a variety of pictorial, plastic, and textile media. But even more than in the case of music, I tend to use such materials more for illustration than for analysis.

The quarter-long focus on specific regions and their literature is certainly not the only way to overcome the dilemmas of teaching about Africa. The more general lesson that it does, perhaps, offer, is the importance of engaging African cultures through their own productions as much as possible. Of course it is evident how much such engagement is mediated across very wide gaps between Africa and ourselves, especially in the transcription and translation of vernacular oral texts, to say nothing of the secondary materials and lectures upon which I ultimately expect my students to base their "independent" interpretations of these works. It is easy—and to some extent even necessary—to continue "deconstructing" any effort at incorporating Africa into the culture of our university classrooms. All that I can argue in defense of my own approach is that it provides students with some access to African modes of self-interpretation and a responsible means of articulating their responses to such experiences.

NOTES

1. Tapes of African popular music did work very effectively to clear the lecture platform during one quarter when I regularly found it still occupied by the instructor of the previous class, my late colleague Allan *(Closing of the American Mind)* Bloom.

SUGGESTIONS FOR FURTHER READING AND RESOURCES

I have been able to make arrangements with publishers to photocopy the works preceded by "(op)" (out of print) at the cost of a modest royalty fee added to the price paid by students. Those works preceded by an asterisk are available from me in edited and annotated form as email attachments (address: wwb3@midway.uchicago.edu; please specify word processor type).

Achebe, Chinua. 1959. *Things Fall Apart*. Portsmouth, N.H.: Heinemann.
Achmat, Zakie. 1993. "'Apostles of Civilized Vice': 'Immoral Practices' and 'Unnatural Vice' in South African Prisons and Compounds, 1890–1920." *Social Dynamics* 19, 2: 92–100.
*Bleek, Dorothea F. 1924. "Mantis Steals Ticks' Sheep." In *The Mantis and His Friends: Bushman Folklore Collected by W.H.I. Bleek and Lucy C. Lloyd*. Cape Town: T. M. Miller.
Bozzoli, Belinda. 1991. *Women of Phokeng: Consciousness, Life Strategy, and Migrancy in South Africa, 1900–1983*. Portsmouth, N.H.: Heinemann.
(op) Brink, André. 1983. *An Instant in the Wind*. London: Fontana Paperbacks.
Cissé, Souleymane. 1987. *Yeelen*. San Francisco: California Newsreel.
Comaroff, Jean, and John Comaroff. 1991. *Of Revelation and Revolution: Christianity, Colonialism, and Consciousness in South Africa*. Chicago: University of Chicago Press.
Cope, Trevor, ed. 1968. *Izibongo: Zulu Praise Poems*. Oxford: Clarendon Press.
Dieterlen, Germaine. 1957. "The Mande Creation Myth." *Africa* 27, 2: 124–137.
Griaule, Marcel. 1965. *Conversations with Ogotemmeli: An Introduction to Dogon Religious Ideas*. London: Oxford University Press.
Hampaté Ba, Ahmadou. 1987. *The Fortunes of Wangrin*. Ibadan, Nigeria: New Horn Press.
Hanson, John, and David Robinson. 1991. "Umar Tal Biographies." In *After the Jihad: The Reign of Ahmad Al-Kabir in the Western Sudan*. East Lansing: Michigan State University Press.

*Hunter, Thomas C., trans. with annotations. 1976a. "The Jabi Ta'rikhs." unpubl.

———. 1976b. "The Jabi Ta'rikhs: Their Significance in West African Islam." *International Journal of African Historical Studies* 9, 3: 435–446.

Jackson, Michael. 1982. "Mande Fabori and the Animals." In *Allegories of the Wilderness: Ethics and Ambiguity in Kuranko Narratives*. Bloomington: Indiana University Press.

Johnson, John William. 1992. *The Epic of Son-Jara*. Bloomington: Indiana University Press.

Kourouma, Ahmadou. 1981. *The Suns of Independence*. New York: Holmes & Meier.

Kouyaté, Dani. 1994. *Keïta: L'Héritage du Griot*. San Francisco: California Newsreel.

La Guma, Alex. 1967. *A Walk in the Night and Other Stories*. Evanston, Ill.: Northwestern University Press.

Laye, Camara. 1987. *The Dark Child*. New York: Farrar, Straus and Giroux.

Mofolo, Thomas. 1981. *Chaka*. London: Heinemann.

Mudimbé, V. Y. 1988. *The Invention of Africa: Gnosis, Philosophy, and the Order of Knowledge*. Bloomington: Indiana University Press.

Niane, D. T. 1965. *Sundiata: An Epic of Old Mali*. London: Longman.

Said, Edward. 1978. *Orientalism*. New York: Pantheon Books.

(op) Scheub, Harold, and Nongenile Mazithathu Zenani. 1972. "Sikhuluma." In *African Folklore,* ed. Richard M. Dorson. Garden City: Doubleday, 528–561.

Schmitz, Oliver, and Thomas Mogotlane. 1988. *Mapantsula*. San Francisco: California Newsreel.

———. 1991. *Mapantsula: The Book* (screenplay and interview). Fordsburg, S. Africa: COSAW.

Sembène, Ousmane. 1986. *God's Bits of Wood*. Portsmouth, N.H.: Heinemann.

Zenani, Nongenile Mazithathu, and Harold Scheub. 1992. *The World and the Word: Tales and Observations from the Xhosa Oral Tradition*. Madison: University of Wisconsin Press.

17

CONCEPT MAPPING AND COUNTRY ADOPTION AS TOOLS FOR TEACHING ABOUT AFRICA

CYRIL KOFIE DADDIEH

So geographers in Afric maps
with savage pictures fill the gaps
And o'r unhabitable downs
Placed elephants for want of towns.
—*Jonathan Swift (cited in Martin and O'Meara 1986: 9)*

Teaching African politics to the typical North American college student is both a daunting task and a humbling experience. Too often, students come to their first day of class with either embarrassingly little knowledge about the continent or, just as likely, plenty of preconceived or distorted notions. I was recently reminded of what the instructor is up against in a conversation I had with a colleague who volunteers at a local public library. She told of her encounter with a mother who came in with her son, who was probably in sixth or seventh grade, and asked for help finding information about "the government of Africa." The mother seemed baffled when my colleague inquired about the particular African country in whose government her son was interested. It was apparently news to her that Africa had more than one government, that, indeed, there were over fifty different countries, each with its own form of government. My colleague and I concurred that this episode was symptomatic of a much larger problem that is sometimes exacerbated by local libraries and school systems even with the best of intentions. For instance, my colleague said that one of the things that had attracted her to volunteer was that she had taken her children to the library on a number of occasions and noticed that there were displays under the rather positive and promotive banner headline "Discover Other Cultures." The displays featured such countries as Spain, Portugal, Brazil, a couple of Middle Eastern countries (her own area of interest) and then, revealingly, a sign pointing users to the huge continent of Africa.

Like my own experiences, my colleague's library encounter underscores the rather pronounced tendency among too many North American students to treat Africa as one monolithic country. Such diminution of Africa is one of the challenges facing all of us as educators. Perhaps a recitation during each class session of "Africa is not a country, it is a continent" might be an appropriate starting point. In any case, her experience reveals that the practice of "filling the gaps" in their knowledge that cartographers once routinely employed—a practice Swift captured in his early–eighteenth-century rhyme reproduced at the beginning of this chapter—is alive and well. The teaching of Africa is simultaneously a struggle to overcome centuries of "filling in the gaps" and a struggle to tear down distortions and misinformation in order to rebuild knowledge. To prepare for such a task, I highly recommend Dorothy Hammond and Alta Jablow's (1992) *The Africa That Never Was* to other instructors.

I have found an interesting and effective way to begin the twin process of dismantling and rebuilding. On the first day of class, before even one word has been uttered about the contents of the course and associated learning objectives, I give each of my students a sheet of paper with Africa encircled in the middle of the page. Students are asked, in this important first learning experience, to put down anything they know about Africa. To encourage those students who invariably display those blank stares all too familiar to instructors, I tell them to write down anything that comes to mind when they hear the word "Africa." Just as important, I ask students to organize their information, ideas, and imaginings in any manner they see fit. That is, they are allowed to adopt any schematic approach that is familiar or comfortable. The idea, of course, is to see whether students treat these ideas as discrete categories or can connect them in some holistic or comprehensive fashion. As a final step, they are asked to summarize their thoughts in a short paragraph or two. It is imperative that all students in the class participate in this exercise.

Following the exercise, I collect the concept maps and invite students to share with the class the kinds of things they wrote. Africa is circled on the board, replicating what students had on their sheets. As students identify the things they wrote and their schematic approach to those ideas, I write them on the board. When all students have had a chance to participate, I lead a discussion of these ideas and imaginings articulated by students.

Students' performance shows some variation; even the best students are able to put down only a few salient ideas or items. A few may claim that they do not know anything about Africa—precisely why they are taking the course—or that they cannot think of anything to write. All too often the recorded items tend to reflect ideas or images from television, documentary programs, and popular films. As such, they border on the superficial, revealing a general lack of in-depth knowledge about Africa.

Typical responses are jungles, hunger, famine, refugees, conflict, beautiful landscape, wars, safari, wildlife, lions, tigers, elephants, rhinos, zebras, overpopulation, starving children, female genital mutilation, pygmies, poverty, heat. The artistically inclined are likely to mention colorful clothes, beautiful masks and carvings, and so on. Students are generally oblivious to the fact that, as David Lamb (1984) reminds his readers in *The Africans,* there are few jungles left in Africa, and the heat there is actually less oppressive than on a summer's day in Philadelphia or Washington. Also worth emphasizing, as Lamb does, is Africa's sheer size and scale. That a population of North American students normally accustomed to time zones and travel can miss this point is astonishing. Here is an opportunity to impress upon students that Africa spans seven time zones and that it takes longer to travel from Dakar, Senegal, in the west to Nairobi, Kenya, in the east than to fly from New York to London. Students are surprised to learn that Africa is roughly four times the size of the continental United States.

The key phrase is "impress upon." A good way to help students absorb information about time and scale is to ask them if they have taken any trips in North America or to Europe or if they have relatives who have taken such trips. I then ask how long these trips generally took. I ask them how they think Africans travel or the kinds of structures in which they live; how many have seen live elephants, tigers, lions, and so on; and how many think African children live with these animals all the time. I can then reveal that most Africans and my students' age cohorts in Africa have never seen lions, tigers, and elephants either in the wild or in the zoo, the latter being few and far between. Students are incredulous when I relate one of my fondest memories: As a seventeen-year-old high school exchange student in Ripon, Wisconsin, my host family, upon learning that I had never seen any of these so-called African animals, decided to rectify this monumental deprivation by arranging for me to visit the Barnum Bailey Circus Museum in Baraboo, Wisconsin. I learned a great deal about Africa in the jungle of the American Midwest.

On a more serious note, the items in the students' catalog reflect tragedies and problems rather than progress or accomplishments. There is little indication of heroic struggles and figures, of a richly textured and varied culture, of dynamic change. Even when political figures are mentioned by name, Idi Amin, Emperor Bokassa, Mobutu Sese Seko, and Samuel Doe appear far more often than Nelson Mandela, Winnie Mandela, Archbishop Desmond Tutu, Amilcar Cabral, Dr. Julius Nyerere, or Dr. Kwame

Nkrumah. The prevalence of negative stereotypes is revealed by the fact that although more notorious heads of state such as Amin, Bokassa, and Doe are gone from the scene, they are easily recalled and spoken about as though they are still in power.

Equally typical is the inability of all but a few students to identify a mere handful of African countries. Those most likely to be identified by those few students are Egypt, South Africa, Rwanda, Kenya, Nigeria, Somalia, and Liberia. Again, for the most part, these names seem to have been more indelibly etched on the memory of North American students because they have become metaphors for the African malaise—genocide, civil wars, famine, dictatorships, brutal suppression, human rights violations, Islamic fundamentalism, and so on—or because they are good tourist destinations, places meant for safaris or pyramid gazing.

Also, at this stage, the organization of whatever ideas students may have about Africa betray another challenge for the teacher: a lack of organizational sophistication. Most students provide a simple list of ideas or images without the slightest hint that there may be interesting connections among items. Invariably, most students appear to be unaware that North American "safaris" to East Africa may have implications for environmental and population issues in Kenya, for instance, let alone for domestic, regional, and international politics. Beneficial at this point is a discussion on the positive and negative effects of such tourism. Who suffers and who benefits from the standard approach to tourism? Is there a way for tourism of any kind, including safaris, to benefit both the local community and the environment? Since regional integration is among the concerns of my courses, I provide a brief tease by indicating how the skewed distribution of benefits from tourism played a role in the dissolution of the East African Community.

To take another example, famine grabs more headlines than chronic malnutrition and undernourishment. The latter, however, are far more significant silent killers and deserve serious attention by students. When our overview discussion turns to economic development, and especially structural adjustment programs (SAPs) as the new framework of policy formulation, I generally identify the main features of SAPs—devaluation, privatization, removal of subsidies, retrenchment of government workers, and so on. I then ask students to think about the connections between such measures and state-society relations and politics. I am able to demonstrate through examples that recent economic policies have had differential impacts on social groups and stimulated opposition by an emerging civil society of student organizations; teachers' and faculty associations; farmers' organizations; and trade union, environmental, and women's movements as well as business and professional bodies and church groups. Within a relatively short period, civil society has achieved remarkable success in prying open sufficient political space for individual and collective self-expression. These changes have led both to the grudging acceptance of political pluralism by regimes once sworn to protect against such "retrograde" steps and to subsequent transition elections in much of Africa.

Thus this concept mapping exercise provides an opportunity to begin to lay out the central concerns of the course and allows the instructor to orient students toward critical thinking along interrelational rather than atomistic or discrete lines. Through such an interdisciplinary exploration, aided by the concept maps, a class can raise the larger political, economic, agricultural, ecological, historical, cultural, international, and regional issues as well as pursue investigations of class, gender, and ethnicity. It is important to keep in mind that these overview discussions should be followed by substantive discussions during the course of the term. At this stage the course does not make any presumption of prior knowledge about Africa. The effort here is to concentrate students' collective thinking on Africa early on and to raise their expectations. To do this properly, it is best to devote the entire first week of classes to the exercise unless the instructor has a block of about an hour and a half to two hours to devote to it in one session. In order to promote experiential learning and assess how well students are catching on to this novel way of thinking about Africa, it is probably useful to break the class into groups and have them brainstorm after about an hour and a half and have another run, this time in groups, at the exercise.

Whatever the outcome of this exercise, during the final concept mapping exercise, which is administered at the end of the course, virtually all students should be able to fill the sheet with relative ease. Their performance should evidence greater sophistication both in terms of knowledge and organization. Most students ask for additional sheets or continue on the back of the page. The instructor is likely to see students making all kinds of intriguing and interesting interconnections among the items on the map.

Besides providing an exit snapshot of a student's overall intellectual development in the course, the final exercise has an encouraging side benefit. It is helpful regarding what I have called "the last-quarter problem" or "the lack of cumulative knowledge" problem. As any instructor can attest, there is an almost pervasive loss of nerve among North American students when it comes to the final examination. They seem to feel a psychological need to ask the question, "Is the final cumulative?" To which I have developed a stock answer: "Is knowledge cumulative?" However, I cannot be so unfeeling as to require that students study for every subject covered by the course in an entire semester. Imagine the relief on students' faces when they hear the almost magical words, "It will cover only the material in the last quarter of the semester." Still, they could not measure up in the final exercise without an overarching or cumulative understanding of Africa. So how does the instructor get students to perform? Invariably, I have to build some incentives into the course by assigning points for the final mapping exercise.

Another challenge facing the instructor is that the typical North American student who is embarking on a study of Africa for the first time seems bewildered by the inordinately large number of countries that make up the continent. As instructors, we seek to ease their anxieties by providing a learning experience that makes students sophisticated generalists—able to speak insightfully to African issues and become critical consumers of news about or coming out of Africa rather than experts of specific countries—while cautioning against making overly broad or sweeping generalization about this vast and varied continent. In this case, it may be asked, what is a student to do? I have found that students feel a lot more reassured if they can become reasonably familiar with at least one country, albeit from afar. Again, the best way to bring some of the issues to life is to relate them to concrete or country-specific experiences. Thus I have often coupled concept mapping with an exercise that I call the Adopt-a-Country project.

This exercise is designed to encourage students to participate even more actively in the process of discovery. Each student comes to develop an affinity for his or her adopted country through close and regular monitoring and information gathering using available newspaper and Internet sources on a regular, weekly basis. The student becomes the class or resident expert on the adopted country. In addition to calling on students to relate issues that come up in class to their adopted country's experiences, I make absolutely clear that this exercise is integral to the requirements of the course. A half-hour may be set aside each week to have students brief the class about their findings. The information gathered eventually becomes the basis for a term paper on the adopted country to be submitted at the end of the course.

This project used to be a tougher assignment for students at smaller colleges and universities like my own with limited library holdings of foreign newspapers, journals, and periodicals but has become relatively easier to accomplish thanks to the Internet. The number of Web sites for Africa is growing by leaps and bounds. Students now have access to an increasing number of local newspapers on the Web.

By exchanging ideas about particular countries, all students learn a great deal more about Africa in general and about their own adopted countries in particular. The country-adoption portion of this approach to teaching and learning about Africa provides the fillers that help to enrich and refine the general knowledge that may have existed at the beginning of the course. This portion of the course can be a very empowering experience as well as an effective way to accomplish the objective of giving the course concreteness and grounding. However, I have learned that students do not devote appropriate attention to it unless I assign weight to it in the overall grading scheme.

The concept mapping and country-adoption exercises offer a compelling companion approach to the study of Africa. When juxtaposed, the initial and final mapping exercises should provide a rich source of information and a powerful visual illustration of the intellectual growth of the students in the course. They also pay greater dividend by impelling students to think about knowledge in cumulative as well as interrelational terms.

SUGGESTIONS FOR FURTHER READING AND RESOURCES

PRINTED MATERIAL

Aryeetey-Attoh, Samuel, ed. 1997. *Geography of Sub-Saharan Africa.* Upper Saddle River, N.J.: Prentice-Hall.

Gordon, April A., and Donald L. Gordon, eds. 1996. *Understanding Contemporary Africa,* 2nd ed. Boulder: Lynne Rienner.

Hammond, Dorothy, and Alta Jablow. 1992. *The Africa That Never Was: Four Centuries of British Writing About Africa.* Prospect Heights, Ill.: Waveland Press.

Harden, Blaine. 1990. *Africa: Dispatches from a Fragile Continent.* Boston: Houghton Mifflin.

Khapoya, Vincent B. 1998. *The African Experience,* 2nd ed. Englewood Cliffs, N.J.: Prentice-Hall.

Lamb, David. 1984. *The Africans.* New York: Vintage Books.

Martin, Phyllis M., and Patrick O'Meara, eds. 1986. *Africa,* 2nd ed. Bloomington: Indiana University Press.

Ramsay, F. Jeffres, ed. 1997. *Africa,* 7th ed. Guilford, Conn.: Dushkin.

Ungar, Sanford J. 1986. *Africa: The People and Politics of an Emerging Continent.* New York: Simon & Schuster.

WEB SITES

Africa 2000 Media Group Home Page. http://www.africa2000.com/. A somewhat radical site interspersing fact and opinion, but thought-provoking topics are covered.

Africa Online. http://www.Africaonline.com/. This Java-enabled site focuses mainly on Ghana, Kenya, and Côte d'Ivoire.

Harvard African Studies. http://icg.harvard.edu/~africa/links.html. Another excellent site from Harvard that lists hundreds of links to sites of African interest.

Iafrica.com. http://www.iaccess.za/. A South African site that is commercial in nature but does have interesting information.

Index on Africa. http://www.fellesraadet.africainfo.no/africaindex/index.html. This is an excellent site from Norway that lists links to many different sites grouped by country.

USAID in Africa. http://www.info.usaid.gov/regions/afr/. Official USAID and U.S. government information regarding African countries.

The Washington Post. http://www.washingtonpost.com/wp-srv/inatl/africa.html. Information is somewhat sporadic and sparse, mainly related to headline news in Africa.

18

AFRICAN INTELLECTUALS AND THE RECONCEPTUALIZATION OF AFRICA

PHILIP S. ZACHERNUK

We are not accustomed to the notion of African intellectuals. Intellectuals are most readily associated in North American students' minds with the likes of Freud or Friedan, voices of a literate, "modern" culture. Africans, in contrast, are more typically placed in some ill-defined exotic landscape marked variously by poverty, violence, tribalism, and underdevelopment. When Africans are seen as the producers of modern culture, the readiest connection is to the realms of art, literature, and dance. Even well-known African leaders such as Nelson Mandela are identified as politicians rather than intellectuals. A minority of students more informed about matters African willingly accept that the world or the West might look to Africa to invigorate its arts, and that we should care about Africa's fate, but they also tend to assume that serious ideas flow from us to Africa—that it remains the fate of Africans to learn about modern problems and their solutions from the West.

The course described in this chapter is meant to unsettle some of these ideas. More constructively, it attempts to develop a sense of what African intellectuals think about and why. By looking at a select group of African thinkers who addressed the problems of colonial rule and of Africa's engagement with modern forces, students confront evidence that undermines what they thought they knew. They quickly start to discover not only that African intellectuals exist but that they have a long tradition of reflecting critically on questions in ways that dissolve the presumed gap between Africa and the West.

Students arrive in my classes holding many long-established notions about Africa: that modern empires divided it into the colonizers and the colonized; that the basic result of colonial rule was to destroy and demean African cultures; that Africans can be grouped together as a single community opposed to foreign control. Africanists have long been at pains to stress the resilience of African societies against colonial and postcolonial oppression. More recent scholarship places this cultural productivity in a rather more complex, less Manichaean context.

Imperial power, we now see, was incomplete, negotiated, and often frustrated. The relation of the colonizer to the colonized was marked not only by oppression but also, sometimes, by mimicry, common interests, and shared agendas of modernization. Africans were not only divided among themselves, they also maintained diverse connections beyond colonial circuits, notably within the black Atlantic. All these themes resonate with the spirit of this course. The attraction of a course in African intellectual history, however, is not that it offers a vehicle for preaching about the latest scholarly trends. Rather, by working their way through over a century of African thought, set in its changing contexts, students can use this material to discover why their received notions about modern African culture will not serve. Some kind of more flexible and open-ended approach to the material is required to deal with the intricate contradictions and shifts of meaning they find. Many students are left with the need to examine their assumptions about the African past and to rethink their perceptions about "Africa."

I make clear early on which African intellectuals are the subject of this course and which are not, also that my choice is not the only possible or necessarily best one. We look at Africans writing in European languages about questions that arise from the advent of colonial rule. We do not, thus, tend toward the anthropological study of, say, Mande concepts of justice. We explore a set of writings that are held together by a common set of questions and that also obviously cross-fertilize and develop as something recognizable as a tradition of thought. The material I have chosen seeks answers to such questions as, Who are the Africans? What has colonial rule done to Africa? How can Africa develop? Where should Africans seek inspiration? This focus gives the course some integrity and momentum as it develops, and it makes one of my points easier to make (no doubt at the expense of establishing other points less effectively): A historical community of African intellectuals has developed a tradition of response to problems of our times, and we can learn about it and from it.

These grand ambitions are pursued in a one-term course that is straightforward and accessible to nonspecialist fourth-year students. Some exposure to intellectual history and textual criticism is often adequate preparation; many students have done well with no previous classes in African history. The syllabus is still, of course, undergoing refinement in content as I find better material. In my initial (and only scripted) lecture I try to develop the relevance of African intellectuals in our current postmodern climate.[1] If Western thinkers are now facing the many failures of modernism, colonial subjects have had to face the dark side of modernism for much longer, not least in the forms of racism and imperial subjugation. I also try to lay out some useful tools for our inquiries, stressing the need to undertake intellectual history within concrete contexts. I have used in the past Jean and John Comaroff's (1991) *Of Revelation and Revolution* as an introductory text, asking for a written, critical evaluation. Several of the Comaroffs' concerns serve well to set up the course, especially their discussion of hegemony, their attention to the complexities of an early colonial setting, and their argument about the colonization of consciousness. Students have returned mixed reviews on how useful this text turned out to be in the long run, but in the short term it fits nicely as a place to start.

I try to minimize preliminaries, preferring that students appreciate my meaning by grappling with the rather hefty reader I have compiled. There are a few published readers that anthologize African writing, but they are either too long, too focused on politics alone, or too broad in scope to work for this course. I have instead gathered material from several of these anthologies, adding some more recent article literature. The reader runs in rough chronological order around select themes, beginning with "the Atlantic context," treating mid–nineteenth-century ideas about Africa in Europe and especially African America. This section involves some explicit and obnoxious racist literature, which is sometimes difficult to discuss, but secondhand descriptions are inadequate to convey the extremity and power of these ideas. The balance of the course examines different writers or groups of writers in context, ranging from early elites in West and South Africa to Pan-Africans of the early twentieth century in Africa and America, the exponents and critics of Negritude, feminist nationalists of the World War II era, African socialists of the independence era, critics of postcolonial society, the Black Consciousness movement, and finally current assessments of the achievements and the agenda of African intellectuals. The scope of texts shows how this intellectual tradition involves the black Atlantic as well as Europe, although Africans occupy their own places within the wider discourse on Africa.

My specific choice of authors and themes has been governed in part by available material and will probably never be either final or fully satisfactory. I have long since forsworn the idea of a comprehensive or even fully representative selection; I consider it more important to find material that both interests students and connects in interesting ways with other readings. In the latest version of the course, my list of intellectual figures included Africanus Horton, Edward W. Blyden, D.D.T. Jabavu, and Pixley Seme (early elites); W.E.B. Du Bois, J. E. Casely Hayford, and Marcus Garvey (early Pan-Africanists); Leopold Senghor (Negritude); Funmilayo

Ransome-Kuti and Constance Cummings-John (women nationalists); Julius Nyerere, Kwame Nkrumah and Ayi Kwei Armah (African socialism); Frantz Fanon and Amilcar Cabral (radical critics); Steve Biko (Black Consciousness); Ngugi wa Thiong'o, Kwame Appiah, and Abiola Irele (contemporary critics).[2]

In each section, secondary treatments of the relevant historical period furnish the all-important sense of context. Often the secondary selections are biographies of the writer in question. Where the writer is not dealt with extensively, short biographies, from various historical dictionaries of Africa generally or of individual African states, are useful. Much of this secondary literature itself forms part of the story, as we sometimes use contemporary champions of, say, Fanon to set his context or nationalist historians of the 1960s to detail the lives of early elites. Students are thus obliged to develop a doubled sense of the primary tradition within the various phases of Africanist scholarship. In the contemporary period, these strands come together.

The format within the classroom is simple and sometimes a bit awkward to animate in the early weeks, but over the course of the term it gathers a certain momentum of its own. The basic idea is that students learn the material by talking about it in structured discussions. The students are divided into groups; with classes of twenty to twenty-five I have formed five groups. Two groups are assigned for each reading, although all members are expected to arrive with the material digested. I do not encourage group presentations. Groups allow me to adjust to changing enrollments and also allow students some flexibility in their schedules (as each group decides within itself which member will do what when). I also use the groups to organize smaller discussions or debating teams within the class. Presentations, however, are done by individuals. A member of the first group is responsible for presenting a precis of the specified article, to remind his or her classmates what the reading was about, and encouraging an in-depth understanding of the reading. Making clear the difference between a precis and a summary or description takes some time and effort; I usually provide a model precis of the first one or two texts and point out where early presentations fall into the latter modes until the point is made. The responsibility of the presenter from the second group changes over time. In the early weeks, the task is to criticize the precis offered by the first group, filling in the gaps or making the points that were missed. This works well to hone the precis writing, as students vie to go uncorrected. Once this idea settles in, the second group's assignment shifts to supplying questions, observations, or discussion starters based on the readings. This is a wide-open assignment, inviting students to compare that week's material or to look back at previous material to find emergent themes. I also supply questions in the syllabus to suggest some lines of inquiry, although I try to avoid dominating the agenda. Students welcome these guides early on; as momentum builds, discussions are more directly shaped by student input.

This structure of presentation, criticism, and discussion is essential to the course. It is through this process that students discover, and indeed often begin to empathize with, the dilemmas and problems of African intellectuals. They begin to see why certain kinds of positions were offered at certain times and how circumstances and contemporary ideas limited possibilities. The sessions on Negritude illustrate this well. The core materials are two essays by Leopold Senghor, set in context by an excerpt from Janet Vaillant's biography of him and Abiola Irele's essay "What Is Negritude?" These are augmented by Ezekiel Mphahlele's critical "Negritude Revisited."[3] Initially, students are either attracted to Negritude because of a prior attraction to Afrocentrist ideas or find it laughably obsolete. But when discussions oblige students to put these ideas in the context of imperial ideas about race and Pan-African agendas, appreciations change. Negritude, we remember, was born in the decades before World War II, when culture and race were still seen as closely linked. Other readings on Pan-African appeals, and the nineteenth-century works of Edward Blyden, serve to remind students of how normal assumptions of racial solidarity once were. The idea of an essential African aesthetic bond emerges as a powerful idea for its time (among, at least, colonial elites), an effective inversion of imperial European denigrations of African accomplishment that nonetheless draws support from other Europeans' appreciation of African arts. As students understand this process of inversion, we move on to consider Senghor's slightly later argument that Negritude represents an "antiracial racialism" and an element of an emergent universal "humanism." This draws out consideration of how and why such constructions of black against white can become obsolete, or at least open to question, as they clearly have among postmodernists. This new appreciation of the power and appeal of Negritude also often leads toward more open and informed discussion of contemporary Afrocentrist appeals. Others might like to build on this with a section on Afrocentrism incorporating, perhaps, works by Cheikh Anta Diop and Molefi Asante.

At the very least, this course leaves students much more adept at presenting and discussing texts and ideas because it involves little else. But the course content tends to have a more profound effect. The broad flow of topics brings students to compare different definitions of Africa around the Atlantic across a century. Divergent Pan-African agendas, the differential appeal of Negritude, the conflict between nationalist leaders and their putative compatriots organized as women or labor unions—these episodes taken together effectively highlight that definitions of Africa and Africans have never been settled or uncontested. Students leave the course unable to use or hear these words without pausing to think: Whose Africa? Which

Africa? Tracing Africans' discourse about this idea also leaves them sharply aware that a long line of intellectuals within Africa have something to say about how they might answer such questions.

NOTES

1. Useful places to draw inspiration on this connection include Fred Cooper and Ann Laura Stoler, *Tensions of Empire* (Los Angeles: University of California Press, 1997); Patrick Williams and Laura Chrisman, "Colonial Discourse and Post-Colonial Theory: An Introduction," in *Colonial Discourse and Post-Colonial Theory: A Reader,* ed. P. Williams and L. Chrisman (New York: Columbia University Press, 1994); Kwame Anthony Appiah, *In My Father's House* (New York: Oxford University Press, 1992).

2. These references for my primary texts should point toward some useful sources and give a sense of readings that work for length and theme: Africanus Horton, "West African Countries and Peoples" (1868), in *Black Nationalism in Africa 1867,* ed. Davidson Nicol (New York: Africana, 1969), 17–41; Edward W. Blyden, "Christianity, Islam, and the Negro Race" (1888), in Mutiso and Rohio (1975: 260–283); D.D.T. Jabavu, "Native Unrest," and Pixley ka Isaka Seme "The Regeneration of Africa," in *From Protest to Challenge: A Documentary History of African Politics in South Africa 1882–1964,* vol. 1, ed. T. Karis and G. M. Carter (Stanford: Hoover Institution Press, 1972), 69–71, 118–125; Casely Hayford, *Ethiopia Unbound* (1911; repr. London: Cass, 1969), 161–197; W.E.B. Du Bois, "Africa," "Reconstruction of Africa," "Not 'Separatism,'" "The Pan-African Congress," "My Mission," "Manifesto of the Second Pan-African Congress," "Pan-Africa and the New Racial Philosophy," in *The Seventh Son: The Thought and Writings of W.E.B. Du Bois, Vol. II,* ed. Julius Lester (New York: Random House, 1971), 187–209; Marcus Garvey, "Africa for the Africans," and "The Future as I See It," selections in *Voices from the Harlem Renaissance,* ed. Nathan Huggins (New York: Oxford University Press, 1976), 35–41; Funmilayo Ransome-Kuti, "The Status of Women in Nigeria," *Journal of Human Relations* 10 (1961): 67–72; LaRay Denzer, "Constance A. Cummings-John of Sierra Leone," *Tarikh* 7 (1981): 20–32; Leopold Senghor, *On African Socialism,* trans. Mercer Cook (New York: Praeger, 1964), 67–84, 92–103; Kwame Nkrumah, "Some Aspects of Socialism in Africa," in *African Socialism,* ed. W. H. Friedland and C. G. Rosberg (Stanford: Stanford University Press, 1964), 259–263; Kwame Nkrumah, "African Socialism Revisited," in Cartey and Kilson (1970: 200–208); Julius Nyerere, "Ujamaa: The Basis of African Socialism," in *Africa's Freedom,* ed. Nyerere et al. (London: Unwin, 1964), 67–77; Ayi Kwei Armah, "African Socialism: Utopian or Scientific?" *Presence Africaine* 64 (1967): 6–30; Amilcar Cabral, "National Liberation and Culture," in Langley (1979: 703–721); Frantz Fanon, *The Wretched of the Earth,* trans. C. Farrington (New York: Grove Press, 1968), 206–248; Steve Biko, "Black Consciousness and the Quest for a True Humanity," in *Steve Biko: I Write What I Like,* ed. A. Stubbs (New York: Harper Row, 1978), 87–98; Ngugi wa Thiong'o, *Moving the Centre: The Struggle for Colonial Freedoms* (London: James Currey, 1993), 60–75; Appiah, *In My Father's House,* 3–27, 173–180 (see also note 1).

3. Leopold Senghor, "What Is Negritude?" in Mutiso and Rohio (1975: 83–84); Leopold Senghor, "Negritude: A Humanism of the 20th Century," in Cartey

and Kilson (1970: 179–192); J. G. Vaillant, *Black, French, and African: A Life of Leopold Sedar Senghor* (Cambridge: Harvard University Press, 1990), 87–116; Abiola Irele, "What Is Negritude," in *The African Experience in Literature and Ideology* (Bloomington: Indiana University Press, 1990), 67–88; Ezekiel Mphahlele, "Negritude Revisited," in *The African Image* (London: Faber and Faber, 1974), 67–95.

SUGGESTIONS FOR
FURTHER READING AND RESOURCES

Asante, Molefi, and Abu S. Abarry, eds. 1996. *African Intellectual Heritage.* Philadelphia: Temple University Press.

Cartey, Wilfred, and Martin Kilson, eds. 1970. *The African Reader: Independent Africa.* New York: Vintage.

Comaroff, Jean, and John Comaroff. 1991. *Of Revelation and Revolution: Christianity, Colonialism, and Consciousness in South Africa,* vol. 1. Chicago: University of Chicago Press.

Langley, J. A., ed. 1979. *Ideologies of Liberation in Black Africa.* London: Rex Collings.

Mutiso, Gideon-Cyrus M., and S. W. Rohio, eds. 1975. *Readings in African Political Thought.* London: Heinemann.

19

"THE COUNTRY OF AFRICA": KEEPING THE AFRICAN SURVEY COURSE LIVELY AND INTERESTING

MISTY L. BASTIAN

After a decade of lecturing in an Africa survey course program (that of the University of Chicago, described by Ralph Austen in Chapter 16) and on my own as a liberal arts faculty member, I have seen very little change in college students' general knowledge of the continent, particularly when this is their first course on Africa. That is, most North American undergraduates seem to know very little about the continent and only a few of them evince any real curiosity about Africa. Indeed, our students often consider the continent to be what one of my most memorable undergraduate writers once described as "the country of Africa, where wild animals live, along with some people." This youthful vision of Africa as a single country, the natural home of wild animals—where people live almost at the sufferance of other mammals—comes to our students from a number of sources, most of which African and Africanist scholars find doubtful, to say the least.

I am not suggesting here that the culture that has provided me with students has been unchanged in the decade between 1986 and 1997, however. When I began teaching at the University of Chicago, students would point to *National Geographic* or to remembered episodes of the television nature program *Wild Kingdom* as the wellsprings of their knowledge about Africa. Today my undergraduate students admit to the influence of the Discovery channel over *Wild Kingdom,* and *The Lion King*'s cartoon and zoomorphic representation of African life seems to have taken the place of *National Geographic*'s exotic bodies and photographed scenery—displacing along with them the differently cartoonish and zoomorphic Tarzan films that members of my own generation watched on Saturday afternoons. Africa as a thriving, ethnically variable, culturally sophisticated, and enormous region thus remains largely "undiscovered" for North American undergraduates, and the shallow quality of their knowledge means that teachers of university-level survey courses about Africa generally have to begin with very basic material and can only infrequently hope to instruct as they might wish.

The purpose of this short chapter is to suggest some ways that my fellow academic laborers in the vineyard can keep their obligatory survey courses fresh—since, as we all know, the bored lecturer rarely takes any pleasure in his or her work or gives any sense of excitement about the material to the students temporarily under his or her care. To this purpose, I will talk about a small number of exercises and other activities that I have worked into my own Africa survey, along with some general suggestions for maintaining a fresh perspective on the continent—both for the sake of our students, who can so easily be frightened away from what they already only hesitantly approach, and for our sake as active scholars who would like to bring the new and cutting-edge material into our classes that we read and think about for our own research and learning agendas. The basic point, of course, is that we should model "lifelong learning" for our students, whatever we teach, and that is better modeled when we are actually engaged in the process. The survey course, one of our regionalist staples, can be an excellent forum—with a little patience and a certain amount of preparation—for exposing both the undergraduate student and ourselves to current academic approaches to Africa.

CHALLENGING STUDENTS
TO READ AND WRITE ABOUT AFRICA

Having heard my academic colleagues of all disciplines decry the fact that our students no longer enjoy reading—and, sometimes, suggest that students no longer know how to read—I determined to use ethnographic and literary texts extensively in the survey. Many wonderful books have been written by Africans and Africanists about African societies, and our students lose an important avenue into understanding continental issues when they are discouraged from reading about them in a scholarly fashion. Students' unconscious prejudices against Africa are also confirmed when African questions are not raised in the authoritative voice that most Westerners associate with books and "book knowledge." Although my students frequently complain about the number and complexity of the readings they find on my survey syllabi, they do not leave the survey course under the impression that African or Africanist scholarly work is shoddy or second-rate. This sentiment may not be the most popular one expressed in this volume, but by dealing with challenging texts and difficult authors, students can better learn to respect the cultures that produced such works—or the cultures that inspired them.

It is especially important to bring texts by African authors to the notice of our students—and not only literary texts. I teach the survey as a 200-level anthropology course, and both my students and I are fortunate to have available so many excellent ethnographies written by African anthropologists. For example, I use Ifi Amadiume's (1987) *Male Daughters, Female Husbands* and David Iyam's (1995) *The Broken Hoe* to illustrate gender and political-economic transformations in southeastern Nigeria during the past century. Both contain significant information on past agricultural production and present commodity trade, as well as clear case studies of transformations in junior-senior and male-female relations. For students, an early introduction not only to African scholarship but, in the case of Amadiume, to female African scholarship is salutory and prepares them for a picture of the continent that is not based solely on "traditions," village life, and below-subsistence economics.

Still in Nigeria, Olutunde Lawuyi's (1997) excellent article on Yoruba taxi drivers and their sloganeering is now widely available—along with a number of other important pieces on African popular culture, several by African scholars—in Barber (1997). Material on urban-based popular culture tends to be very effective in shaking up student preconceptions, partially because it calls forth familiar referents: dance music, media, fashion as well as other forms of commodity consumption, sexuality, and all aspects of "modern" technology. (See Masquelier's Chapter 4, this volume, on ways to integrate popular music into the African studies classroom.) Although his work is particularly difficult, I sometimes use Achille Mbembe's shorter pieces (notably Mbembe and Roitman 1995 and Mbembe 1997) to invoke the movement of urban West African life. If set alongside a film like *Quartier Mozart* (Bekolo 1992), even this most postmodern of African political theorists can make a good deal of sense to students already surprised to learn that Cameroon has skyscrapers—or, at least, according to Mbembe and Roitman (1995: 333), the outward facades of such buildings.

To sweeten the substantive reading even further, I might bring into class articles from Nigeria's sensationalist press, giving students a glimpse into what African people their own age are reading and talking about as well as watching and listening to. Although local African newspapers may not be readily available to every teacher of the survey, it is possible to find magazines and tabloids printed for an African immigrant audience in North

America and Europe. Most major urban centers have magazine shops that feature these newspapers and magazines. At least one of the magazines, *USAfrica*, has a Web site as well (http://www.usafricaonline.com/). These examples of print and virtual media represent African people as transnational actors and as professionals in a world that our students know well. They also offer an interesting way for students to reconsider the news they watch on their television sets and (perhaps) read in the so-called mainstream press.

Of course, students must also write as well as read, and working through related sets of readings makes the development of synthetic essays easier. (See the appendix to this chapter for a sample of essay questions.) I tend to approach every survey course with a larger theme in mind and set readings in relation to that theme. For example, in past years I have based whole courses on ethnographies and novels that explore gender relations around the continent, materials that take a critical look at African political economies, or scholarly works dealing with arts and aesthetics in three societies in West Africa. Other themes that I intend to work into future survey courses include African conceptions of youth and aging, mythologies and religious practice, and various African societies' ideas about personhood. (Clearly, these themes are ones that interest me professionally and personally. The reader should develop his or her own set of general themes for the survey if this approach seems useful.)

These themes are broad enough that many current monographs as well as many works of fiction can fit into them, and students can be engaged by connections between readings or films and their own, large questions about human existence. Although I always give students a choice of essay topics for each section of the survey, including ones that require only an engagement with the assigned texts, I make a point of putting in at least one topic per section that allows students to compare their own experiences with those of their African counterparts. These topics are both popular and useful for integrating North American experience into a larger, global frame— surely one of the desired ends for any "non Western" course.

SEEING AND BEING IS BELIEVING: FILM AND ROLE PLAYING IN THE SURVEY

Beyond the required and supplementary texts I assign for the survey, I also make sure that students receive visual and aural information on Africa. The best images available, in my opinion, are those generated by African filmmakers and other media specialists. I have already mentioned Bekolo's *Quartier Mozart* (1992) as one of the films I use in the survey, but I would more generally suggest that African studies teachers familiarize themselves with many of the available African feature-length films and begin to show them to and discuss them with their classes. (California Newsreel is the premier purveyor of these films for classroom teaching in North America, and most, but not all, of the films I mention are available for rental or purchase from this company.)

Since North American students tend to live in an extremely image-oriented culture, their viewing of sophisticated representations of African life, made by African actors and directors, can again have a positive impact on how they begin to reconstruct their vision of the continent. Next to making a trip to the continent or African home-stays (which I advocate but realize most of our students will not experience during their tenure with us), what students see and hear of the continent can make the strongest impression on them.

For example, in Souleymane Cissé's 1987 film *Yeelen* (Brightness), students can listen to Bambara being spoken while they also see Mande material culture and the microenvironments of Mali; they are also required to follow a coming-of-age narrative that relates to local understandings of magic, proper forms of sexuality, and myth. In *La vie est belle (Life is rosy)*, a Zairian film directed by Benoît Lamy (1987), the class can consider how a popular musical form came to dominate Kinshasa's social and cultural life as well as what the quest for money and luxuries requires of African urbanites in the late twentieth century. The many films of Ousmane Sembène, unfortunately rather more difficult to obtain for classroom viewing than others previously mentioned, can help direct survey students to issues such as class formation on the continent, gender, and specific incidents in West African history. A film like *Udju azu di Yonta* (The blue eyes of Yonta) (Gomes 1991), the revolutionary *Sambizanga* (Maldoror 1972), or *These Hands* (M'mbugu-Schelling 1992) can demonstrate the power of African women's presence behind—and in front of—a camera as well as move students to discuss disparities between elites (whether colonial or local) and ordinary Africans, liberation struggles and their aftermaths, and the dignity of women's labor under difficult circumstances. I would also suggest Ngozi Onwurah's beautiful documentary *Monday's Girls* (1993) for anyone looking to discuss gender, initiation, and contemporary African life in his or her survey.

For teachers who would like to know more about the social and artistic contexts of African filmmaking, Ukadike's *Black African Cinema* (1994) is, in my opinion, the most lucid and interesting monograph available. Ukadike's text is probably not appropriate for most undergraduate teaching—unless the class focuses specifically on African film—but offers very useful background for the Africanist scholar who wishes to bring these films knowledgeably into his or her classroom setting and, indeed, into his or her research.

Besides film and the use of music in the survey, I have also experimented with various role-playing exercises in an attempt to break down the division that North American students often make between the African "other" and themselves. Some of these exercises have been more successful than others, for various reasons. I will discuss only one such role-playing exercise here. It was both successful and troubling. For that reason, it makes an interesting example for other teachers not only to emulate but also as an inspiration for (and cautionary tale about) freshening materials already present on Africa survey syllabi.

In the fall semester of 1995, I decided to invent a role-playing exercise for the Africa survey, based on a text I had previously taught very successfully and enjoyed discussing with my classes, Cohen and Odhiambo's (1992) *Burying SM: The Politics of Knowledge and the Sociology of Power in Africa.* For those unfamiliar with this work, Cohen and Odhiambo offer a view of competing discourses around the burial and, indeed, the life of S. M. Otieno, an important figure in Kenyan legal circles. Because a number of perspectives about the funeral and the deposition of Otieno's corpse are represented in the monograph and because the book revolves around a legal battle, I thought it would be exciting and instructive for my students to re-create the courtroom scenes when Otieno's widow, Virginia Wambui Waiyaki Otieno, and his patriclan, Umira Kager, disputed publicly about who had jurisdiction over the body and its burial. This case brought forward issues of gender; "traditional" versus "modern" notions of the person and the person's biography; and the position of the African state in what might originally appear to be highly individualistic, local disputes. As these were themes that resonated more generally with my major themes for the semester—political economy and social transformation—an exercise on *Burying SM* seemed to give students the best possible context for embodying and displaying their newfound knowledge about the continent.

The students were randomly selected to be part of one of three groups: Umira Kager (meant to represent rural, patriclan interests), what I called "the supporters of Wambui" (who were meant to represent the urban, progressivist elements in the dispute), and the *Raia,* or "ordinary Kenyans," who took varying positions during the trial. One student was randomly selected to act as the judge, and two others were selected by the students to act as the legal counsel for the mock trial.

On our first day of this group work, I was asked by a small group of students if they could opt out of their respective groups and constitute themselves as a jury for the trial. This seemed a reasonable request, so I gave them a new assignment—to take careful note of the groups' preparations and to decide, by the trial's end, on a winner from the evidence presented in class. I was also asked by each group if its members could "elect" certain people to represent important players in *Burying SM*—notably clan elders, Wambui herself, and key witnesses from among *Raia.* Again, this seemed reasonable, and the groups began to coalesce around these pivotal figures. Interestingly, my relatively diverse class began to split along ethnic lines as it considered the roles available within our emerging legal drama: The lawyers were all Euro-American, the primary roles within Umira Kager were taken up by African American men with its "silent majority" Euro-American, *Raia* chose all of its witnesses from among the Euro-American participants, the jury seemed to be run by an African American woman who rarely spoke in class, and Wambui was impersonated by a young Ghanaian woman who had already shown herself to be a class leader in other contexts.

As an anthropologist, I am always engaged by group formation and dynamics, but I did not really consider how what was going on in my classroom was taking on the characteristics of what was occurring outside of it. I was too interested in how students would represent a set of African dilemmas about modernity and "tradition" to notice, right away, that they were engaged in developing another subtext altogether. This was, as I mentioned before, fall 1995—and a highly publicized trial, with racial overtones, was drawing to its conclusion in Los Angeles, California. Of course, I was very aware of how the O. J. Simpson murder trial was being represented to various constituencies around the United States, and my very notion of putting on a mock trial probably came out of the juridical atmosphere of the moment. (Most teachers will use whatever has recently attracted student interest to illustrate points from their assigned texts. I consider this a useful teaching mode.)

However, what I did not expect was that my students would read into Wambui and Umira Kager's story an internal narrative that reflected their own ambivalences toward race and the state in the United States—and would attempt to enact those ambivalences cathartically in my African survey classroom. This, in fact, was what happened when we went past the research phase, where students developed their cases from both *Burying SM* and Cohen and Odihambo's Luo ethnography *Siaya* (1989), and into the mock trial itself.

The trial was meant to take one class period, but the students had been so thorough in their research and so passionate in their presentation that only Umira Kager had an opportunity to present its case during the first class. *Raia* participants were a very noticeable presence during this phase of the trial—disrupting the proceedings again and again to comment on and criticize what was happening. The jury remained largely silent but watchful. The next class period fell, astonishingly, on the very day that the Simpson jury handed down its verdict, and all my students entered the classroom in various stages of surprise or jubilation. As soon as the supporters of Wambui began to present their case, I could see that, in some way, Wambui stood for members of the class as a figure unjustly deprived of all her rights, not allowed to mourn her husband properly, pressured by the state to give up her freedom to satisfy the retrograde forces of Umira Kager. Even Umira Kager, with the exception of its lawyers, seemed to lean toward the woman representing Wambui during her testimony. All the lawyers, including Wambui's, became the target of *Raia*'s distaste. At the end of the testimony, the jury deliberated for ten minutes and announced its verdict: Wambui could do, in our classroom, what she was not allowed to do in Kenya—bury her husband on their communal property.

In retrospect, the SM trial exercise enabled the students to "talk" about racial categories in a disguised fashion. Some Euro-American students came up to me after class to complain that the trial had not been done "properly"; the wrong person had won. They blamed the jury, which they said was biased in Wambui's favor all along. (This small but vocal group included students assigned to the supporters of the Wambui group, by the way.) Some of my African American and African students, including members of the Umira Kager group, were equally verbal and self-congratulatory about the trial. At the time I was disappointed, feeling that the African issues I was most interested in had been hijacked by North American current events and used by my students only as a mirror for themselves—much as Africa has been used by the West time and again. However, as the class progressed after this relatively early event, I noticed that some of the tensions I expected in the class were diffused. People worked together, not always harmoniously but productively, on topics raised by the survey material. And we were even able, on the last day of class, to discuss frankly a racial incident on campus that had caused some of the African American students great pain. Several students told me afterward they had wanted to talk about the incident earlier but had not had enough class time to do so.

The Africa survey course in North America can never be completely free of the problematic history of racial categories. Just as we try to contextualize the continent's historical and social diversity to help our students envision an Africa that is not a monolithic "country" filled with wild animals, we also have to remember how difficult it is for them to remove the cultural lenses with which they look at the material we present. My class's experience of "Nairobi, California," is a very useful reminder of how powerful our own cultural lives are, and how encompassing. Perhaps the best we can do is make students a little more aware of the world outside their own society rather than try to force the survey to do too much for too many. It is possible that students from that survey course will always think of Wambui as a female O. J. Simpson, but the fact that they remember something about an African struggle over identity and rights in the face of state intervention is meaningful in their broader education. The survey is still a powerful tool and one that we should treat carefully and respectfully as teachers at the university level. It can repay us, and not only with students who know where Nelson Mandela lives or a chance to read new material in our academic disciplines but also with insights into our own societies and the meaningful struggles of our students and ourselves over our own identities and concerns.

APPENDIX A: SAMPLE ESSAY
QUESTIONS FOR PAST SURVEY COURSES

- In all three of the texts covered in this part of the course—Deng's *The Cry of the Owl,* Amadiume's *Male Daughters, Female Husbands,* and Nwapa's *Efuru*—experiences of spirituality are shown to be important—even central—to African peoples' everyday existence. Using material from at least two of the texts, discuss some aspect of this spirituality (e.g., ancestorhood, connection with certain deities) and show how it impinges on Dinka and/or Igbo people's daily lives.
- Clearly, when we think about who "makes art" in Mande, we first think of the *nyamakalaw.* What is the nature of the art that *nyamakalaw* make? For this question, you should discuss what types of implements and artifacts can be characterized as art in these societies. This means that you also have to discuss Mande aesthetics—the criteria by which Mande people construct things as artful and beautiful. (Example: Is usefulness part of Mande aesthetics? How do you know?) Use specific examples from all the works we read/saw/heard/talked about for this section of the course—which means you should be able to talk about songs, pottery, and even fishnets as well as blacksmithing and Komo masks; you might refer to sorcery or even bodily transformations as art forms (but be sure to say why they could be considered such). Finally, you should also think about whether the work of *horon* can be characterized as art in terms of Mande aesthetics. Why or why not?
- The Sundiata epic, Soyinka's autobiographical *Aké,* and Beyala's novel *Loukoum* have one obvious commonality: the main character of each is a young man engaged in an attempt to discover more about society and his own place in it. Using these three works as the base for your essay, consider how these young men learn about a number of important, even universal, topics: notably power, sexuality, and mortality. Are there experiences here that you feel are strictly West African? Are there other experiences that anyone in the West could relate to? What is the difference between these types of experience? Which two young men would have the most to say to each other, do you think? Why? Give very specific, textual examples for this essay. (Hint: a really excellent essay will probably also deal, if only peripherally, with the films *Yeleen* and *Quartier Mozart.*)

SUGGESTIONS FOR
FURTHER READING AND RESOURCES

PRINTED MATERIAL AND FILMS

Amadiume, Ifi. 1987. *Male Daughters, Female Husbands: Gender and Sex in an African Society.* London: Zed Books.
Barber, Karin, ed. 1997. *Readings in African Popular Culture.* Bloomington: Indiana University Press.

Bekolo, Jean-Pierre (Cameroon). 1992. *Quartier Mozart*. In French with English subtitles. San Francisco: California Newsreel.

Beyala, Calixtha. 1995. *Loukoum: The "Little Prince" of Belleville*. London: Heinemann.

Cissé, Souleymane (Mali). 1987. *Yeelen* (Brightness). In Bambara with English subtitles. San Francisco: California Newsreel.

Cohen, David William, and E. S. Atieno Odhiambo. 1989. *Siaya: The Historical Anthropology of an African Landscape*. Athens: Ohio University Press.

———. 1992. *Burying SM: The Politics of Knowledge and the Sociology of Power in Africa*. Portsmouth, N.H.: Heinemann.

Gomes, Flora (Guinea-Bissau). 1991. *Udju azu di Yonta* (The blue eyes of Yonta). In Criolo with English subtitles. San Francisco: California Newsreel.

Iyam, David Uru. 1995. *The Broken Hoe: Cultural Reconfiguration in Biase Southeast Nigeria*. Chicago: University of Chicago Press.

Lamy, Benoît (Zaire). 1987. *La vie est belle* (Life is rosy). In French and Lingala with English subtitles. San Francisco: California Newsreel.

Lawuyi, Olatunde Bayo. 1997. "The World of the Yoruba Taxi Driver: An Interpretative Analysis." In *Readings in African Popular Culture*, ed. Karin Barber. Bloomington: Indiana University Press.

Maldoror, Sarah (Angola/Guadaloupe). 1972. *Sambizanga*. In Portuguese and local languages with English subtitles.

Mbembe, Achille. 1997. "The 'Thing' and Its Doubles in Cameroonian Cartoons." In *Readings in African Popular Culture*, ed. Karin Barber. Bloomington: Indiana University Press.

Mbembe, Achille, and Janet Roitman. 1995. "Figures of the Subject in Times of Crisis." *Public Culture* 7, 2: 323–352.

M'mbugu-Schelling, Flora (Tanzania). 1992. *These Hands*. In Swahili and Kimakonde with English subtitles. San Francisco: California Newsreel.

Niane, D. T. 1965. *Sundiata: An Epic of Old Mali*. London: Longman.

Onwurah, Ngozi (Nigeria/U.K.). 1993. *Monday's Girls*. In Waikiriki and Nigerian English with English subtitles. San Francisco: California Newsreel.

Soyinka, 'Wole. 1989. *Aké: Years of Childhood*. New York: Harper Collins.

Ukadike, Nwachukwu Frank. 1994. *Black African Cinema*. Berkeley: University of California Press.

About the Contributors

Ralph A. Austen is professor of African history, cochair of the Committee on African and African American Studies, and chair of the Committee on International Relations at the University of Chicago. He is the author or editor of *African Economic History* (1987); *In Search of Sunjata: The Mande Epic as History, Literature, and Performance* (1998); and (with Jonathan Derrick) *Middlemen of the Cameroon Rivers: The Duala and Their Hinterland, ca. 1600–ca. 1960* (1988).

Misty L. Bastian is assistant professor of anthropology at Franklin and Marshall College. She has published extensively on gender, popular culture and the media, religious practice, fashion, and the "predatory state" in Nigeria. She is currently a senior fellow at the Harvard Center for the Study of World Religions and an AAUW American Fellow (1998–1999).

Bill Bravman teaches African history at the University of Maryland, College Park, where he has codeveloped a course in the fundamentals of reading, writing, analysis, and research design for new majors. He is the author of *Making Ethnic Ways: Communities and Their Transformations in Taita, Kenya, c. 1800–1950* (1998).

Cyril Kofie Daddieh is director of black studies and associate professor of political science at Providence College in Rhode Island. He is coeditor of and contributor to the forthcoming *State Building and Democratization in Africa* and author of numerous articles.

229

Dickson Eyoh is associate professor of political science and African studies and director of the African Studies Program, University of Toronto. He is most concerned with African and Africanist discourses on development and culture, identity, and nation-state construction in Africa. He has published in specialist journals such as *Research in African Literature, African Studies Review,* and *Journal of Contemporary African Studies.*

Tamara Giles-Vernick is assistant professor of history at the University of Virginia. She is currently working on a book on the Mpiemu people entitled *Vines of the Past: Environmental and Cultural History of the Sangha Basin of Equatorial Africa.* She has published articles in *Ethnohistory* (American Society of Ethnohistory prize for best article in the field, 1997) and *Environmental History.*

Rosalind I. J. Hackett is the Lindsay Young professor of the humanities at the University of Tennessee, Knoxville. She teaches in the Department of Religious Studies and is also an adjunct in the Department of Anthropology. She has published numerous articles and three books on different aspects of religion in Africa. She is currently working on "Nigeria: Religion in the Balance" for the U.S. Institute of Peace.

Elizabeth Isichei is professor of religious studies at the University of Otago, New Zealand. She taught in African universities for sixteen years and has published many books and articles on Africa. Her most recent books are *A History of Christianity in Africa* (1995) and *A History of African Societies to 1870* (1997). She was awarded a D. Litt (Canterbury, NZ) for her writings on Africa and is a fellow of the Royal Society of New Zealand.

Curtis A. Keim teaches African history and politics at Moravian College, Bethlehem, Pennsylvania. His research focuses on central Africa, especially the precolonial societies of northeastern Congo and the impact of colonialism on those societies. He is also interested in the way that Westerners have viewed Africa over the past two centuries.

Corinne A. Kratz teaches African studies and anthropology at Emory University. Her work concerns performance theory and analysis, ritual, the cultural politics of ethnic identity and gender relations, marriage arrangements, and the politics of representation in museums and other sites of cultural display. She relates these diverse topics through a culture and communication framework. Her primary research has been in Kenya.

Jack Livingston is a Ph.D. candidate in geography at the University of Kansas. His dissertaion concerns the political ecology of conservation policy in the British colonial West Indies. He has taught introductory physical geography and human geography at the University of Kansas and Emporia State University.

Sandra J. MacLean is a research fellow at the Center for Foreign Policy Studies and assistant professor in the International Development Studies Program at Dalhousie University. Her research interests include civil society and NGOs, democratization, "new" security issues, and the "new" regionalism. She has published on these topics in the *Canadian Journal of Development Studies, New Political Economy,* and the *Journal of Contemporary African Studies.*

Adeline Masquelier is assistant professor of anthropology at Tulane University. Her current focus is on reformist Islam in Niger and France. She has published several articles on spirit possession in academic journals and has also contributed essays on healing, clothing, and Islamic identities to edited books. Her interests include medicine, gender, commodization, and ritual processes in the postcolonial world. She is currently finishing a book on *bori.*

Garth Myers is an assistant professor at the University of Kansas with a joint appointment in the Departments of Geography and African/African-American Studies. His research focus is on the political, cultural, and historical geography of development in eastern Africa. Myers's teaching interests include the human and physical geography of Africa, the geography of African development, introductory human geography, social theory in geograpy, and colonialism in Africa.

Katherine Orr is assistant director of the Center for Foreign Policy Studies at Dalhousie University and teaches in the Political Science and International Development Studies programs. She has published on peacebuilding in Bosnia (*International Insights,* 1997) and peacebuilding and African organizations (with Timothy Shaw and Sandra MacLean) in Klass van Walraven (ed.), *African Organisations and Peace-building* (1998).

Jane L. Parpart is professor of history, international development studies, and women's studies at Dalhousie University. She has published extensively on women, the state, class, and development in Africa and the third world. Her most recent edited collections are, with Marianne Marchand, *Feminism/Postmodernism/Development* (1995) and, with Marysia Zalewski, *The "Man" Question in International Relations* (1998).

Benjamin C. Ray is professor of religious studies and holder of the Daniels Family NEH distinguished teaching professorship at Dartmouth College. He has published an introductory textbook, *African Religions: Ritual, Symbol, and Community* (1976) and a research monograph, *Myth, Ritual, and Kingship in Buganda* (1991). For the past several years he has curated a number of exhibitions of African art for the Bayly Museum at the University of Virginia.

L. Natalie Sandomirsky is professor of foreign languages and African area studies at Southern Connecticut State University, New Haven. She teaches French language and literature, and western and central African literature courses. She is working on language issues in West Africa, regarding both literary works and education, beginning in the 1970s with Ahmadou Kourouma's fiction. She is also studying the new South African models for language problems and education.

Timothy M. Shaw is professor of political science and international development studies and director of the Center for Foreign Policy Studies at Dalhousie University. He is the editor of the International Political Economy series at Macmillan. He has published extensively on African foreign policy, international political economy, international development, as well as NGOs and civil society, and more recently on new security issues and peacebuilding in Africa.

Sarah Signiski is completing a master's degree in geography at the University of Kansas with a focus on remote sensing applications.

Aimee Stewart is an MA student in geography at the University of Kansas. She is focusing on remote sensing.

Kearsley Stewart teaches in anthropology and women's studies at the University of Georgia. She is carrying out Ph.D. research (for the University of Florida) on adolescent sexuality and HIV/AIDS in Uganda. In addition, she is the field anthropologist for a joint clinical research project in Atlanta (Centers for Disease Control/Emory University) to investigate adherence to the new drug therapies for HIV/AIDS.

Robert G. White is professor of government and politics at Humboldt State University. He has been actively involved in H-Africa and the potential of the Internet for teaching, research, and communication. He has been exploring the potential impact of the implementation of the Leland Initiative for Internet connectivity in Kenya, Ethiopia, Eritrea, and Uganda. He is a member of the Royal African Society.

Philip S. Zachernuk is assistant professor of history at Dalhousie University. His forthcoming book *Colonial Subjects* suggests a new approach to the intellectual history of colonial society in southern Nigeria. Currently he is examining history writing in colonial West Africa, exploring how colonial African intellectuals produced historical knowledge between the influences of indigenous practices, imperial imperatives, and black Atlantic inspirations.

INDEX

4951

About the Book

Some of the best college and university teachers in the field describe projects and assignments that have worked effectively for them in teaching African studies in a variety of disciplines.

The authors present a wide range of approaches: from preparing African cuisines as a way to understand people-environment relations to using the Internet to develop a virtual art history exhibit; from viewing an African film or assigning a novel to broaden students' grasp of social context to challenging students to draft their own development projects in order to better appreciate village-level society and economy. Six chapters are devoted to ways of handling such particularly sensitive subjects as ethnicity in Africa, the slave trade, AIDS, and female genital mutilation.

Each chapter includes topics that enlivened class discussion and a list of supplementary readings.

Misty L. Bastian is assistant professor of anthropology at Franklin and Marshall College. Her research interests focus on gender and popular media in Africa, as well as new African diasporas and global popular cultures. **Jane L. Parpart** is professor of history, women's studies, and international development studies at Dalhousie University. Her most recent book is *The "Man" Question in International Relations,* coedited with Mary Zalewski, and she has written extensively on women, gender, and development in Africa.